Fidelity & Freedom

Fidelity & Freedom

EX CORDE ECCLESIAE AT TWENTY-FIVE

Edited by Stephen M. Hildebrand and
Sean O. Sheridan, TOR

FRANCISCAN UNIVERSITY PRESS

Franciscan University Press
1235 University Boulevard
Steubenville, OH 43952
740-283-3771

Distributed by:
The Catholic University of America Press
c/o HFS
P.O. Box 50370
Baltimore, MD 21211
800-537-5487

Library of Congress Cataloging-in-Publication Data
Names: Hildebrand, Stephen M., 1973– editor. | Sheridan, Sean O., editor. | Franciscan University of Steubenville, sponsoring body.
Title: Fidelity and freedom : Ex corde ecclesiae at twenty-five / edited by Stephen M. Hildebrand and Sean O. Sheridan, TOR.
Description: Steubenville : Franciscan University Press, 2018. | Includes index. | Includes papers presented at three symposia hosted by Franciscan University of Steubenville to commemorate the 25th anniversary of the promulgation of St. John Paul II's Ex corde Ecclesiae, held from November 2014 through March 2015.—ECIP introduction.
Identifiers: LCCN 2017043528 | ISBN 9780996930567
Subjects: LCSH: Catholic Church. Pope (1978-2005 : John Paul II). Ex corde ecclesiae—Congresses. | Universities and colleges (Canon law)—Congresses. | Catholic universities and colleges—United States—Congresses.
Classification: LCC KBU3054 .F53 2018 | DDC 378/.0712—dc23
LC record available at https://lccn.loc.gov/2017043528

Text and Cover Design: Kachergis Book Design

Printed in the United States of America.
ISBN: 978-0-9969305-6-7

CONTENTS

ABBREVIATIONS

CCC — *Catechism of the Catholic Church*, 2nd ed. (Washington, DC: United States Catholic Conference, 2000)

CCE — Congregation for Catholic Education

CIC — *Codex Iuris Canonici auctoritate Ioannis Pauli PP. II promulgatus* (Vatican City: Libreria Editrice Vaticana, 1983); English translation from *Code of Canon Law*, Latin-English ed., New English trans. (Washington, DC: Canon Law Society of America, 2012).

EcE — John Paul II, apostolic constitution *Ex corde Ecclesiae*, August 15, 1990: *Acta Apostolicae Sedis* 82 (1990): 1475–509. Translation in English by National Conference of Catholic Bishops in *Origins* 20, no. 17 (October 4, 1990): 265–26. See also Committee on Catholic Education, United States Conference of Catholic Bishops, *Catholic Mission and Culture in Colleges and Universities: Defining Documents: 1965–2014* (Washington, DC: United States Conference of Catholic Bishops, 2014), 69–89, http://w2.vatican.va/content/john-paul-ii/en/apost_constitutions/documents/hf_jp-ii_apc_15081990_ex-corde-ecclesiae.html.

The Introduction and Part I of *EcE* are cited by paragraph number (e.g., *EcE*, 19). Part II, "General Norms" does not have paragraph numbers but article and section numbers (e.g., *EcE*, art. 2, §5).

FR — John Paul II, encyclical *Fides et ratio*, September 14, 1998: *AAS* 91 (1999): 5–88, http://w2.vatican.va/content/john-paul-ii/en/encyclicals/documents/hf_jp-ii_enc_14091998_fides-et-ratio.html.

FOREWORD

The great higher educational venture that we know as the "university"—in all its various forms—rightfully springs forth "from the heart of the Church." The beginnings of our contemporary higher education institutions are found in the medieval period and the learned teachers who were engaged by diocesan bishops to teach at cathedral schools. From those early beginnings, colleges and universities developed and flourished through the centuries.

The number of Catholic colleges and universities multiplied to serve the emerging population of Catholics, which in many cases was underserved because higher education was often not available to the group. Established to educate their students and also to form them as men and women of faith, Catholic universities were often seen as somewhat removed from the rigors of secular academia. After World War II, during a period when many Catholic colleges and universities were established and experienced substantial growth, some Catholic educators began to advocate for mitigating the role of faith at these institutions while emphasizing their academic rigor and research capabilities to compete more directly with their secular counterparts.

Many Catholic universities agreed with this plan, but others chose to remain rooted in their role as institutions of higher learning that were in fact Catholic. I am blessed to serve as the president of Franciscan University of Steubenville, which was established as a Catholic university always faithful to the Church. In 1946, the Franciscans, Third Order Regular of the Province of the Most Sacred Heart of Jesus, accepted the invitation of Most Reverend John King Mussio, the first Bishop of the Diocese of Steubenville, to found the College of Steubenville to serve the higher educational needs of the people of the Ohio Valley. Over the past seventy years, the university has continued to grow into what we now know as Franciscan University.

Foreword

In 1974, when he became the fourth president of what was then the College of Steubenville, Fr. Michael Scanlan, TOR, sought to make Christ the center of life on campus—academics, student life, finances—with a heightened emphasis on the college's Catholic identity. Not everyone embraced Father Mike's ideas at first, particularly because other Catholic universities were moving in the opposite direction. Many were skeptical about the plan, while others said it simply could not be done.

But Pope John Paul II, himself an educator, provided a road map for Catholic universities in his 1990 apostolic constitution *Ex corde Ecclesiae*. Franciscan University embraced the challenge it set forth.

John Paul II maintained that a Catholic university is a community of scholars that advances the various branches of academic studies. But it is also an educational institution that advances the principles of Catholicism as a defining component of what it was established to be as a "Catholic university." Consequently, as John Paul II urged, Catholic ideals are to be part of the daily activities of a Catholic university.

The emphasis on the university as "Catholic" promotes its dual purpose. It does so by educating. It does so through participation of members of the university community in the sacraments. It also does so by promoting the teachings of the Catholic Church. The community of a Catholic university is unique because of its focus on Christ. John Paul II said:

> A Catholic university pursues its objectives through its formation of an authentic human community animated by the spirit of Christ. The source of its unity springs from a common dedication to the truth, a common vision of the dignity of the human person, and ultimately, the person and message of Christ, which gives the institution its distinctive character. As a result of this inspiration, the community is animated by a spirit of freedom and charity; it is characterized by mutual respect, sincere dialogue and protection of the rights of individuals. It assists each of its members to achieve wholeness as human persons; in turn, everyone in the community helps in promoting unity, and each one, according to his or her role and capacity, contributes towards decisions which affect the community, and also towards maintaining and strengthening the distinctive Catholic character of the institution.[1]

1. *Ex corde Ecclesiae*, 21.

Still, some questioned whether a higher education institution could be both Catholic and a university, and others said it simply could not be done.

When I became president of Franciscan University in 2013, I knew that we were quickly approaching the twenty-fifth anniversary of the promulgation of *Ex corde Ecclesiae*. As an institution that aspires to always remain faithful to the Church, it seemed appropriate for us to celebrate that anniversary. It is my great honor to present to you the essays submitted for three symposia celebrating the twenty-fifth anniversary, collected under the title *Fidelity and Freedom: Ex corde Ecclesiae at Twenty-Five*. This dialogue about the issues related to education in a Catholic university was intended to lead us deeper into the principles embodied in *Ex corde Ecclesiae*. I am grateful to all the distinguished contributors who engaged us in our discussions.

We who participate in this great endeavor known as a Catholic university do so in response to the Lord's Great Commission to the Apostles, set forth in the final verses of Matthew's Gospel: "Go, therefore, and make disciples of all nations, baptizing them in the name of the Father, and of the Son, and of the holy Spirit, teaching them to observe all that I have commanded you. And behold, I am with you always, until the end of the age" (Mt 28:19–20). As we strive to embrace this mandate, I invite you to engage the dialogue presented in this volume.

Sean O. Sheridan, TOR

Fidelity & Freedom

Introduction

Stephen M. Hildebrand

Between November 2014 and March 2015, Franciscan University of Steubenville hosted three symposia to commemorate the twenty-fifth anniversary of the promulgation of St. John Paul II's *Ex corde Ecclesiae*. Under the general title of "Fidelity and Freedom," each of the symposia was organized around a particular theme. The first symposium was titled "Academic Freedom and Revealed Truth" (November 14 and 15, 2014), the second "The Dialogue of Faith and Reason" (March 6, 2015), and the third "Engaging the Culture" (September 18 and 19, 2015). At each symposium, both theoretical and practical issues were addressed, and from numerous perspectives. Most of the participants were faculty from various universities, but bishops and university presidents were also involved.

The papers given at these symposia form the heart of this collection of essays, although the contributions here are ordered according to a different principle than that which guided the organization of the symposia. After Part I, "*Ex corde Ecclesiae*," which contains an introductory review of the contents and drafting process of *Ex corde Ecclesiae*, comes the collection of symposium essays. Part II, "Academic and Cultural Questions," contains essays on the various theological, canonical, and cultural issues that both preexisted the publication of *Ex corde Ecclesiae* and received significant attention afterward. Part III, "Pastoral and Practical Reflection," presents the views of two bishops and three university presidents on the meaning of *Ex corde Ecclesiae* for universities, small and large, and for the Church.

Within Part II, essays hit upon various important themes. Peter F. Ryan, SJ, in "The Catholic University and the Idea of Academic Freedom" offers a critical analysis of the dominant view that a university, by definition, cannot submit to any external authority, such as that of the Magisterium of the Catholic Church. He argues that by such a definition, none of the purportedly Catholic universities could distinguish themselves as Catholic; that without a bond with the Magisterium, such universities will inevitably become more secularized; and that academic freedom need not be construed in such a way that it is at odds with the Catholic mission of Catholic universities.

Terrence W. Tilley's "Academic Freedom, Divine Revelation, and Catholic Universities" begins with an analysis of academic freedom as defined by the American Association of University Professors. Tilley argues that this "procedural" version of academic freedom is necessary but not sufficient, and to it must be added some important factors: freedom is the freedom to teach and research in one's area of expertise, and freedom to investigate given proposals presumes a body of knowledge from which the investigation is conducted (at sea, one cannot replace a whole ship at once, but rather stands on the deck to replace a plank). From academic freedom, Tilley moves to revelation. Here he offers a definition of revelation (God's self-manifestation through symbolic communication), a way of understanding it (not ahistorical and propositional but symbolic and historically conditioned), an explanation of its relation to faith (actual, as opposed to virtual, revelation cannot be had without faith, and only the symbols of actual revelation are subject to theological examination), and a statement of its implications (exploration of the symbols of God's revelation is proper to theologians; exploration requires clear distinctions of activities, e.g., *appraising* and *adjudicating*; and theologians as such cannot dispute the fact of revelation but only its particular symbolic expression). The final section of Tilley's essay presents the Catholic university as an "open circle": it presumes that the Catholic intellectual tradition centers the circle but invites everyone, no matter the faith or discipline, into it.

Reinhard Hütter's essay, "Academic Freedom and Revealed Truth: Applying the Spirit and Letter of *Ex corde Ecclesiae* to Catholic Universities in Contemporary America," begins by outlining the difficult situation in which most Catholic universities find themselves: on the one hand, the commodification of education and economic hardship has created intense pressure, especially for universities without large endowments, to compete with (and often to assimilate to) non-Catholic universities. On the other hand, Catholic universities, small and large, wealthy and not, have been subject to an inexorable movement toward secularization. Hütter goes on to elucidate the "imperious claims of secular reason" and the view of academic freedom that corresponds to it, and to contrast this view of freedom with that authentic freedom that attends a true university (marked by the quest of universal knowledge and the unity of knowledge). Academic freedom is not merely freedom from interference—which can, by itself, degenerate into indifference—rather, academic freedom exists where inquiry is ordered to truth and universal knowledge, the whole truth about nature, man, and God. Thus revealed truth makes possible an even deeper and more authentic freedom—it perfects freedom.

In "The Dialogue between Faith and Reason in a Catholic University," Susan K. Wood, SCL, unfolds the idea that the university is the place where the Church does its thinking. She first analyzes the relationship between faith and reason, and holds that faith, following the more personalistic emphasis of Vatican II over the more propositionalist emphasis of Vatican I, is above all personal adherence to God. Faith is a "first-order primary experience," and the articulation of, reflection on, and communication of it requires reason. Sr. Wood sees an analogy between the relationship between faith and reason on the one hand, and the sacred and the secular on the other. This latter interaction and engagement are the hallmarks of a Catholic university, wherein secular knowledge becomes the "sacrament" and witness to the ultimate mystery and presence of God.

Scott W. Hahn argues in "How the New Evangelization Fits with Catholic Higher Education" against the prima facie impression that the new evangelization would have no place at the Catholic university and for the conclusion that it is in fact necessary for its flourishing. He begins with an explanation of what the new evangelization is: it is not mere proselytizing, but the constant interior renewal and ever deepening conversion of not only individuals but also the whole of culture and the social order above all through the witness and personal influence, as Newman has it, of committed Catholics. While American academics responded rather indifferently to the recent papal calls for the new evangelization—Avery Cardinal Dulles, SJ, was the exception—Hahn argues that the Catholic university is a privileged place for the new evangelization. What better place for young Catholics, under the mentorship of experienced and committed Catholic faculty, staff, and administration, to grow as disciples in the commitment of their wills, minds, and hearts to God and engage the contemporary culture and present the Gospel to it in an intellectually persuasive manner?

Anne Hendershott begins "In Service: Shaping the Culture, Serving the Church" by recalling the well-known essay of John Tracy Ellis that acutely criticized faculty at Catholic universities for their low level of scholarship and intellectual excellence. Hendershott sees the likewise famous Land O'Lakes statement as the fulfillment of Ellis's call, but many of the Catholic universities that had embraced Land O'Lakes lost their Catholic identities, and *Ex corde Ecclesiae* called for the renewal of universities' authentically Catholic character. Hendershott reports the hostile and hyperbolic (to the point of absurdity) reaction of administrators and faculty at many Catholic universities. Some openly dissented from *Ex corde*, while others were quietly unfaithful. Hendershott then points out that many Catholic colleges have essentially given "cover" to the secular culture, even where it is most opposed to the teaching and practice of the Catholic Church, for example, on reproductive rights and same-sex marriage. Among a long list of examples, the various connections and forms of cooperation between some Catholic universities and Planned Parenthood are particularly striking. Far from serving the Church and illuminating the truth about life and marriage, many at Catholic institutions with the support of these universities have been coworkers in the culture of death. Hendershott concludes her essay with a call for Catholic universities to resist the danger of sentimentality and to be places where Catholicism is vitally present and where individuals are dedicated to the search for truth. Only then will they be able to wage the inevitable culture wars.

The essay by James J. Conn, SJ, "Canonical Issues and US Catholic Universities: Twenty-Five Years since *Ex corde Ecclesiae*," is the last of Part II. After recounting the story of his own life and vocation, especially as they intersected with Catholic schools and universities, Fr. Conn turns to an analysis of two canons (810 and 812) and their respective implementation by the Particular Norms of the United States Conference of Catholic Bishops (USCCB). Canon 810 §1 declared the criteria for appointment and removal of teachers: appropriate qualifications and integrity of doctrine and probity of life. Fr. Conn explains the *ratio* here—participation in the Church's mission requires a critical mass of committed Catholics. Canon 810 §2 offers the correlate of §1: the bishops have the right and duty to be vigilant of universities' observance of the principles of Catholic doctrine. Fr. Conn then turns to Canon 812, on the *mandatum*, whose *ratio* is the right of the faithful to authentic Catholic teaching. In each of these cases (810 §1 and §2, and 812), Fr. Conn analyzes the Particular Norms of the USCCB and in each of the cases judges these norms to be significantly flawed. He concludes his essay with a list of model statutes whereby Catholic universities, through self-regulation, would accomplish the implementation of the spirit of *Ex corde Ecclesiae* and the canons that pertain to it.

Part III includes essays by bishops and university presidents. These contributions are clearly informed by personal invaluable experience and provide a series of pastoral and practical insights. The essay by Jeffrey Monforton, Bishop of Steubenville, "The Bishop and the Catholic University: Cultivating Dialogue and Cooperation," begins with a reflection on the bishop. Bishop Monforton stresses the obedience that a bishop owes to the Lord and his obligation to evangelize the people under his care. Turning to the Catholic university, Bishop Monforton emphasizes that the Catholic university is not to be an ivory tower, but rather participates in the daily life of the local Church by freely sharing the truth of Jesus Christ. At the foundation of the relationship between the bishop and the university are dialogue and cooperation. The university can expect from the bishop effective communication and encouragement, and the bishop can expect from the university that it will help in the task to evangelize and will contribute to the life of the local Church.

Mark L. Bartchak, Bishop of Altoona-Johnstown, focuses on the two questions indicated in the title of his essay, "Reflections on the Dialogue between Faith and Reason and the Relationship of a Diocesan Bishop with Local Catholic Universities." His exploration of faith and reason begins with the *New Catholic Encyclopedia* and culminates in John Paul II's *Fides et Ratio.* Throughout he stresses the imperative to search for the truth and the integration of knowledge arrived at by faith on the one hand, and reason on the other. In the second part of his essay,

Bishop Bartchak recounts some of his experiences with the two colleges in his diocese, St. Francis University in Loretto and Mount Aloysius in Cresson. Both colleges focus on the professional formation of students and so have a service orientation. Bishop Bartchak expresses a deep appreciation for this orientation while stressing the need to overcome the compartmentalization of knowledge. A prominent theme in this second part is the need for dialogue between the presidents of universities and local bishops. A canon lawyer, Bartchak closes his contributions with some reflections on two of the *Ex corde Ecclesiae*'s General Norms, one on academic freedom and the other on the communication between the university and the bishop.

Richard Jusseaume, president of Walsh University in northeast Ohio, tells the story of his university and effort to implement *Ex corde Ecclesiae* in "The Heart of the Matter." He begins with the history of Walsh, a small Catholic college founded in 1958 by the Christian Brothers, that in its early years was marked by a strong Catholic identity in curriculum and culture, but that by 2001, the year Jusseaume became president, had lost much of it: "No nuns—no cassocks—no prayer before classes—fewer required theology classes—no dedicated chapel—no vocations—and no branding tied to Catholic origins." Although the implementation of *Ex corde Ecclesiae* had begun on the campus of Walsh in the 1990s with discussion groups and dialogue, Jusseaume decided in 2001 to return to the founding mission and Catholic identity of the university. Through scholarships and tuition discounts, he drew Catholic students, and through the promotion of various devotions and a free-standing chapel, he grew a Catholic culture. Jusseaume took the oath of fidelity and worked with his local bishop, Thomas Tobin, to get his theology faculty comfortable with the *mandatum*. Eventually, he made the *mandatum* a condition of employment for theologians. In a short excursus on academic freedom, Jusseaume stresses the goods that one is free to enjoy with the commitment of faith, but in such a way that discussion remains open, with no subject off limits and no opinions silenced. Jusseaume concludes his essay with a description of present challenges. He writes of a crisis of leadership among Catholic university presidents, many of whom have capitulated to a hostile government and a hostile culture. In this context, *Ex corde Ecclesiae* is not threatening but inspirational and helpful—through it God has granted increase to Walsh University.

In "*Ex corde Ecclesiae* at the University of Mary," James P. Shea, president of the University of Mary in Bismarck, North Dakota, offers an account of the implementation of *Ex corde Ecclesiae* at his university. Before turning to his main subject, however, he makes the point that every university without exception operates by first principles and has "faith" commitments of a sort, whether they be the materialist naturalism that animates many secular universities or those of the Christian view of the world that animated the original universities. Msgr. Shea makes the point that, both metaphysically and historically speaking, Christianity has preserved and deepened the educational ideal of the ancients, and the Catholic university's faith commitments, its acceptance of coherent first principles, make genuine intellectual activity possible. The second part of his essay focuses on the University of Mary's efforts to become an instance of the ideal outlined in the first part. This is being achieved through intellectual formation for faculty; through the grounding of the School of Health Sciences, for example, in the Catholic vision of the human person; through hiring for mission; and through the promotion of a Catholic moral and spiritual life. Msgr. Shea concludes his essay with a call for Catholic universities to see Catholic identity not as a burden or impediment to intellectual excellence, but as an intellectual advantage that will enable them, unlike their secular counterparts, to respond to the most profound intellectual tasks and to enable their students to become wise, good, whole, mature, and intelligent.

In the final essay in the volume, "Embracing the Gift of *Ex corde Ecclesiae* to Challenge the Culture," Sean O. Sheridan, TOR, describes the way that Franciscan University of Steubenville has embraced the apostolic constitution as a gift and so has been equipped with the tools to challenge the culture and change the world. Fr. Sheridan organizes his essay around several teachings of *Ex corde Ecclesiae*. First, the Catholic university is to be a community centered on Christ. Teachers, students, and administrators all strive in their various roles at the university to grow in holiness and communion with Christ. Second, the faculty of a university have the obligation not only to teach but also to preach the Good News. The faculty of a Catholic university should have the opportunity, through prayer and the participation in the sacraments, to integrate faith and life as well as Christian wisdom and professional competence. At Franciscan University, this happens in numerous ways: faculty participation in the university's faith and sacramental life, faculty advisors to households, faculty participation in mission trips, faculty advisors to clubs, and so on. Third, a Catholic university, while above all a university, must be about the pastoral care of the members of the community. Fr. Sheridan singles out, among the many possible examples of this at Franciscan, the instances of pastoral care in residence halls, each of which has the Blessed Sacrament reserved and a chaplain who is available for spiritual direction and, as the case may be, for sacramental confession. Finally, all members of the university family are evangelizers, for all are called to ongoing conversion to Christ and must live out the faith in all aspects of life.

If Catholic universities do not connect faith with daily life, if we fail to infuse academics, residence life, athletics, student activities, and the like with the truths of the Catholic faith, then we are unwittingly reducing our God-given and constitutionally guaranteed right to "freedom of religion" to a mere "freedom of worship," thereby buying into the very premise of secularism. In fact, if the culture—and, ultimately, all men and women of faith—do not embrace the teachings of the Church—the absolute truths of the faith—and maintain the voice of faithful Catholics in the public square, the potential arises for much more serious consequences than secularism and relativism. We run the risk of rejecting Christ himself, and at that point our lives become meaningless.

Fr. Sheridan sees Franciscan as a university that, in striving to be faithful to *Ex corde Ecclesiae*, follows the example of the earliest universities that embraced the search for truth in the dialogue between faith and reason and recognized that its source is God himself.

After the final essay from the symposia is an appendix, also by Fr. Sheridan. Drawn from his dissertation on *Ex corde Ecclesiae*, it offers practical suggestions for the implementation of the apostolic constitution, with a focus on five objections raised against it: (1) that norms cannot be applied to universities because they have no juridical status; (2) that Catholic identity cannot be realized at all levels of a university; (3) that a university cannot rightly give preference to Catholics in hiring; (4) that there are contractual problems with Canons 810 and 812; and (5) that a university should be independent of the local and universal Church.

Although the many contributions to this volume are varied, there are nonetheless some common themes to recognize and important issues to ponder further. Academic freedom is one. Although handled differently by each contributor, one common thread is that academic freedom cannot merely mean the lack of constraints on free inquiry, what Tilley calls "procedural freedom" or what Hütter calls "freedom from interference." All the authors who discuss academic freedom qualify it in some way. Ryan qualifies it by emphasizing the instrumental character of freedom and its connection to truth, a point that Hütter also stresses. Tilley qualifies it by calling to mind the importance of expertise in subject matter and the practical point that one cannot call into question everything at once but needs a place to stand, so to speak, from which one may inquire into this question or that. Jusseaume understands faith not to limit freedom, but to make it possible. Faith makes one free to enjoy the good of having a guide through endless historical and intellectual complexities and cultural difficulties. And Shea makes the point, at least by implication, that absolute freedom would be impossible, for one must start with some kind of faith, some sort of first principles.

Ex corde Ecclesiae's statement on academic freedom appears often in this volume:

> freedom in research and teaching is recognized and respected according to the principles and methods of each individual discipline, so long as the rights of the individual and of the community are preserved within the confines of the truth and the common good.[1]

Freedom is here viewed as lack of constraint, and the rights of the individual and community as well as the truth and the common good can impose legitimate limits on research and teaching. One might think, for example, of the dignity of the human person as limiting or constraining a sociologist's freedom to conduct research: for starters, a researcher cannot make persons the subjects of experiments without their permission. Or, again, a biologist studying the nutritional value of grapefruits would not be free, for the sake of research, to confiscate all the grapefruits from the school cafeteria. Aside from the fact that this would be stealing property, the common good demands that food stuffs not be altogether ordered to biological experiments above consumption

1. *EcE*, art. 2, §5.

and nourishment. Of course, in certain circumstances one may—rather, one must—conduct experiments on grapefruits, but the freedom to do so is obviously and reasonably qualified and limited.

"Freedom," however, can mean more than the lack of constraint or interference; it can denote the ability, the freedom, to enjoy a good. Moreover, these two types of freedom can be inversely proportional. That is, the ability to enjoy a good comes at the cost of the ability to do what one wishes. Let me illustrate with a simple example.[2] If I would like the freedom to enjoy the good of playing in an orchestra, I must surrender my choice to the conductor. I lose the choice to play what I wish, when I wish, how I wish, and so on. But in surrendering this free choice, I get to enjoy a new, higher, communal good—beautiful music—that I could not, that I am not free to, enjoy by myself. We see a similar trade-off not only in marriage and religious life but also in the Christian life itself. One makes a choice to surrender some choices in order to be free to enjoy the wonderful goods of the Christian life, or of married life, or of religious life. Thus to place oneself under authority—whether of an orchestra conductor, a teacher, a coach, a university president, or God himself, to mention only a few examples—can be liberating, for those under authority, because and insofar as they are under the authority, they are enabled to enjoy the goods that the authority makes possible, goods that could not otherwise be enjoyed.

Here we can see Ryan's point on the instrumental character of freedom (freedom in the sense of free choice or free inquiry rather than the ability to enjoy a good). We can also see Tilley's point that to enjoy the good of doing theology, one must accept revelation and surrender the choice to entertain lines of thought that deny it. I cannot keep the choice to deny revelation and do theology any more than I can keep the choice to date and get married. More broadly still, we can see Hütter's point that academic freedom is not merely the negative freedom of interference but the ability of a community of human persons to realize the essence of a university. We are free to know, and to know in a "philosophical way," in such a way that we enjoy universal knowledge.

Commitment to the Catholic faith without a doubt places constraints on those who teach and research at a Catholic university, con-

2. I borrow this example from Victor Austin, *Up with Authority* (New York: T&T Clark, 2010).

straints that colleagues at secular universities would not have. And yet this loss of freedom is nothing to lament, for when one chooses to surrender this freedom in the commitment of faith, one is liberated to enjoy those very goods for which freedom exists in the first place.

A second important theme emerges when one compares the essays of Hütter and Tilley, and it is a theme especially relevant to the considerations raised by the two bishops: the manner in which one understands revelation will, in turn, determine the role of the Magisterium in revelation as well as the its role in relation to Catholic universities. This all seems abstract, but let us begin with the different ways in which Hütter and Tilley make sense of propositions and revelation.[3]

For Tilley, the propositions of Scripture or of the Church's authoritative teachings cannot be identified in any simplistic way with revelation. He speaks of "revealed truth" but not of "revealed truths," for this latter way of speaking betrays an incorrect view of the ways in which propositions relate to revealed truth. Revelation is not the delivery of divine propositions into the human mind. It is better to say that revelation is mediated through symbols, which have their meaning in a particular historical context and a particular "web of meanings." Virtual revelation becomes actual only when it is received in faith and made concrete by the expression of revelatory symbols, and it is the task of theology to discern which symbols should be used to express faith and which symbols still effectively communicate. Theologians cannot dispute that God reveals, but they may propose new symbols and sentences that express that revelation.

In this understanding of revelation, the role of the Magisterium would not be to pass on a set of propositions identified with revelation. Rather, the Magisterium adjudicates among the appraisals of symbols that are generated by theologians. As Tilley understands *Ex corde Ecclesiae*, theologians have a responsibility to present the adjudications of the Church (official Church teaching) and the arguments for these adjudications, but they are free also to present, argue for, and agree with dis-

3. Sr. Wood also considers the relationship between propositions and revealed truth, but from the vantage point of Vatican II's *Dei Verbum*. *Dei Verbum* subsumes the teaching of Vatican I's *Dei Filius*, which tended to be more propositional, into a more personalist view of faith. Assent and submission of mind and will are taken up into a framework of total commitment of self to God.

sident appraisals, though without advocating that students accept the theologian's own position. One might say that in Tilley's understanding of revelation and the relation of propositions to revelation, magisterial adjudications bear less weight, for they could never be identified with revelation itself and could not rightly be considered "revealed truths," the very expression of which involves a linguistic and theological impossibility.

Hütter takes a more traditionally Thomistic view of propositions, seemingly informed from the doctrine of analogy. Revealed truth is essentially testimony about God from God that necessarily takes propositional form. The specification of revealed truth in propositions is received from Scripture and tradition interpreted by the Magisterium. Although necessarily propositional, revealed truth remains transcendent. Transcendence is not compromised by propositionality but conveyed by it. For Hütter, the exercise of that freedom whereby the university comes into existence, whereby universal knowledge is had, is inconsistent with a "flight from the testimonial propositionality of revealed truth." Instead, authentic academic freedom is realized in fidelity to the propositions of Scripture and tradition as authoritatively specified by the Church. Thus Hütter differs from Tilley on revealed truth and propositions—and, as a consequence, also on the role of the Magisterium in the Catholic university—as well as the relationship of individual theologians to the Magisterium.

This difference between Tilley and Hütter is instructive, for it reveals that differences over mandates and oaths of fidelity and disagreements over the role of bishops and theologians in the life of the university and the Church are to be explained at a more fundamental level. Such differences and disagreements could only be resolved by tending to the underlying discrepancy in theologies of revelation. The same is true of the tense and uneasy relationship between so many bishops and so many theologians: often they are operating with competing theories of revelation and the place of propositions in this revelation.

I would like to draw attention to one final theme that several of the essays engage. It goes without saying that in a discussion of the identity of Catholic universities, the Land O'Lakes document will be a constant reference point. Yet it is interesting how many of the questions for Catholic universities have shifted since then. In the mid-1960s, there were Catholic universities competing with their secular counterparts, but this collection of essays indicates that things have moved in a different direction. One can see the whole shift in miniature in the interesting career and personal "conversion" of James Conn, SJ, but it is also evident especially in the essays of Anne Hendershott, Scott Hahn, the university presidents, and the bishops. There is far more attention on forming students in the richness that the Catholic faith and tradition has to offer, on preparing them to face an increasingly secular world, and on enlisting their help in the Church's engagement with an increasingly hostile culture.

At one point in the discussion, it becomes clear that smaller and larger Catholic universities, both of which were represented in the symposia, are moving in different worlds. Richard Jusseaume persuasively made the case, born out by his own experience with Walsh University, that small, struggling Catholic colleges will not be able to turn their fortunes around by imitating the larger Catholic universities, who have more or less been able to compete with secular schools but often at the cost of a loss in their Catholic identity. Rather, Jusseaume insists that the road to vitality for these institutions is to embrace what sets them apart—their Catholic identity. Only this will give them something to offer students, something that cannot be had at secular (or some of the larger Catholic) universities.

It is our hope that this collection of essays will be the beginning of a conversation about the role and identity of Catholic universities in our time. Even after twenty-five years, *Ex corde Ecclesiae* has only just begun to have its effect.

PART I

Ex corde Ecclesiae

[1]

The Message and Drafting Process of *Ex corde Ecclesiae*

Sean O. Sheridan, TOR

On August 15, 1990, the Solemnity of the Assumption of the Blessed Virgin Mary, Pope John Paul II promulgated the long-anticipated document on Catholic universities. The apostolic constitution was given the incipit *Ex corde Ecclesiae*, "Born from the Heart of the Church," to acknowledge the significant role that Catholic universities fulfill in the Church.[1] John Paul II identified what it means for a university to be Catholic and issued General Norms to supplement the provisions of the code of canon law that pertain to Catholic universities.[2] He challenged Catholic universities and those associated with their mission to deliver more effectively the Church's message. For example, he encouraged those who teach at Catholic universities "to be witnesses and educators of authentic Christian life, which evidences attained integration between faith and life, and between professional competence and

This chapter is drawn from the author's previous work. See "*Ex corde Ecclesiae*: A Canonical Commentary on Catholic Universities, 'From the Heart of the Church' to Catholic Universities" (JCD diss., Catholic University of America, 2009).

1. John Paul II, apostolic constitution *Ex corde Ecclesiae* (hereafter *EcE*) 1, August 15, 1990: *Acta Apostolicae Sedis* 82 (1990). Translation in English by National Conference of Catholic Bishops in *Origins* 20, no. 17 (October 4, 1990): 265–76. See also Committee on Catholic Education, United States Conference of Catholic Bishops, *Catholic Mission and Culture in Colleges and Universities: Defining Documents: 1965–2014* (Washington, DC: United States Conference of Catholic Bishops, 2014), 69–89.

2. *EcE*, arts. 1–7.

Christian wisdom."[3] He charged bishops with being more actively involved in Catholic institutions within their dioceses and to foster close personal and pastoral relationships with Catholic universities. The Holy Father argued that the relationship between a Catholic university and its diocesan bishop should be "characterized by mutual trust, close and consistent cooperation and continuing dialogue,"[4] with the bishop actively participating in the life of each Catholic university within his diocese.

Like *Sapientia Christiana*, its predecessor on ecclesiastical universities and faculties, *Ex corde Ecclesiae* was promulgated as an apostolic constitution. Morrisey submits:

> Apostolic constitutions may be considered the most solemn form of legal document issued by the Pope in his own name. They deal with doctrinal or disciplinary matters, but are issued only in relation to very weighty questions. They are now generally reserved for acts of the Pope related to important matters regarding the Church universal or a particular Church, such as the erection of dioceses.[5]

Although more emphasis has been placed on the doctrinal significance of an apostolic constitution since the pontificate of Pope Paul VI, "there is no doubt that an apostolic constitution is essentially a legislative text."[6] Martens provides a thoughtful summary of the various types of issues with which popes have dealt by means of apostolic constitutions.

> A closer analysis of the topics of [the eleven apostolic constitutions that Pope John Paul II promulgated] shows that these major apostolic constitutions constitute important legislation: the promulgation of the 1983 Code of Canon Law, new norms for ecclesiastical universities and faculties and for catholic universities, the organization of the diocese of Rome, norms for the vacancy of the see of Rome and the election of a new Pope are just a few examples. The most important aspects of the postconciliar reform were promulgated by

3. *EcE*, 22.

4. *EcE*, 28.

5. Francis G. Morrisey, *Papal and Curial Pronouncements*, 2nd ed., ed. Michel Thériault (Ottawa: St. Paul University, 2001), 14–15.

6. Ibid., 17; idem, "Papal and Curial Pronouncements: Their Canonical Significance in Light of the 1983 Code of Canon Law," 108.

Paul VI in the form of apostolic constitutions: an example is liturgical law. The erection of new dioceses and other such changes in the life of a particular Church or the erection of ecclesiastical provinces are usually achieved through an apostolic constitution. Some teaching documents are promulgated with an apostolic constitution, such as the Catechism of the Catholic Church, or the dogma of the Assumption of Mary.[7]

Ex corde Ecclesiae consists of two main parts preceded by an introduction. Part I, "Identity and Mission," is more theological in nature and addresses the development of Catholic universities and the role that they play in society. With regard to the "Identity of a Catholic University," *Ex corde Ecclesiae* is subdivided into the following sections: "Nature and Objectives," "The University Community," and "The Catholic University in the Church." The section "The Mission of Service of a Catholic University" is subdivided as follows: "Service to Church and Society," "Pastoral Ministry," "Cultural Dialogue," and "Evangelization."[8]

Part II's General Norms are divided into seven articles: Article 1, Nature of These Norms; Article 2, Nature of a Catholic University; Article 3, Establishment of a Catholic University; Article 4, University Community; Article 5, Catholic University within the Church; Article 6, Pastoral Ministry; and Article 7, Cooperation.[9] Transitional Norms are included and encompass four brief articles.[10]

The promulgation of *Ex corde Ecclesiae* followed a lengthy period of discussion among members of the Catholic university communities, bishops throughout the world, and hierarchical representatives of the Holy See. This process demonstrates that the Church affords great esteem and respect to Catholic universities and their representatives and is grateful for the ministry that each of these universities provides. Pope John Paul II stated that "the mission that the church, with great hope, entrusts to Catholic universities holds a cultural and religious meaning of vital importance because it concerns the very future of humanity.

7. Kurt Martens, "Nature of Authority of Roman Documents," *CLSA Proceedings* 69 (2007): 139.

8. *EcE*, 12–49. See James H. Provost, "The Canonical Aspects of Catholic Identity in the Light of *Ex corde Ecclesiae*," *Studia canonica* 25 (1991): 156. See, generally, Antonio Mantineo, *Le Università Cattoliche nel Diritto della Chiesa e dello Stato* (Milan: Dott. A. Giuffrè, 1995), 43–78.

9. *EcE*, arts. 1–7. See Provost, "Canonical Aspects of Catholic Identity," 156.

10. *EcE*, arts. 8–11.

The renewal requested of Catholic universities will make them better able to respond to the task of bringing the message of Christ to man, to society, to the various cultures."[11]

A Brief Review of the Contents of *Ex corde Ecclesiae*

Part I: Identity and Mission

The Identity of a Catholic University

The portion of *Ex corde Ecclesiae* dedicated to identity of a Catholic university is subdivided into three parts that deal with the Catholic university's nature and objectives, community, and role in the life of the Church.

It describes the Catholic university as an "academic community" that seeks to protect and advance the dignity of the human person through research, teaching, and other activities in communities at the local, national, and international levels. In pursuing these activities, the Catholic university also has institutional autonomy and guarantees academic freedom, "so long as the rights of the individual person and of the community are preserved within the confines of the truth and the common good."[12]

Each Catholic university, being Catholic, must embrace the following essential characteristics:

1. A Christian inspiration not only of individuals but also of the university community.

2. A continuing reflection in the light of the Catholic faith upon the growing treasury of human knowledge, to which it seeks to contribute by its own research.

3. Fidelity to the Christian message as it comes to us through the Church.

4. An *institutional commitment* to the service of the people of God and of the human family in their pilgrimage to the transcendent goal which gives meaning to life.[13]

11. *EcE*, Conclusion.
12. *EcE*, 12. See Mantineo, *Università Cattoliche*, 54–55.
13. *EcE*, 13. See "The Catholic University in the Modern World," in *American Catholic*

Consequently, Catholic ideals should permeate the entirety of a Catholic university's activities. "Being both a university and catholic, it must be both a community of scholars representing various branches of human knowledge and an academic institution in which Catholicism is vitally present and operative."[14] Certainly, research is an important activity in a Catholic university and includes "(a) the search for an integration of knowledge, (b) a dialogue between faith and reason, (c) an ethical concern and (d) a theological perspective."[15]

The Catholic university promotes the integration of knowledge, and as a result the dialogue between faith and reason in search for truth. The "vital interaction of two distinct levels of coming to know the one truth leads to a greater love for truth itself, and contributes to a more comprehensive understanding of the meaning of human life and of the purpose of God's creation."[16] Moreover, the dignity of the human person as well as the ethical and moral implications of the methods and the discoveries of research are to be reflected in all academic research.[17] Theology plays a role in informing such research, and it is affected by the results of such research. Thus, "because of its specific importance among the academic disciplines, every Catholic university should have a faculty, or at least a chair, of theology."[18] And it is "through research and teaching [that] the students are educated in the various disciplines so as to become truly competent in the specific sectors in which they will devote themselves to the service of society and of the church, but at the same time prepared to give the witness of their faith to the world."[19]

The denomination of a university as "Catholic" is foundational to its identity and purpose. "A Catholic university is identified as Catholic because of its purpose and means. Its purpose or end is holiness, sanctification; and the means to that end are the sanctifying (primarily sacramental) activities, the teachings and the unifying authority of the

---

Higher Education: Essential Documents, 1967–1990, ed. Alice Gallin (Notre Dame, IN: Notre Dame University Press, 1992), 37.

14. *EcE*, 14.

15. *EcE*, 15, emphasis original.

16. *EcE*, 17.

17. *EcE*, 18, emphasis original.

18. *EcE*, 19.

19. *EcE*, 20.

Catholic Church as manifested in an authentic context of higher education."[20]

The community of a Catholic university is unique, for it is united in its focus on Christ through which it expresses its Catholic identity and mission.

> A Catholic university pursues its objectives through its formation of an authentic human community animated by the spirit of Christ. The source of its unity springs from a common dedication to the truth, a common vision of the dignity of the human person, and ultimately, the person and message of Christ, which gives the institution its distinctive character. As a result of this inspiration, the community is animated by a spirit of freedom and charity; it is characterized by mutual respect, sincere dialogue and protection of the rights of individuals. It assists each of its members to achieve wholeness as human persons; in turn, everyone in the community helps in promoting unity, and each one, according to his or her role and capacity, contributes towards decisions which affect the community, and also towards maintaining and strengthening the distinctive Catholic character of the institution.[21]

Numerous people participate in the community of a Catholic university. The community includes teachers, students, directors, and administrators, as well as members of a religious congregation and laypeople. Within the context of these various roles, each member of a university community has duties within the university community. For example, "all teachers are to be inspired by academic ideals and by the principles of an authentically human life."[22] Students come to a Catholic university to pursue truth and meaning in their lives, enabling them to more deeply live a Christian way of life. "They should realize the responsibility of their professional life, the enthusiasm of being the trained 'leaders' of tomorrow, of being witnesses to Christ in whatever place they may exercise their profession."[23] Directors and administrators seek to promote the university community through their ministry of service.[24]

Ex corde Ecclesiae also recognizes that although many Catholic uni-

20. Daniel Pilarczyk, "A Catholic University and Its Trustees," *Origins* 31, no. 21 (November 1, 2001): 362.

21. *EcE*, 21.

22. *EcE*, 22.

23. *EcE*, 23.

24. *EcE*, 24, emphasis original.

versities were originally founded by institutes of consecrated life, members of the laity have today increasingly assumed more prominent roles in these institutions.

The future of Catholic universities depends to a great extent on the competent and dedicated service of lay Catholics. The church sees their developing presence in these institutions both as a sign of hope and as a confirmation of the irreplaceable lay vocation in the church and in the world, confident that lay people will, in the exercise of their own distinctive role, "illumine and organize these (temporal) affairs in such a way that they always start out, develop, and continue according to Christ's mind, to the praise of the Creator and the Redeemer."[25]

Moreover, the Catholic university community extends to men and women of different faith traditions and also to those who may not profess any religious beliefs. Yet the training and experience provided to these individuals also further the ministerial outreach of a Catholic university.[26]

A Catholic university maintains ties with both the local and the universal Church, with a special bond with the Holy See. "One consequence of its essential relationship to the Church is that the institutional fidelity of the university to the Christian message includes a recognition of and adherence to the teaching authority of the Church in matters of faith and morals."[27] And all Catholic members of a Catholic university community are required to maintain communion with the Church, while non-Catholic members of the Catholic university community must respect the Catholic nature of the university.[28]

Bishops also play a special role in promoting a Catholic university. Consequently, they should maintain a close and personal relationship with Catholic universities and foster ongoing dialogue. "Even when they do not enter directly into the internal governance of the University, Bishops 'should be seen not as external agents but as participants in the life of the Catholic University.'"[29]

Theologians and the study of theology have a particularly important

25. *EcE*, 25.
26. *EcE*, 26.
27. *EcE*, 27.
28. *EcE*, 27.
29. *EcE*, 28.

role in the life of a Catholic university, and they ought to be encouraged in their endeavors.

> [Theologians] serve the church through research done in a way that respects theological method. They seek to understand better, further develop, and more effectively communicate the meaning of Christian Revelation as transmitted in Scripture and Tradition and in the Church's Magisterium. They also investigate the ways in which theology can shed light on specific questions raised by contemporary culture. At the same time, since theology seeks an understanding of revealed truth whose authentic interpretation is entrusted to the bishops of the Church, it is intrinsic to the principles and methods of their research and teaching in their academic discipline that theologians respect the authority of the bishops and assent to Catholic doctrine according to the degree of authority with which it is taught. Because of their interrelated roles, dialogue between Bishops and theologians is essential; this is especially true today, when the results of research are so quickly and so widely communicated through the media.[30]

Thus a Catholic university is not an isolated entity. Rather, each Catholic university is to be a significant participant in the life of the Church on both the local and universal levels. The Church is also an important participant in the life of the Catholic university and in how it functions and educates its students.

The Mission of Service of a Catholic University

Although each Catholic university will pursue its mission according to its own charism, "the basic mission of a University is a continuous quest for truth through its research, and the preservation and communication of knowledge for the good of society."[31] As part of its mission, a Catholic university "prepares men and women who, inspired by Christian principles and helped to live their Christian vocation in a mature and responsible manner, will be able to assume positions of responsibility in the Church."[32] A Catholic university also helps society through its research to address current problems in the world.

30. *EcE*, 29.
31. *EcE*, 30.
32. *EcE*, 31.

Included among its research activities, therefore, will be a study of serious contemporary problems in areas such as the dignity of human life, the promotion of justice for all, the quality of personal and family life, the protection of nature, the search for peace and political stability, a more just sharing in the world's resources, and a new economic and political order that will better serve the human community at a national and international level.[33]

Representatives of a Catholic university must be prepared to "speak uncomfortable truths which do not please public opinion"[34] if it is necessary to protect the good of society. A Catholic university conveys ethical and religious truths that seek to protect the dignity of the human person. "In this way a University can contribute further to the development of a true Christian anthropology, founded on the person of Christ, which will bring the dynamism of the creation and redemption to bear on reality and on the correct solution to the problems of life."[35] A Catholic university likewise participates in the Church's mission of social justice to contribute to the development of society and the development of emerging nations.[36] To assist with achieving these goals, a Catholic university should foster cooperation among the various academic disciplines within the university as well as with various local, national, and international private and public associations and entities.[37]

In connection with the many contributions that Catholic universities make to society, "they have the full right to expect that civil society and public authorities will recognize and defend their institutional autonomy and academic freedom; moreover, they have the right to the financial support that is necessary for their continued existence and development."[38] Pastoral ministry at a Catholic university combines the members of the university community with the opportunity to integrate their faith into their daily lives. Pastoral ministry ought to influence all aspects of the life of a Catholic university, with numerous opportunities throughout the day for prayer and reflection. "Catholic members of this community will be offered opportunities to assimilate

33. *EcE*, 32, emphasis original.

34. *EcE*, 32.

35. *EcE*, 33.

36. *EcE*, 34.

37. *EcE*, 35, 37.

38. *EcE*, 37.

Catholic teaching and practice into their lives and will be encouraged to participate in the celebration of the sacraments, especially the Eucharist as the most perfect act of community worship."[39]

Pastoral ministers help members of the Catholic university community to become more aware of the struggles of the poor and those that society has forgotten. They prepare students for active participation in the Church, as well as for their chosen vocation, whether it is to be married or to remain single, to be ordained or to be consecrated as a religious. Spiritual associations are developed for students to assist pastoral ministers with these endeavors.[40]

A Catholic university provides a setting for dialogue between the Gospel and the culture in which the university is located. "Through this dialogue a Catholic University assists the Church, enabling it to come to a better knowledge of diverse cultures, discern their positive and negative aspects, to receive their authentically human contributions and to develop means by which it can make the faith better understood by men and women of a particular culture."[41] It is important for the Catholic university to engage the culture so as to promote the dignity of the human person and a sense of being responsible to that which transcends all other things. Connected with this respect for the human person is the dignity of the family as the basis for all human cultures.[42]

Of importance in this area is how Christian thought engages the natural and human sciences at a Catholic university, especially as these sciences address philosophical and ethical questions that in our times can be complex. "This task requires persons particularly well versed in the individual disciplines and who are at the same time adequately prepared theologically, and who are capable of confronting epistemolog-

39. *EcE*, 39; Monika Hellwig, "What Makes Our Colleges Catholic?," in *Mission and Identity: A Handbook for Trustees of Catholic Colleges and Universities*, ed. Association of Governing Boards of Universities and Colleges, Association of Catholic Colleges and Universities, and Association of Jesuit Colleges & Universities (Washington, DC: AGB Publications, 2004), 48. "Without sacramental worship on campus it will be very difficult to maintain the Catholic character and the Christian inspiration of the whole. Certainly the students will not be afforded a solid experience of incorporation in the Catholic community and its worship without the Eucharist on campus as a central experience of their incipient adulthood."

40. *EcE*, 40–42.

41. *EcE*, 44.

42. *EcE*, 45.

ical questions at the level of the relationship between faith and reason."[43]

Lastly, the Catholic university's dialogue with culture can serve ecumenical and interreligious purposes as well. "It does so to further the search for unity among all Christians. In interreligious dialogue it will assist in discerning the spiritual values that are present in the different religions."[44] "Each Catholic university makes an important contribution to the Church's work of evangelization."[45] In all aspects of its educational mission, the Catholic university ought to engage in evangelization to assist the Church in her mission.

Part II: General and Transitional Norms

General Norms

Article 1: The Nature of These General Norms

The norms that are embodied in *Ex corde Ecclesiae* are intended to develop further the provisions of the code of canon law and may be amended at the discretion of the Holy See. Contrary to arguments that had been raised about canons dealing with Catholic universities when the revised code was promulgated, the norms of *Ex corde Ecclesiae* "are valid for all Catholic Universities and other Catholic Institutes of Higher Studies throughout the world."[46]

The General Norms direct each episcopal conference to apply them concretely at the local and national levels in compliance with the code of canon law, the applicable law, and the governing documents of the various Catholic universities and other institutes of higher studies within the jurisdiction of the episcopal conference. Any ordinances that an episcopal conference may prepare to implement *Ex corde Ecclesiae* are to be reviewed by the Holy See before they become valid for all Catholic universities in a particular region. To the extent possible, the provisions of these General Norms are to be incorporated into the governing documents of all Catholic universities and other institutes of higher studies.[47]

43. *EcE*, 46.
44. *EcE*, 47.
45. *EcE*, 48.
46. *EcE*, art. 1, §1.
47. *EcE*, art. 1, §§2–3.

Article 2: The Nature of a Catholic University

A Catholic university is simultaneously a university and Catholic. As a university, it "is a community of scholars representing various branches of human knowledge. It is dedicated to research, to teaching and to various kinds of service in accordance with its cultural mission."[48] As Catholic, the university "informs and carries out its research, teaching, and all other activities with Catholic ideals, principles and attitudes. It is linked with the Church either by a formal, constitutive and statutory bond or by reason of an institutional commitment made by those responsible for it."[49]

The Catholic university's Catholic identity is a significant aspect of its composition. Thus the Catholic university is to declare its Catholic identity in its mission statement or other similar public governing document and to guarantee the expression of its Catholic identity.[50] This Catholic identity should pervade all its teaching, research, and other activities through which the university seeks to pursue its mission. Additionally, "freedom in research and teaching is recognized and respected according to the principles and methods of each individual discipline, so long as the rights of the individual and of the community are preserved within the confines of the truth and the common good."[51]

Article 3: The Establishment of a Catholic University

A Catholic university may be established by various groups or individuals. For example, the Holy See, an episcopal conference, or a diocesan bishop can establish a Catholic university.[52] Additionally, a religious institute or other public juridic person can establish a Catholic university, provided that the diocesan bishop gives his consent thereto.[53] In these instances, the statutes of the newly established Catholic university must be approved by the competent ecclesiastical authority.[54] Other ecclesias-

48. *EcE*, art. 2, §1.
49. *EcE*, art. 2, §2.
50. *EcE*, art. 2, §3.
51. *EcE*, art. 2, §5.
52. *EcE*, art. 3, §1.
53. *EcE*, art. 3, §2.
54. *EcE*, art. 3, §4.

tical or laypersons may also establish a Catholic university. In such cases, however, the consent of the competent ecclesiastical authority is required before the university may identify itself as a Catholic university.[55]

Article 4: The University Community

The university community bears the primary responsibility for promoting the Catholic identity of the university. Responsible persons include university authorities, such as the chancellor and the board of trustees or an equivalent governing body. Nevertheless, this responsibility is shared with other members of the university community. "It is shared in varying degrees by all members of the university community; and therefore calls for the recruitment of adequate university personnel, especially teachers and administrators, who are both willing and able to promote that identity."[56] Of particular importance in this regard is the quality of those who teach at the university and their respect for Catholic doctrine, which the competent ecclesiastical authority observes in compliance with canon law.[57]

Because the Catholic identity of the institution is of such significance, all teachers and administrators are to be informed about the university's Catholic identity at the time of their appointment. They should also be advised of the implications of the university's Catholic identity for their teaching, research, and administrative responsibilities.[58]

Article 4, Section 3 of the General Norms reiterates the need for all Catholic teachers to be faithful to Catholic doctrine and for teachers of the theological disciplines to have a mandate to teach from the competent ecclesiastical authority:

> In ways appropriate to the different academic disciplines, all Catholic teachers are to be faithful to, and all other teachers are to respect, Catholic doctrine and morals in their research and teaching. In particular, Catholic theologians, aware that they fulfill a mandate received from the Church, are to be faithful to the Magisterium of the Church as the authentic interpreter of Sacred Scripture and Sacred Tradition.[59]

55. *EcE*, art. 3, §3.
56. *EcE*, art. 4, §1.
57. *EcE*, art. 4, §1.
58. *EcE*, art. 4, §2.
59. *EcE*, art. 4, §3.

Students, teachers, and other members of the administration of a Catholic university who are not Catholic must respect the Catholic identity of the university. Additionally, the General Norms require that a majority of teachers be Catholic and that any non-Catholic teachers within the institution should not be allowed to constitute a majority.[60]

Formation in the Church's social teachings and ethical decision making is to be provided as a component of the academic and professional development of the students of a Catholic university. Additionally, classes in Catholic doctrine must be made available in the curriculum for all students.[61]

Article 5: The Catholic University within the Church

A Catholic university participates in both the local and the universal Church. As a result, a Catholic university must remain in communion with the Church and with the bishops of the region in which the Catholic university is located. In appropriate ways, the Catholic university also contributes to the work of the Church with regard to evangelization.[62]

The diocesan bishop has the responsibility to oversee a Catholic university located within his diocese and to take appropriate action when necessary.[63] The Catholic university assists in this function by periodically reporting to the competent ecclesiastical authority regarding its activities along with other relevant information.[64]

Article 6: Pastoral Ministry

Pastoral care is to be provided for all members of the Catholic university community.[65] To assist with carrying out this obligation, "a sufficient number of qualified people—priests, religious and lay persons—are to be appointed to provide pastoral ministry for the university community, carried on in harmony and cooperation with the pastoral activities of the local Church under the guidance or with the approval

60. *EcE*, art. 4, §4.
61. *EcE*, art. 4, §5.
62. *EcE*, art. 5, §1.
63. *EcE*, art. 5, §2.
64. *EcE*, art. 5, §3.
65. *EcE*, art. 6, §1.

of the diocesan Bishop."[66] But these are not the only persons who are to engage in pastoral ministry, as "all members of the university community are to be invited to assist the work of pastoral ministry and to collaborate in its activities."[67]

Article 7: Cooperation

The General Norms also call for cooperation at various levels to promote research and teaching among Catholic universities and ecclesiastical universities and faculties. Cooperation should also occur with other educational institutions, both public and private.[68] If consistent with the teachings of the Catholic Church, Catholic universities may also participate in government programs to promote justice and the development of the human person.[69]

Transitional Norms

The Transitional Norms indicate that the provisions of *Ex corde Ecclesiae* would be effective for each Catholic university on the first day of their 1991 academic year.[70] Additionally, the enforcement of *Ex corde Ecclesiae* was entrusted to the Congregation for Catholic Education, which was also responsible for developing directives to assist with its implementation.[71] The Congregation for Catholic Education received competence to suggest changes to *Ex corde Ecclesiae* in the event that it was appropriate to do so.[72] *Ex corde Ecclesiae* abolished any prior particular laws or customs that were currently in effect at the time that the apostolic constitution was promulgated. Any privileges contrary to the provisions of *Ex corde Ecclesiae* were also abolished.[73]

66. *EcE*, art. 6, §2.
67. *EcE*, art. 6, §2.
68. *EcE*, art. 7, §1.
69. *EcE*, art. 7, §2.
70. *EcE*, art. 8.
71. *EcE*, art. 9.
72. *EcE*, art. 10.
73. *EcE*, art. 11.

The Drafting Process

The drafting process for *Ex corde Ecclesiae* was particularly extensive, with significant input in and opposition to its promulgation by theologians and representatives of Catholic universities. In her book that embodies documents pertinent to Catholic higher education from 1967 to 1990, editor Alice Gallin, OSU, gives a succinct historical time line of the various drafts that led to the promulgation of *Ex corde Ecclesiae*.[74] Gallin reported that, as early as 1980, the Congregation for Catholic Education began to work on a document that would regulate Catholic colleges and universities in a manner similar to how *Sapientia Christiana* addressed ecclesiastical universities and faculties.[75] Suggesting the need for further explanation of Canons 807 to 814 of the revised code of canon law, Gallin submitted that "the first draft circulated for consultation was that done in the same year, 1983; it went only to certain 'periti' for their review. Following some revision in the text, a draft was then circulated to all bishops and university presidents in 1985; this draft became known as the 'Schema.'"[76]

Gallin reported that the Association of Catholic Colleges and Universities gathered the comments that the Catholic university presidents had made to the 1985 Schema, and in consultation with the United States Catholic Conference submitted them to the Congregation for Catholic Education in February 1986. In 1988, the congregation shared with all participants another draft of the document[77] and invited further consideration in anticipation of an April 1989 meeting in Rome to discuss the revised document. "Ninety rectors or presidents of universities and forty bishops chosen by their national conferences met in Rome

74. Alice Gallin, "Point and Counterpoint: *Ex Corde Ecclesiae* 1985–1990," in *American Catholic Higher Education*, 189–90.

75. Ibid., 189. Cf. Francis Joseph Hoffman, *The Apostolic Constitution Ex corde Ecclesiae and Catholic Universities in the United States of America*, Canon Law Studies 567/95 (Rome: Pontificium Athenaeum Sanctae Crucis, 1996), 103: "For the purpose of this study the document has its origins in March of 1981, when a plenary meeting of the Sacred Congregation for Catholic Education reviewed a first, rudimentary draft of it."

76. Gallin, *American Catholic Higher Education*, 189. See "Draft Schema of a Pontifical Document on Catholic Universities (April 1985)," in ibid., 191–214. See also Hoffman, *Apostolic Constitution*, 106.

77. "Revised Draft Schema for a Pontifical Document of Catholic Higher Education (November 8, 1988)," in Gallin, *American Catholic Higher Education*, 323–80.

for eight days of discussion and debate … In addition to the delegates, about forty persons were there as periti or guests of the Congregation."[78] From this group, fifteen persons were selected to return to Rome in September 1989 to consider comments that might be submitted in response to a further revised draft of the document that resulted from the April 1989 meeting.[79] Thereafter, Pope John Paul II promulgated the apostolic constitution *Ex corde Ecclesiae* on August 15, 1990.

Despite the objections that had been raised to the implementation of *Ex corde Ecclesiae* since its promulgation, Gallin offered words of praise for the consultation process that occurred during the drafting of the document.

> *This extensive process was in itself a source of confidence in the outcome … When the final apostolic constitution, Ex Corde Ecclesiae, was issued in September 1990, such confidence was rewarded. Apart from the norms (already in the Code of 1983), there was little to cause anxiety and much to enable and inspire those in higher education.* The implementation of the "norms" was handed to the national conferences of bishops. Thus, it will be many years before the process will be completed.[80]

Accordingly, because of the significance of the consultation process, it is appropriate to offer a brief review of each of the draft documents leading to the promulgation of *Ex corde Ecclesiae.*

The April 1985 Proposed Schema

The April 1985 Proposed Schema of the document on Catholic colleges and universities was somewhat unique in that it offered a preliminary description of the early components of the consultation process and an explanation of the format for the document.[81] The document itself consisted of two major sections, the Proemium and the Norms.

78. Gallin, "Point and Counterpoint," 190.

79. "Revised Draft Schema for a Pontifical Document on Catholic Higher Education (July 1989)," in Gallin, *American Catholic Higher Education*, 395–412.

80. Gallin, "Point and Counterpoint," 190, emphasis added. See also Hoffman, *Apostolic Constitution*, 107.

81. Congregation for Catholic Education (CCE), "Proposed Schema for a Pontifical Document on Catholic Universities," *Origins* 15, no. 43 (April 10, 1986): 706–11. See also CCE, "Draft Schema of a Pontifical Document on Catholic Universities (April 1985)," in Gallin, *American Catholic Higher Education*, 191–93.

Proemium of the 1985 Schema

The Proemium consisted of fifty-one paragraphs that described Catholic colleges and universities from both historical and theological perspectives. The major subdivisions of the Proemium were: I, Reasons for a Pontifical Document; II, Church and University; III, Actual Situation of the Catholic Universities; IV, Nature of the Catholic University; V, The Ecclesial Function of the Catholic University; VI, Role of the Catholic University in Society; and VII, Opportuneness of Some Fundamental Norms for Catholic Universities.

The Proemium also included several significant themes that would continue to be recognized through the promulgation of *Ex corde Ecclesiae*: the importance of a Catholic education in our time and culture;[82] the Church's right to establish Catholic universities;[83] a description of the nature of a Catholic university;[84] the duty of the members of the Catholic community to promote and protect the Catholic identity of the university;[85] the Catholic university's role in preparing people to live out their Catholic faith in society;[86] and the Catholic university as a place to study the interaction between faith and science[87] and faith and culture.[88]

Norms of the 1985 Schema

From a more canonical perspective, the Norms of the 1985 Proposed Schema contained forty-nine articles that were divided into the following categories: Chapter I, "Nature and Objectives of the Catholic University"; Chapter II, "The Catholic University within the Church"; Chapter III, "Various Types of Catholic University"; Chapter IV, "The Academic Community"; Chapter V, "Catholic Orientation of the Curriculum"; Chapter VI, "University Pastoral Care"; Chapter VII, "Plan-

82. CCE, "Proposed Schema of a Pontifical Document," 1.

83. Ibid., "Proemium," 5. Hoffman, *Apostolic Constitution*, 110.

84. CCE, "Proposed Schema of a Pontifical Document," 12–16. Hoffman, *Apostolic Constitution*, 110–11.

85. CCE, "Proposed Schema of a Pontifical Document," 21.

86. Ibid., "Proemium," 25. Hoffman, *Apostolic Constitution*, 111–12.

87. CCE, "Proposed Schema of a Pontifical Document," 32–35.

88. Ibid., "Proemium," 36–38: "The Catholic university presents itself as a place particularly adapted and fully suited to contribute to this dialogue between culture and faith."

ning and Cooperation"; and Chapter VIII, "Other Ecclesial Activities in the University and Cultural Milieu." "Just as the canons in the 1983 Code, the Norms are a mixture of exhortations, descriptions, and prescriptions."[89]

Early formulations of the Norms embodied in *Ex corde Ecclesiae* were also present in the 1985 Draft Schema and included the following: the Church's right to establish and to govern Catholic universities;[90] the need for the consent of the competent ecclesiastical authority to identify a university as "Catholic";[91] the nature of the relationship between a Catholic university and the local ordinary and the episcopal conference;[92] the limits on academic freedom;[93] the need for a Catholic university to set forth its Catholic identity in its governing documents;[94] the need for a Catholic president of a Catholic university;[95] the qualifications for teachers at a Catholic university;[96] the need for non-Catholic teachers and students to respect the teachings of the Catholic Church;[97] the need for a faculty or chair of theology;[98] the mandate to teach the theological disciplines;[99] and pastoral care at a Catholic university.[100]

Response to the 1985 Schema

Hoffman noted that the 1985 Proposed Schema was received with great interest, and as a result the Congregation for Catholic Education extended the deadline for comments about the Schema to be submitted to the end of 1987.[101] The responses of the Catholic colleges and universities in the United States to the 1985 Schema were varied. According to Gallin, "most of those responding would find it more advantageous to the work of the Church in American Higher Education if this kind

89. Hoffman, *Apostolic Constitution*, 113.
90. CCE, "Proposed Schema of a Pontifical Document," art. 4.
91. Ibid., "Norms," art. 6.
92. Ibid., arts. 8–9.
93. Ibid., art. 10.
94. Ibid., art. 19.
95. Ibid., art. 25.
96. Ibid., art. 26.
97. Ibid., art. 27.
98. Ibid., art. 30.
99. Ibid., art. 31.
100. Ibid., arts. 33–37.
101. Hoffman, *Apostolic Constitution*, 115.

of juridical document were not issued at all."[102] Gallin further noted that "many do however express satisfaction at the objective of the document—that is, to give strong support to the ministry exercised by Catholic religious and laity in the field of Catholic higher education around the world."[103] It is in these responses, however, that the theme began to emerge that the situation of Catholic higher education in the United States is unique and cannot be adequately regulated in an ecclesiastical document.[104]

The reaction to the Proemium was fairly positive, primarily with suggestions on how to further elaborate on the theological principles embodied therein. Gallin noted a specific objection to the Proemium's ecclesiology primarily displayed in the use of the terms "church" and "Church." It was also suggested that "the whole of the Proemium needs to be rewritten in such a way that the 'universality' of the institution referred to as 'a Catholic university' is tempered by recognition of the remarkable diversity among the institutions and the cultures in which they exist."[105] Objections were also raised about the specific mention of non-Catholic teachers and students and their respective roles in a Catholic university.[106]

As was the case throughout the drafting process, the Norms of the document received little positive critique. They were described as "simply unenforceable,"[107] "highly unsatisfactory,"[108] and "self-contradictory."[109] Gallin argued that "the real crux of the document is perceived by many

102. Alice Gallin, "Synthesis of Responses from 110 Catholic Colleges and University Presidents on Proposed Schema for a Pontifical Document on Catholic Universities," *Origins* 15, no. 43 (April 10, 1986): 697–704, reprinted in *American Catholic Higher Education*, 259–65.

103. Gallin, "Synthesis of Responses," 701.

104. Ibid.

105. Ibid., 702.

106. Ibid. See, e.g., "The criterion for accepting them into faculties should be their commitment to the goals of the university, not their personal membership in a church. We are strengthened in our faith through their presence, and we hope they are equally assisted by ours."

107. Ibid. "Article 9 is simply unenforceable; how does the bishop now see that the individuals in his diocese 'observe the principles of Catholic doctrine?'"

108. Ibid., 703. "The attempt to identify different types or categories of Catholic universities (*Norms*, Chapter III) proves to be highly unsatisfactory."

109. Ibid. "*Norms*, Chapter IV, Article 26 is, of course, self-contradictory."

to be the assertion of a power on the part of the bishop to control theologians (*Norms*, Chapter IV, Article 31) and to assure 'orthodoxy' in their teaching."[110] The Norm to which Gallin pointed here was the mandate to teach the theological disciplines embodied in Article 31 of the 1985 Schema. Yet the specific critique later asserted about Article 31 recognized that this requirement was already embodied in Canon 812 of the code of canon law. "To repeat it here by itself could give rise to a false understanding. One must read a particular canon within the context of the whole code, its history, and its nature as canon law—a very different concept from American civil/constitutional law."[111]

Although the "Synthesis of Responses Received from U.S. Catholic College and University Presidents to the Pontifical Document on Catholic Universities" provided significant detail about the various concerns raised to the 1985 Draft Schema, responses were also submitted by numerous other associations and bodies throughout the world. For example, the Board of Trustees for the Association of Catholic Colleges and Universities submitted its own response,[112] as did the presidents of fourteen leading Catholic universities in North America.[113] Although Gallin summarized well the arguments of the Association of Catholic Colleges and Universities and its member universities, it is not clear whether she included the observations of the Fellowship of Catholic Scholars[114] in her comments.

In a March 15, 1986, statement at the Catholic University of America, Monsignor George Kelly, then president of the Fellowship of Catholic Scholars, summarized the reaction of the association to the 1985 Draft Schema. Although Kelly did not offer comments directed to specific portions of the 1985 Draft Schema, he did endorse the document and encouraged the Congregation for Catholic Education to move forward

110. Ibid.

111. Ibid.

112. "Response of the Board of Directors of the Association of Catholic Colleges and Universities on 'Proposed Schema for a Pontifical Document on Catholic Universities,'" in Gallin, *American Catholic Higher Education*, 273–78.

113. "Statement of Presidents of Leading Catholic Universities of North America on the Schema for a Proposed Document on the Catholic University," in Gallin, *American Catholic Higher Education*, 279–83.

114. See George Kelly, "Vatican's Proposed Higher Education Schema Supported," *Origins* 15, no. 43 (April 10, 1986): 704–5.

with the promulgation of a document that would govern Catholic universities. "The Fellowship of Catholic Scholars feels privileged to join those parents, colleges and scholarly committees such as those of the American Catholic Philosophical Association in encouraging the Congregation for Catholic Education in Rome to proceed apace with their initiative."[115] Kelly also summarized the need for such a document.

> It is inconceivable that a school at any stage of education can call itself Catholic without simultaneously relating itself to the magisterium of the church. In the last analysis, magisterium is the only guarantor of Catholicity for a parish, a religious order or a university. If colleges advertise themselves as Catholic and parents subsidize these institutions on this basis, there must be a guarantee of Catholicity beyond the good intentions of the college administrators.[116]

Hoffman maintained that "the response written by the President of the Fellowship of Catholic Scholars (FCS) provided an optimistic, positive, and considerably shorter assessment of the *Proposed Schema*. The FCS viewed the *Proposed Schema* as an effort to bring the light of Magisterium back into the Catholic university."[117]

Kelly objected to what he perceived as a gradual movement of Catholic universities toward a secular model. He challenged the arguments that the university's Catholic identity ought to be abandoned in favor of possibly obtaining additional government funding and eliminating any perceived limitation of academic freedom because of the religious affiliation.[118] Hoffman further challenged certain commonly advanced objections.[119]

The Congregation for Catholic Education summarized the responses to the 1985 Draft Schema that had been received from throughout the world.[120] An overview of the responses noted,

115. Ibid., 704.

116. Ibid.

117. Hoffman, *Apostolic Constitution*, 121.

118. Kelly, "Vatican's Proposed Higher Education Schema Supported," 705.

119. Hoffman, *Apostolic Constitution*, 123–34.

120. CCE, "Summary of Responses to Proposed Schema for a Pontifical Document on Catholic Universities," *Origins* 17, no. 41 (March 24, 1988): 693–705.

As a general norm (but with important exceptions), larger and more complex institutions are more critical of the draft, while smaller institutions are more accepting. As a general tendency (again with important exceptions), institutions in Asia (except The Philippines), North America, Northern Europe (Belgium, France, Germany, Great Britain, Holland, Switzerland), and some countries in Latin America, are more accepting. A response from an institution that is not canonically established is, in most cases, more critical than a response from an institution that has been so established—especially when the latter assumes that *all* Catholic universities are canonically established, or that the draft only applies to such universities.[121]

Comments of general concern about the 1985 Proposed Schema addressed the following areas: a lack of understanding of the nature of the individual university; the need for a governing document that is different, just as Catholic universities are different from ecclesiastical universities; the importance of academic freedom and tenure as aids to critical thinking; the involvement of civil authorities in governing universities; the limited understanding of the university's role in transmitting secular knowledge; and the need to more clearly define the role of a Catholic university as Catholic.[122]

The themes presented in the Proemium apparently were universally accepted, although suggestions for improvement were provided as well.[123] Nevertheless, "the Norms, in general, receive more criticism—both from those who want them strengthened and from those who ask that they be drastically revised and perhaps reduced to a few basic principles."[124] Specific suggestions for changing the Norms included the following: to distinguish between Catholic universities that are influenced by the Church rather than controlled by the Church, to recognize that the civil requirements in different nations may make illegal certain provisions, to distinguish between exhortations and regulations, to place into context provisions of canon law included in the document, and to identify the specific competent ecclesiastical authority for affected norms.[125] Having considered the numerous and various responses, the

121. Ibid., 697.
122. Ibid., 697–99.
123. Ibid., 701–2.
124. Ibid., 702.
125. Ibid., 702–3.

congregation prepared and distributed for review a November 8, 1988, "Revised Draft Schema for a Pontifical Document on Catholic Higher Education."[126]

The November 8, 1988, Revised Draft Schema

Preceded by an introduction containing seven articles, the 1988 Revised Draft Schema was divided into two parts. The first was titled "The Identity and Mission of Catholic Higher Education," and the second was titled "Norms for Catholic Universities and Other Catholic Institutions of Higher Education."[127]

Hoffman maintained that the 1988 Revised Draft Schema was significantly different from the previous draft.

> First, it is a more finished and refined document and is longer. The expository part is further nuanced and offers a positive vision of the role and potential of the Catholic university in contemporary society. Second, the Norms draw more heavily upon the Code of Canon Law and go beyond those canons specifically treating Catholic universities. The Norms appear to be more flexible because they incorporate language and phrasing which would allow them to be applied, perhaps, in a greater variety of circumstances. Many of the prescriptive norms and norms offering definitions are presented with various possible alternatives.[128]

Next, we turn to a closer examination of the 1988 Revised Draft Schema.

The 1988 Schema

The Identity and Mission of Catholic Higher Education

This first part of the 1988 Revised Draft Schema was subdivided into five specific sections plus a conclusion. Its eighty-two paragraphs addressed the following areas: the Development of Catholic Higher Education, Catholic Higher Education Today, the Nature of a Catholic Institution of Higher Education, the Catholic Institution of the Mission of the Church, and Pastoral Ministry.[129]

126. CCE, "A Draft Document on Catholic Higher Education," *Origins* 18, no. 28 (December 22, 1988): 445–64.

127. Ibid.

128. Hoffman, *Apostolic Constitution*, 137–38.

129. CCE, "Draft Document on Catholic Higher Education," Part I, arts. 8–85, 456–62,

Part I of the 1988 Revised Draft Schema included several significant themes that would continue to be recognized through the promulgation of *Ex corde Ecclesiae*, including: the basic human desire to know the truth;[130] the Church's role in the early establishment of universities;[131] the role of Catholic universities in providing education in the contemporary world;[132] the nature of a Catholic university;[133] the relationship between a Catholic university and society;[134] the Catholic university in service of the Church;[135] the role of theology at a Catholic university;[136] a Catholic university's role in evangelization;[137] the dialogue with culture;[138] the dialogue between faith and reason;[139] the promotion of religious and ethical principles;[140] the progress of peoples;[141] ecumenism and religious dialogue;[142] and pastoral ministry.[143]

Norms for Catholic Universities and Other Catholic Institutions of Higher Education

The second part of the 1988 Revised Draft Schema embodied the document's Norms and was subdivided into seven chapters. Its seventy-two articles were contained within these chapters: "Nature and Objectives," "Various Types of Catholic Institutions of Higher Education," "Catholic University within the Church," "University Community," "University Activities," "Planning and Cooperation," and "Pastoral Ministry."

Early formulations of norms embodied in *Ex corde Ecclesiae* were also present in the 1988 Revised Draft Schema and included the follow-

---

reprinted in "Revised Draft Schema for a Pontifical Document of Catholic Higher Education (November 8, 1988)," in Gallin, *American Catholic Higher Education*, 325–51.

130. CCE, "Draft Document on Catholic Higher Education," Part I, art. 8.

131. Ibid., Part I, arts. 10–12.

132. Ibid., Part I, arts. 16–24.

133. Ibid., Part I, arts. 25–35. See, e.g., Part I, art. 25.

134. Ibid., Part I, arts. 36–37. See, e.g., Part I, art. 36.

135. Ibid., Part I, arts. 38–44. See, e.g., Part I, art. 38.

136. Ibid., Part I, arts. 45–50. See, e.g., Part I, art. 46.

137. Ibid., Part I, arts. 51–52. See, e.g., Part I, art. 52.

138. Ibid., Part I, arts. 53–57. See, e.g., Part I, art. 53.

139. Ibid., Part I, arts. 58–61. See, e.g., Part I, art. 60.

140. Ibid., Part I, arts. 62–63. See, e.g., Part I, art. 62.

141. Ibid., Part I, arts. 64–67. See, e.g., Part I, art. 64.

142. Ibid., Part I, arts. 69–71. See, e.g., Part I, art. 69.

143. Ibid., Part I, arts. 72–85. See, e.g., Part I, art. 82.

ing: the need for a Catholic university to describe its Catholic identity in its governing documents;[144] the Church's right to establish and maintain Catholic universities;[145] the need to comply with civil requirements;[146] the need for permission to use the term "Catholic" in its title;[147] the relationship with the local Church;[148] the joint mission of the university community to promote Catholic identity;[149] the need to inform teachers of the university's Catholic identity at the time of hiring;[150] the need for teachers to be outstanding in integrity and pedagogical skills;[151] the need for a mandate to teach the theological disciplines;[152] the need for a theology faculty;[153] the need for cooperation among Catholic universities;[154] and the need for pastoral care for the university community.[155]

Recommendations from the Delegates of the 1989 Meeting

In April 1989, select Catholic university presidents, bishops, and experts met in Rome to address the 1988 Revised Draft Schema. They submitted recommendations to the Congregation for Catholic Education for consideration in drafting a further revised pontifical document on Catholic higher education.[156]

Recommendations about the nature of the 1988 Revised Draft Schema were similar to comments submitted previously. Again, it was suggested that the emphasis of a document on Catholic universities should be placed on positively encouraging Catholic universities in their mission rather than establishing norms to govern their operation.

144. Ibid., Part II, art. 7.

145. Ibid., Part II, art. 8.

146. Ibid., Part II, art. 9.

147. Ibid., Part II, art. 10.

148. Ibid., Part II, art. 25.

149. Ibid., Part II, art. 30.

150. Ibid., Part II, art. 38.

151. Ibid., Part II, art. 40.

152. Ibid., Part II, art. 41.

153. Ibid., Part II, art. 50.

154. Ibid., Part II, arts. 55–63. See, e.g., Part II, art. 59.

155. Ibid., Part II, arts. 64–72. See, e.g., art. 65.

156. Catholic Higher Education Congress, "Ten Recommendations," *Origins* 19, no. 01 (May 18, 1989): 16. For a discussion of how the 1988 draft was considered at the Catholic Higher Education Congress and the Ten Recommendations were prepared, see Hoffman, *Apostolic Constitution*, 144–47.

The document on the Catholic university should be positive, inspirational, and future-oriented. It should serve to encourage university people in the important mission of the Catholic university for the world and for the Church. It should be written according to academic standards and maintain a world perspective, sensitive to the richly diverse cultures that are the Catholic university's milieu. Whatever normative principles are included in the document should be few in numbers, general in nature, and interpreted and applied in accord with principles to be developed by regional bishops' conferences, taking into account regional laws and institutional status.[157]

Rather than advocating a mutual responsibility for promoting a Catholic university's Catholic identity, it was recommended that the responsibility belongs mainly to the university. "The maintenance and strengthening of the Catholic identity of the university is primarily the responsibility of the university, a responsibility that calls for the attraction of faculty and staff who respect that identity and are both willing and able to promote it."[158] It was also recommended that the episcopal conferences should designate competent canon and civil lawyers to review and comment on the propriety of the document before its promulgation.[159] The committee agreed that bishops "should not be seen as external agents, but as participants in the life of the Catholic university."[160] Again, they recommended that canons from the revised code of canon law should not be repeated in the document's norms.[161] Additionally, while acknowledging that "Catholic theology that is taught should be faithful to the magisterium of the Church," it should also be open to research in the hope for a deeper comprehension of theology.[162]

Pope John Paul II also addressed the participants in the April 1989 conference and encouraged them in their endeavors both as members of the conference and in their involvement with Catholic universities.[163]

157. Catholic Higher Education Congress, "Ten Recommendations," n. 1.

158. Ibid., 5. See Hoffman, *Apostolic Constitution*, 145–46.

159. Catholic Higher Education Congress, "Ten Recommendations," 16, n. 6. See Hoffman, *Apostolic Constitution*, 146.

160. Catholic Higher Education Congress, "Ten Recommendations," 16, n. 7.

161. Ibid., 16, n. 8: "no repetition of such pertinent canons is necessary or appropriate in this document."

162. Ibid., 16, n. 9. See Hoffman, *Apostolic Constitution*, 146.

163. "Address, Pope John Paul II to International Meeting on Catholic Higher Education (Rome, April 25, 1989)," in Gallin, *American Catholic Higher Education*, 385–93.

The fruit of such a deeper understanding should be a new "harmony": a closer and more faithful collaboration between the episcopate, the religious families, the ecclesial offices and the faithful on the one hand, and the universities and other Catholic institutions on the other; this will ensure that each activity undertaken within the ambience of these universities is in harmony with the Catholic nature of the institution. You and your universities should be proud of the title "Catholic," as suggested in the eloquent words of Paul VI: "While equal to other universities in academic efforts and quality, and like them also in patterns and attainments, a Catholic university must not be afraid to be seen as different and original because of what can be called its baptism: this is a stimulus rather than a burden, which does not separate it from the world of culture, but rather enables it to enter this world with a more friendly and honest posture, not for vainglory but for the commitment of converting it."[164]

With the additional input from the April 1989 conference and upon further study, the congregation prepared an additional revised schema that would be discussed among select conference representatives at a subsequent meeting.

The July 1989 Revised Draft Schema

The Congregation for Catholic Education released a July 1989 Revised Draft Schema[165] for consultation purposes and input from the Catholic university community. Like the earlier drafts, it consisted of two major parts. Part I was dedicated to the "Identity and Mission of a Catholic University," while Part II embodied "*Normae Generales*."

The Identity and Mission of a Catholic University

Part I of the 1989 Revised Draft Schema consisted of four major divisions: the Identity of a Catholic University,[166] the Catholic University in Society,[167] the Catholic University in the Church,[168] and the Mission of the Catholic University.[169] Part I contained forty-six paragraphs that,

164. Ibid., 329, para. 10.

165. CCE, "Revised Draft Schema for a Pontifical Document on Catholic Higher Education (July 1989)," in Gallin, *American Catholic Higher Education*, 395–412.

166. Ibid., 396–400, paras. 3–21.

167. Ibid., Part I, arts. 22–28.

168. Ibid., Part I, arts. 29–36.

169. Ibid., Part I, arts. 37–46.

like earlier draft schemas, provided a theological background for the General Norms that followed.

Themes included within Part I of the 1989 Revised Draft Schema that would be carried through to the promulgation of *Ex corde Ecclesiae* included: the essential characteristics of a Catholic university;[170] the university as a place to promote the dialogue between faith and reason;[171] the importance of theology,[172] the university community,[173] and pastoral ministry[174] at a Catholic university; the interaction between a Catholic university and society;[175] a Catholic university's role in the Church;[176] a Catholic university as the place for dialogue between faith and culture;[177] and a Catholic university's role in evangelization.[178]

Normae Generales

The General Norms were divided into seven articles, each of which was subdivided into two to three sections: Article 1, "The Nature of a Catholic University"; Article 2, "The Establishment of a Catholic University"; Article 3, "The University Community"; Article 4, "University Activities"; Article 5, "Pastoral Ministry"; Article 6, "Cooperation"; and Article 7, "The Catholic University within the Church."

Ex corde Ecclesiae provisions that were also addressed in the General Norms included: the inclusion of a university's Catholic identity in its governing documents;[179] the establishment of a Catholic university;[180] the shared responsibility for promoting Catholic identity;[181] the need for non-Catholic university employees to respect Catholic Church teach-

170. Ibid., Part I, art. 4.

171. Ibid., Part I, art. 8.

172. Ibid., Part I, art. 9.

173. Ibid., Part I, arts. 11–15.

174. Ibid., Part I, arts. 17–21. See, e.g., Part I, art. 18.

175. Ibid., Part I, arts. 22–28. See, e.g., Part I, art. 22.

176. Ibid., Part I, arts. 29–36. See, e.g., Part I, art. 29.

177. Ibid., Part I, arts. 37–42. See, e.g., Part I, art. 37.

178. CCE, "Revised Draft Schema for a Pontifical Document on Catholic Higher Education (July 1989)," in Gallin, *American Catholic Higher Education*, 405–6, paras. 43–46.

179. CCE, "Revised Draft Schema for a Pontifical Document on Catholic Higher Education (July 1989) Part II: Normae Generales," in Gallin, *American Catholic Higher Education*, 406, art. 1, §2.

180. Ibid., Part II, art. 2, §1–2.

181. Ibid., Part II, art. 3, §1.

ing;[182] the need to inform new employees of the university's Catholic identity;[183] the need for theologians to be faithful to the Magisterium;[184] the need for pastoral ministry;[185] the need for cooperation among various universities;[186] and a Catholic university's ties to the local Church.[187] Conspicuously absent from the General Norms of the 1989 Revised Draft Schema were several key provisions that are also addressed in the code of canon law. For example, these General Norms did not address the need for a mandate from the competent ecclesiastical authority to teach the theological disciplines,[188] and the need for a Catholic university to have a department of theology or at least a chair of theology.[189] Perhaps the drafters of the 1989 Revised Draft Schema were persuaded by the arguments of the university presidents, bishops, and experts that it would not be necessary to reiterate within a pontifical document on Catholic universities provisions of the code of canon law without placing them in the larger context of the code.

In any event, the 1989 Revised Draft Schema was the final draft document on Catholic universities released for comment and review prior to the actual promulgation of *Ex corde Ecclesiae* in 1990.

182. Ibid., Part II, art. 3, §2.

183. Ibid., Part II, art. 3, §3.

184. Ibid., Part II, art. 4, §2.

185. Ibid., Part II, art. 5.

186. Ibid., Part II, art. 6.

187. Ibid., Part II, art. 7.

188. Cf. *Codex Iuris Canonici auctoritate Ioannis Pauli PP. II promulgatus* (Vatican City: Libreria Editrice Vaticana, 1983), c. 812. "Those who teach theological disciplines in any institutes of higher studies whatsoever must have a mandate from the competent ecclesiastical authority." English translation from *Code of Canon Law*, Latin-English ed., new English trans. [reprint] (Washington, DC: CLSA, 2012). All subsequent English translations of canons from this code are from this source unless otherwise indicated.

189. Cf. *CIC*, c. 811.

PART II

Academic and Cultural Questions

[2]

The Catholic University and the Idea of Academic Freedom

Peter F. Ryan, SJ

In 1994, Fr. Theodore Hesburgh edited a collection of essays by members of Notre Dame's faculty and administration titled *The Challenge and Promise of a Catholic University*. In the initial essay, Hesburgh proclaims, "A great Catholic university must begin by being a great university that is also Catholic."[1] He argues that if the Catholic Church wants to be a part of the university world in modern times, she must play by the rules that govern that world. "The best and only traditional authority in the university is intellectual competence: this," he affirms, "is the coin of the realm." He concludes that the university cannot be subject to any external authority, including the Magisterium.[2]

Fr. Richard McBrien expounds a similar position. He wholeheartedly subscribes to the view expressed in a 1976 position paper of the National Catholic Educational Association on academic freedom in Catholic colleges and universities:

This essay was previously published as "The Catholic University and the Idea of Academic Freedom," in *The Nature of Catholic Higher Education: Proceedings of the Eighteenth Convention of the Fellowship of Catholic Scholars*, ed. Anthony J. Mastroeni (Steubenville, OH: Franciscan University Press, 1996), 133–56.

1. Theodore M. Hesburgh, "The Challenge and Promise of a Catholic University," in *The Challenge and Promise of a Catholic University*, ed. Theodore M. Hesburgh (South Bend, IN: University of Notre Dame Press, 1994), 5.

2. Ibid.

Freedom from outside constraints is the very breath of life for a college and university. An authentic Catholic institution of higher learning must be free to be Catholic. If the integrity and freedom of the academy is attacked, undermined by "an academic law of the Church," the Church will be the first to suffer. Its enemies will contend derisively that truth cannot be upheld and defended without resort to penalties and outside sanctions, confirming for some the suspicion that Catholic institutions cannot be true universities.[3]

Fr. Richard McCormick deplores the idea of understanding the Catholicity of a Catholic university "in terms of a rigid, narrowly defined orthodoxy," which he sees as a threat to academic freedom.[4] As an example of such an unenlightened outlook, he cites *Veritatis Splendor* 116:

It falls to them [bishops], in communion with the Holy See, both to grant the title *Catholic* to church-related schools, universities, health-care facilities and counseling services, and, in cases of serious failure to live up to that title, to take it away.[5]

Those who govern the overwhelming majority of the Catholic colleges and universities in this country share the view of academic freedom espoused by Frs. Hesburgh, McBrien, and McCormick. I critique two presuppositions that make it impossible for them to identify the features that distinguish a university precisely as Catholic: first, the assumption that the Magisterium should not be the final arbiter of what counts as Catholic in a university, and, second, the assumption that we should find the value of such specifically Catholic elements as sacraments mainly in their capacity to open our eyes to the goodness of the secular world, which is already "grounded in grace." I then argue that unless the connection of Catholic universities with the Magisterium is reestablished, they will inevitably become ever more secularized. Finally, I outline an approach to academic freedom capable of supporting the specifically Catholic mission of our institutions of higher education.

3. Richard P. McBrien, "What Is a Catholic University?," in Hesburgh, *Challenge and Promise of a Catholic University*, 161–62.

4. Richard A. McCormick, "What Is a Great Catholic University?," in Hesburgh, *Challenge and Promise of a Catholic University*, 165.

5. Ibid., 165–66, quoting John Paul II, *Veritatis Splendor* 116, August 6, 1993 (emphasis added).

The Problem of Identifying What Makes a University Catholic

The problem of determining what it means for a university to be Catholic cannot be resolved by arguing, as McBrien does, that Catholic identity, at least at Notre Dame, is obvious from the many symbols and expressions of Catholicism, most notably the many well-attended masses.[6] Although Catholic symbols, the mass itself, and an emphasis on social justice are essential, they are by no means sufficient to sustain a university's Catholic character. Ralph McInerny explains: "A university is chiefly concerned with the mind and imagination. If the faith has no influence on what goes on in the classrooms and laboratories, studios and stages, of the university, the university is not Catholic."[7]

Recognizing that more than externals are needed, McBrien spells out three essential requirements of a Catholic university, attributes that in and of themselves are hard to dispute. But he adds a caveat to each one that effectively contradicts the claim that it establishes Catholic specificity.

He first points out that the Catholic university "identifies itself with the Catholic tradition and with the wider Catholic community," but quickly adds that the whole Church, and not just the Magisterium, is charged with the task of interpreting that tradition.[8] He claims that only someone with a "faulty ecclesiology" would hold that it is the particular role of the Magisterium, rather than of the whole People of God, to determine what counts as Catholic.[9] McBrien is right to insist that the People of God are authorized to interpret the tradition, but he wrongly implies that they can carry out that function apart from the Magisterium. The People of God as such do not authentically interpret the tradition whenever a Catholic, a group of Catholics, or even a group of Catholic theologians claims that an interpretation is Catholic; they do so only when the Magisterium speaks on matters of faith and morals. An analogy will illuminate the point. The People of God celebrate

6. McBrien, "What Is a Catholic University?," 154–55.

7. Ralph McInerny, "The Advantages of a Catholic University," in Hesburgh, *Challenge and Promise of a Catholic University*, 182.

8. McBrien, "What Is a Catholic University?," 155–56.

9. Ibid., 159; see also 156.

mass. But they do not do so whenever a group of Catholics gather to share bread and wine, even if they use all the right words and believe that it is a true mass. The People of God celebrate mass only when a validly ordained priest acts as the principal celebrant.

The second characteristic of a Catholic university McBrien identifies is that it "intentionally embraces and attempts to live by Catholic values." But he makes it impossible to understand those values as specifically Catholic by insisting that they are, "at the same time, humane values that can be shared by non-Catholic Christians and by non-Christians alike."[10] More on this point later.

Finally, he argues that the "critical mass" of faculty and administrators needed to keep a university Catholic includes not only committed Catholics, but also "non-Catholics who respect the Catholic tradition and who support the university's intention to be and to remain faithful to that tradition."[11] Those who respect the tradition without placing themselves within it are thus numbered among the critical mass necessary for maintaining the university's identity as specifically Catholic. Without a doubt, certain key non-Catholic "fellow travelers" have done a great deal—in some cases, more than many of their Catholic colleagues—to preserve the Christian character of the universities in which they serve. We should be grateful to them. Yet McBrien insists that even such a broadly conceived critical mass need not constitute a simple majority. He thus implies that a minority that may include many non-Catholics is sufficient to preserve a university's specifically Catholic identity, even when faced with a majority that is hostile to the idea of maintaining it. That would be possible only if the identity at stake were based on a watered-down notion of Catholicism.

Hesburgh fares no better in his effort to identify the distinctive features of a Catholic university. Although he insists that philosophy and especially theology must be afforded a central place and be "in living dialogue" with the other areas of study,[12] he does not clarify what the university's specifically Catholic character means. On the one hand, he does not explain why philosophy, which in and of itself does not presuppose faith, should be central only to a Catholic university. On the

10. Ibid., 155–56.

11. Ibid., 156.

12. Hesburgh, "Challenge and Promise of a Catholic University," 6–7.

other hand, he never explains how promoting theology would necessarily have the effect of preserving Catholic identity. For theology can only function as a university's specifically Catholic integrating principle if it is specifically Catholic theology. And Hesburgh's account gives no basis for assuming that the theology promoted would necessarily be Catholic, for he effectively detaches university theology from the Magisterium by suggesting that the only standards for judging theology are internal to the academy and by seeing the Magisterium as external.

The Ecclesiological Problem with the Secular Concept of Academic Freedom

The first problematic presupposition of Catholics who adopt the secular concept of academic freedom, then, is ecclesiological: they assume that the Magisterium cannot be the final arbiter of a university's specifically Catholic identity because they hold that any appeal to an external authority compromises academic freedom.

The problem that view poses with respect to a university's Catholic character comes into sharp focus when one considers its implications for the discipline of theology. Again, the question arises as to how theology can serve as a university's Catholic integrating principle when it is divorced from the Magisterium. According to the Catholic understanding, the Magisterium is uniquely competent to propose articles of faith and to settle disputes about it. As Avery Dulles aptly put it, "The successors of Peter, and the bishops in communion with him, are individually and collectively the judges of doctrine."[13]

13. Avery Dulles, lecture to the Pre-Convention Seminar of the Catholic Theological Society of America, June 1995, in "Criteria of Catholic Theology," *Communio* 22 (Summer 1995): 312–13. Dulles adds that "Catholic theology will recognize the differing weight of different ecclesiastical pronouncements ... But even non-infallible teachings deserve to be received with respectful submission of mind." Recall, however, that many teachings widely assumed to be non-infallible because they are not the subject of *ex cathedra* pronouncements are actually taught infallibly by the ordinary Magisterium. The criteria for determining whether a teaching fits into that category are spelled out in *Lumen Gentium* 25. The encyclical *Evangelium Vitae* refers to that passage in notes attached to its declarations about the intrinsic evil of intentionally killing the innocent (no. 57) and of abortion (no. 62) and euthanasia (no. 65) as instances of such killing. The Vatican summary of the encyclical, *Origins* 24 (1995): 729, calls attention to that "significant reference" about

The doctrines on faith and morals promulgated by the teaching authority of the Church, then, serve as first principles for Catholic theology. Thus it is not only academic inquiry that has its own methods and a degree of autonomy, but also faith as well. As Germain Grisez puts it, "The truths of faith make an incontrovertible demand upon the mind of the believer, a demand no more open to denial than that made by facts of experience or evident logical truths."[14] Because authentically Catholic theology strives to deepen our understanding of faith and its practical requirements, it proceeds by definition from those truths.

Does that mean that Catholic theology is incompatible with the idea of academic freedom? Not at all, so long as academic freedom is properly conceived. *Ex corde Ecclesiae* describes it thus:

> "Academic freedom" is the guarantee given to those involved in teaching and research that, within their specific branch of knowledge, and according to the methods proper to that specific area, they may search for the truth wherever analysis and evidence leads [sic] them, and may teach and publish the results of this search, keeping in mind the cited criteria, that is, safeguarding the rights of the individual and of society within the confines of the truth and the common good.[15]

But accepting revelation as it comes to us from the Magisterium is the indispensable starting point of Catholic theological method. As the document puts it:

> Since theology seeks an understanding of revealed truth whose authentic interpretation is entrusted to the bishops of the church, ... it is intrinsic to the principles and methods of their research and teaching in their academic discipline that theologians respect the authority of the bishops, and assent to Catholic doctrine according to the degree of authority with which it is taught.[16]

---

the conditions under which the bishops together with the pope "proclaim infallibly the doctrine of Christ." For a theological explication and defense of that teaching, see Peter F. Ryan, SJ, and Germain Grisez, "Indissoluble Marriage: A Reply to Kenneth Himes and James Coriden," *Theological Studies* 72, no. 2 (2011): 369–415 at 410–12.

14. Germain Grisez, "American Catholic Higher Education: The Experience Evaluated," in *Why Should the Catholic University Survive?*, ed. George A. Kelly (New York: St. John's University Press, 1973), 53.

15. *EcE*, 13, n. 15.

16. *EcE*, 29.

To be sure, Catholic theology includes the creative role of reflecting on Scripture and tradition in order to suggest possible developments of doctrine. But those suggestions must be compatible with previously settled magisterial teachings. There is no reason to assume that creativity is impossible without radical theological dissent.[17]

The Anthropological Problem with the Secular Concept of Academic Freedom

The second problematic presupposition that makes it impossible for Catholics who adopt the secular concept of academic freedom to provide an adequate explanation of what makes a university Catholic has to do with their conception of the relation between nature and grace—the anthropological problem. The difficulty is evident, for example, in Richard McCormick's explanation of the sacramentality of the "Catholic vision" that should distinguish graduates of a great Catholic university. He quotes Michael and Kenneth Himes: "Sacraments are not intrusions into the secular world," but "points at which the depth of the secular is uncovered and revealed as grounded in grace."[18]

One need not view sacraments as somehow opposed to the natural order, or deny the goodness of creation, to find that explanation less than satisfactory. The world is indeed created and sustained by God, and his offer of grace is open to all. But human nature as we know it now is in a fallen condition, and not everyone accepts God's offer of grace. Ignoring those points, McCormick plays down what is specifically Catholic in the sacraments and emphasizes their capacity to help us appreciate the sacredness of the secular. Yet he provides no principle whereby one can distinguish the sacred dimension of the secular order from the sinful. His comment on the passage quoted makes the problem clear:

17. See Germain Grisez, *The Way of the Lord Jesus*, vol. 1, *Christian Moral Principles* (Chicago: Franciscan Herald Press, 1983), 901–2.

18. McCormick, "What Is a Great Catholic University?," 167, quoting Michael J. Himes and Kenneth R. Himes, OFM, *Fullness of Faith: The Public Significance of Theology* (Mahwah, NJ: Paulist Press, 1993), 82.

The "points" to which the brothers Himes refer are persons, places, things that allow us to experience all reality as grounded in God's gracious self-communication (grace). This sacramental vision is impoverished when "the mediation of God's grace is restricted to special rituals which are formally designated as 'sacraments.'" In the Catholic vision, all of reality is sacred, and the seven sacraments seek to "evoke awareness" of this sacredness and ultimacy.[19]

Another aspect of the anthropological problem with which we are concerned is suggested by McBrien's comment that the values that distinguish the Catholic university "are, at the same time, humane values that can be shared by non-Catholic Christians and by non-Christians alike."[20] Of course, one can hardly deny that Catholics can and should have many important values in common with all people of good will, especially with other Christians. But to reduce Catholic values to those that are shared not only with other Christians but also with anyone at all regardless of explicit faith is to suggest that the norm for determining Catholicity is to be found not in the Church but in the secular world. Like McCormick, McBrien seems to assume that the secular world is basically benign, and he too fails to furnish a principle whereby one can distinguish the extent to which the secular order is sacred rather than sinful. We are left with a sort of anonymous Catholicism, which is treated as the very norm of Catholicity, a state of affairs that precludes any possibility of explaining why the anonymous reality in question should be considered Catholic in the first place.

A further dimension of the problem is manifested in Hesburgh's description of what should characterize any great university, even apart from the question of Catholic identity. He writes in glowing terms of a place where

> the values of justice *and charity*, truth and beauty, are both taught and exemplified by the faculty, and where both faculty and students are seized by a deep compassion for human anguishes and are committed to proffer a helping hand, wherever possible, in every aspect of our material, intellectual, spiritual and cultural development.[21]

19. Ibid., 168. For an incisive critique of the Himes book, see Michael J. Baxter, "The Non-Catholic Character of the 'Public Church,'" *Modern Theology* 11, no. 2 (April 1995): 243–58.

20. McBrien, "What Is a Catholic University?," 155–56.

21. Hesburgh, "Challenge and Promise of a Catholic University," 6, emphasis added.

Certainly, any university should be concerned to improve the human condition in ways that pertain to the university's identity as a center of intellectual activity. But Hesburgh goes beyond that, implying that the theological virtue of charity characterizes the university as such, even apart from its specifically religious identity. Both his use of the term "charity" and his description of the activity in question suggest that he is importing Christian meaning into his understanding of even a secular university. Here, too, the secular order is regarded as sacred, as anonymously Christian. It is no wonder that difficulties arise when he attempts to isolate the distinctive features of a Catholic university.

A disinterested observer could not help but regard this baptizing of the secular world by Catholics as ironic. To appreciate that irony, one need only consider the actual character of that world and, more specifically, of American academic culture. In an essay in the Hesburgh volume that echoes themes from his *The Soul of the American University,*[22] George Marsden explains that

> there is a dominant American university culture that dictates the standards for all who want to be recognized as true universities. This dominant university culture, in turn, has distinctly Protestant origins.[23]

Indeed, writes Marsden, "American universities had distinctl anti-Catholic origins." That point becomes clear when one analyzes the characteristics that were supposed to distinguish these universities. They were set up to be nonsectarian and scientific. But Marsden explains that "nonsectarian … meant broadly Protestant," and dedicated to "democratic *moral ideas,*" while "scientific" meant freedom from what was perceived as "sectarian prejudice," the grossest expression of which was thought to be found in Catholicism with its structure of authority. The freedom of scientific inquiry was increasingly assumed to exclude theological commitments in principle.[24]

Some might claim that this shaking off of Christian specificity does not reflect an animus toward Christianity in general and Catholicism

22. George M. Marsden, *The Soul of the American University: From Protestant Establishment to Established Nonbelief* (New York: Oxford University Press, 1994).

23. George M. Marsden, "What Can Catholic Universities Learn from Protestant Examples?," in Hesburgh, *Challenge and Promise of a Catholic University,* 189.

24. Ibid., 189–90.

in particular, but only an honest concern to promote free scientific inquiry. Such an interpretation would be more plausible if American university culture were ideologically neutral. But that has never has been the case. For example, the truth of the opinion that it is possible to find "a scientific basis for shared moral ideals" was merely assumed, not demonstrated. That claim was first denied primarily by Catholics and is now rejected by postmodern critics. Reflection on such points should serve to remind us that universities do not exist in a vacuum, but within a culture characterized by its own specific and sometimes unwarranted presuppositions that are open to criticism even from secular sources.[25]

Grisez identifies some of the assumptions that characterize university culture. It tends, for example, to suppose that supernatural revelation is impossible, and therefore treats religion as a mere matter of opinion based on purely subjective values. It also bases knowledge about reality on the model of empirical scientific research. Thus knowledge is ever revisable, and one can never arrive at a conviction that is not open to refutation at some point in the future. (When theologians embrace that view, they conclude that infallible teaching is impossible.) University culture also tends to treat knowledge as salvific, for it sees man as one more subject of scientific investigation alongside others, and assumes that the increase and application of knowledge about his problems will ensure his perfection. Finally, social sciences tend to exclude freedom by presupposing a deterministic view of history.[26]

Those assumptions are obviously incompatible with Christianity in general and Catholicism in particular. Yet, although none has been corroborated, challenging them in any consistent and forceful manner could elicit the charge that one is blocking free inquiry by introducing matters of faith, which in turn could have the effect of reducing one's credibility in the academy. Concerns about violations of academic freedom tend not to be raised when someone is criticized or persecuted for objecting to the received assumptions of the academic community. They rather tend to arise when a university's specifically Christian or Catholic identity conflicts with those assumptions. That point becomes evident when one considers the phenomenon of political correctness. As McInerny puts it, "If there is anything that characterizes the con-

25. Ibid., 195–96.

26. Grisez, "American Catholic Higher Education," 47–48.

temporary secular university it is the thought police who roam about the campus seeking whom they might silence."[27]

A single example will suffice. McInerny remarks that "the charge of *homophobia* has almost silenced the commonly recognized (and authoritatively taught) truth that homosexuality is a perversion and a sin."[28] McInerny is of course referring to homosexual activity, and the problem he identifies is by no means limited to secular universities. I experienced it myself in a forum at a Catholic college, when an openly homosexual graduate was taking questions and comments from an overwhelmingly sympathetic audience after expounding on the joys and persecutions experienced by the active homosexual on campus. When I gently pointed out that homosexual activity is incompatible with Christian teaching and that living a chaste life, though difficult, is possible with grace and can serve as an opportunity for the homosexual person to grow in holiness, I was almost shouted down by angry members of the audience. Although I was finally allowed to continue, that reaction poisoned the atmosphere and may well have prevented others from making similar points. Such experiences, which unfortunately are not rare on Catholic campuses, illustrate a sad truth about the culture we have borrowed from the secular academy: certain ideas and classes of persons within the university enjoy a practical exemption from criticism, even when the price of maintaining that exemption is to compromise the integrity of the university's Catholic identity.

The Need to Reestablish the Practical Link between Catholic Universities and the Magisterium

Marsden's account of how the great nonsectarian Christian universities lost their religious character could serve as an object lesson for those in policy-making positions at Catholic institutions of higher learning. He points out:

> The shapers of American university culture excluded the more conservative parts of their own cultural heritage. Theology, which was considered divisive,

27. McInerny, "Advantages of a Catholic University," 184.
28. Ibid.

was removed as a reference point in other academic inquiry, so that religious viewpoints, such as there were, had strictly to do with morality.[29]

Without the underpinnings of faith and theology, however, moral unity cannot endure. It did not last any longer in those universities than in the surrounding culture. Lacking a basis in theology, a shared morality does not in any event unite people as Christians, but only culturally. As Marsden puts it, "Morality detached from theological reference … would soon make Christianity as such irrelevant."[30]

The very idea of a nonsectarian Christian university, at least in the sense just considered, is problematic, for it carries the seeds of the destruction of the university's religious identity. It implies a mixed agenda: while Christianity seems to be highly valued, the desire to avoid the consequences of institutional commitment to doctrine overrides any effectual effort to maintain the university's Christian character. Unless a university is willing to clarify the nature of its commitment to Christianity by articulating a clear principle by which it will stand and that will serve as a concrete link to the Christian religion, it will not be equipped to withstand the massive drift of society at large away from Christianity.

The only principle capable of sustaining the specifically Catholic identity of a university is commitment to the fullness of the Christian message as it is handed on through the teaching office of the Church. The broadly Protestant universities had no such principle and were therefore inherently subject to what Marsden calls the "gale-force winds" of secularization.[31] Catholic universities that jettison that principle cast aside their shield against those winds and abandon the heritage and perspective that enable them to engage the culture from a critical distance while making a unique contribution to it.

29. Marsden, "What Can Catholic Universities Learn from Protestant Examples?," 190.

30. Ibid., 190.

31. Ibid., 193.

Institutional Academic Freedom and Concern for Diversity

Some charge that it violates academic freedom to treat religious commitment and the ability to promote the university's specifically Catholic mission as factors that are no less important than academic competence in grounding judgments about hiring faculty and awarding tenure. But academic freedom applies not only to individuals within universities but also to universities themselves. Institutions as well as individuals have the right to define themselves. That is, the right of individuals to do so extends to their establishing institutions, whose character reflects their convictions.

When one considers the concern for the values of diversity and multiculturalism currently professed by virtually every major institution of higher education in this country, one sees that the current effort to promote those values is in some ways self-defeating. For, although individuals within institutions may come from diverse cultures, the cultures themselves are represented only in an extremely fragmented form. Marsden observes:

> As it is typically implemented in the dominant academic culture, multiculturalism amounts not to creating diversity among institutions but rather toward making them all look alike. Particular traditions of institutions, including religious traditions, are expected to give way to representing the variety of currently accepted viewpoints.[32]

He asks whether multiculturalism should not "include concern for the religious heritages that have been at the hearts of most cultures."[33] To deny that it should would reveal not only a bias against religion as such but also a lack of concern for authentic diversity. Thus, even from the standpoint of fostering diversity, Catholic universities would do well to hold fast to their specifically Catholic heritage.

32. Ibid., 192.
33. Ibid.

Academic Freedom within the University

The Catholic university combines the free pursuit of truth with an affiliation with the Catholic Church, which is committed to specific stands on key questions of truth. That raises questions about the autonomy of a Catholic university. Should not any university be free, as Hesburgh and others insist, from authorities that would place restrictions on its quest for knowledge?

Freedom is crucial for the proper functioning of any university, but freedom is always subject to various legitimate restrictions. From within the university, there are requirements of competence for receiving tenure; from without, there are restrictions imposed by accrediting associations to ensure that universities meet certain standards. Neither constitutes an illicit infringement of academic freedom. There is also the effective system of financial limitations placed on universities by the government and ultimately by the public at large on programs they find unacceptable. The legitimacy of this last sort of restriction is implicitly admitted by academics when they appeal to the larger community for funding based on the claim that they perform a public service.

True enough, freedom may sometimes be restricted unduly, but some restrictions on freedom are perfectly legitimate. Freedom, after all, is not an absolute but an instrumental value. The ultimate reason for the existence of a university is not simply *to be free* but rather *to search for and discover truth.* While freedom is generally an indispensable means to that end, sometimes restrictions on freedom can be conducive to it, as the above examples attest. Those restrictions on the freedom of the university tend to be widely accepted because, with the possible exception of the role of the community at large, they are generally recognized as intrinsic requirements of the search for truth.

What about restrictions imposed by Church authority based on the exigencies of Catholic doctrine? Objections to the legitimacy of that form of limitation tend to be based on the contention that such authority is external not only to the university in question but also to the academic project as such.

But is Church authority really external to the university? In one sense it clearly is, since the hierarchy is not a part of the university's formal organizational structure and does not administer it. Yet, in a more profound sense, that authority is internal to the university, inasmuch as those who establish a university as Catholic freely arrange for it to be such. If a university wants to proclaim itself Catholic, then it must measure up to certain objective criteria. Although those standards are not established by the university itself (since *it* does not determine what counts as Catholic), they are internalized by the university in the very intention of its founders to set it up as Catholic.

Is Church authority external to the academic project as such? For the unbeliever who assumes that truth can only be attained through human effort, it cannot help but seem external. As Grisez puts it, "Lacking faith, human reason and experience inevitably view the truths of faith as particular opinions on a controverted question."[34] Limitations based on Church authority therefore strike the unbeliever as arbitrary and inappropriate.

But here we are referring to the *committed* unbeliever. Those who do not believe, or do not fully believe yet have not accepted the antireligious credo of the dominant academic culture, will at least be in a position to realize that they cannot, like George Bernard Shaw, dismiss the Catholic university as a contradiction in terms. For they will acknowledge that neither the possibility of divine revelation in general nor the claims of Catholicism in particular has been disproved. They will therefore not assume that Church authority within the university is necessarily incompatible with the academic project as such.

As for the believer, Grisez explains,

> Faith opens up ... an entire realm of transcendent truth otherwise utterly inaccessible. At the same time faith generates its own critique of the myths that compete with it, myths that are actually projections of the human mind on reality, but which claim acceptance as philosophic critique or scientific truth.[35]

Far from viewing a university's religious commitment as a restriction on freedom, the believer is able to see that faith is not only compatible with the academic project, but also complements and stimulates it.

34. Grisez, "Academic Freedom and Catholic Faith," *NCEA Bulletin* (November 1967): 17, alluding to the 1915 statement of the Committee on Academic Freedom of the American Association of University Professors: "Genuine boldness and thoroughness of inquiry, and freedom of speech, are scarcely reconcilable with the prescribed inculcation of a particular opinion upon a controverted question."

35. Grisez, "American Catholic Higher Education," 52.

Academic Freedom and the Present Situation

It is painfully obvious that many members of Catholic university communities do not agree with the Catholic view of the purpose of life. Some do not believe in God or, if they do, have a completely different understanding of who God is. Some, perhaps many, do not believe that the human person is a unity of body and soul, and that he is called to share Christ's resurrection life and enjoy a fulfillment beyond what this life can offer.

Most students have probably done little thinking about such questions. They may have some religious training and even some faith commitment, but at the same time are likely to have formed their views largely according to the canons of modern secular culture. Although that culture is compatible with some aspects of a Judeo-Christian worldview, it is increasingly hostile to the claims of organized religions such as Catholicism to mediate divine revelation and to speak with authority on controversial questions of social and personal morality. Given that context, how can a Catholic institution of higher education function as a community?

It must be acknowledged at once that there are legitimate differences among members of the university community that should be respected. Indeed, insofar as differences reflect a commitment to truth and a search for meaning, they enrich that community. We need to learn from each other and realize that beneath our differences it is often possible to discover shared values. But the question arises as to what degree of pluralism is possible without surrendering or at least diluting what is specifically Catholic. What common ground can be found in such a situation?

Those who become members of *any* university community should at least agree that knowledge is a value worth pursuing for its own sake. Those who choose to be a part of a *Catholic* community of higher education should also agree on something more. They should share the conviction that it is likewise a value to determine whether there is an overall purpose to life, which, if discovered, should be shared with others as one collaborates in the task of relating the pursuit of knowledge and indeed all other values to that purpose.

That attitude can be required of every member of a Catholic college community. Such an approach respects the intellectual integrity of each individual and challenges him to engage in a mutual search for truth and meaning. It calls everyone to recognize that although knowledge is worth pursuing for its own sake, the search for truth is fully coherent only if it is informed by the hope of finding it and integrating it into the whole of life. The conviction that it is possible to attain truth, then, should not be rejected a priori as incompatible with the search for truth. It is instead the presupposition that truth cannot be found that renders the search futile and precludes the possibility of discerning any meaning in life.

Even if they do not share their university's Catholic faith commitment, members of the academic community should be prepared to understand that commitment not as being incompatible with an absolute openness to truth wherever the search for it may lead, but as expressing the institutional conviction that an open-minded search for truth has led precisely to that commitment. They should not expect that conviction to change but rather to be made manifest. To expect anything else would be to wish that those responsible for the orientation of the college not be true to their own convictions—which is at odds with even the most general respect for truth and value and conscience.

As *Ex corde Ecclesiae* makes clear, the Church recognizes the "academic freedom of scholars in each discipline in accordance with its own principles and proper methods … and within the confines of truth and the common good."[36] So, while academic freedom should prevail, it may not contradict either the principles of Catholic theology or the common good of a university grounded in the Catholic faith.

That understanding of academic freedom is not a restriction on reason, for it must be borne in mind that faith and reason do not conflict. Faith has nothing to fear from reason, nor reason from faith. Both are gifts of God that, in the manner proper to each, mediate truth.[37] Because truth is not self-contradictory, the university's mission to pursue truth through reason is in no way compromised by its commitment to the truths of faith. A contradiction is not even theoretically possible. Only from the perspective of unbelief do contradictions seem possible and even inevitable. But unbelief cannot be vindicated without showing that reason refutes truths of faith, which the person of faith claims cannot be shown.

36. *EcE*, 29.

37. For a rich treatment of these themes, see John Paul II, *Fides et ratio*, September 14, 1998.

This commitment to faith is no mere fideism, however, for the believer employs his reason to explain why claims that contradict faith do not really tell against it. And unless his arguments are refuted, the view that faith hampers reason cannot be sustained. In any case, far from viewing faith as a restriction on his freedom, the person of faith recognizes its value, both in helping him avoid intellectual blind alleys and in opening us new avenues of inquiry that otherwise would have been undiscovered.

As for those responsible for maintaining the university's Catholic character, it is crucial that they do more than preserve a merely juridical link with the Church. Although the approach to the present situation that I have proposed explains how a certain legitimate diversity can exist on the campus of a Catholic university, it does not explain how its Catholic character can be preserved. The need for a university to make its religious commitment concrete is evident from Marsden's observation that the religious identities of the great nonsectarian Christian universities were not lost because those who controlled those institutions directly chose to abandon their institutions' religious identities, but rather as a result of choices that promised to improve those institutions and even to enhance their Christian character by encouraging openness and tolerance. "Schools became more open, more inclusive, and less coercive," he tells us, "all in the name of the Christian spirit of the institutions."[38] He considers in particular the critical area of faculty hiring and points out that

> Once a church-related institution adopts the policy that it will hire simply "the best qualified candidates," it is simply a matter of time until its faculty will have an ideological profile essentially like that of the faculty at every other mainstream university.[39]

Those who adopted that policy in the now-secular universities apparently did not appreciate that inevitability. It is essential that administrators of Catholic universities recognize the danger and make concerted efforts to hire teachers whose lives reflect "an attained integration between faith and life, and between professional competence and Christian wisdom."[40] Otherwise, despite a technical, juridical connection with the Catholic Church, the secularizing of Catholic universities will proceed apace, and their capacity to make their unique contribution will be lost.

38. Marsden, "What Can Catholic Universities Learn from Protestant Examples?," 188.

39. Ibid., 193.

40. *EcE*, 22.

[3]

Academic Freedom and Revealed Truth

Applying the Spirit and Letter of *Ex corde Ecclesiae* to Catholic Universities in Contemporary America

Reinhard Hütter

It was a delight and honor for me to make a contribution to the Fidelity and Freedom Symposia, sponsored and published by the president of the Franciscan University of Steubenville, next to colleagues from the Catholic academy, from Catholic university administration, and from the Catholic Bishops' Conference. It is presumptuous to compare myself to the Apostle Paul, but in this collection of contributions from noted Catholic scholars and administrators, these words of St. Paul force themselves into my mind: "I am the least of the Apostles, unfit to be called an apostle" (1 Cor 15:9; RSV). After all, I have never been a student at a Catholic university; moreover, all my academic degrees come from Protestant university faculties in Germany and one Protestant university divinity school in the United States. And, finally, I only received the *mandatum* in September 2015—after having taught theology for twenty-five years. The occasion for coming under the *mandatum* was the invitation to serve as Paluch Chair of Theology on the pontifical faculty of the University of St. Mary of the Lake/Mundelein Seminary. Although a Catholic since 2004, I taught until the summer of 2016 at an ecumenically oriented but nevertheless Protestant divinity school located at a secular research university famous for a basketball team named after the fallen angels. Only since the fall semester of 2017 have I held a professorship of fundamental and dogmatic theology at the Catholic University of America's School of Theology and Religious Studies. But there are the happy memories of teaching theology for one year in the honors program at Providence College, founded and still run by the Dominican Order, not forgetting the semester in residence at the University of St. Mary of the Lake/Mundelein Seminary as well as a yearlong visiting professorship at the Catholic University of America. Also, in 2009, I was asked to make myself available as a candidate for the presidency of the only Catholic university in Germany. In the process leading up to being elected, I immersed myself deeply into the promise and problematic of Catholic universities in modern secular societies. In the end, it turned out that because of intercontinental system incompatibilities it was impossible for me to take the position. The intellectual preparation was not wasted, however; indeed, the experience continues to be deeply formative. Despite this smattering of experiences in Catholic institutions of higher learning, the following reflections are clearly not those of a longtime, seasoned participant, let alone partisan, in the debates antecedent to *Ex corde Ecclesiae* and those subsequent to it. Rather, what I have to say comes from being a sympathetic and engaged observer. As such, I deem it necessary to put *Ex corde Ecclesiae* into the context of American higher education and acknowledge that, with the exception of few of them, Catholic institutions of higher learning in the United States are uniquely caught between a rock and a hard place. This precarious predicament makes it difficult—and at the same time even more necessary—to receive *Ex corde Ecclesiae* in fullness and to implement it with boldness.

Putting *Ex corde Ecclesiae* into the Contemporary American Context: The Catholic College and Teaching University in America Today—Between a Rock and a Hard Place

Perhaps in earlier years the landscape was different, but it is now undeniable that higher education in the United States is organized along the lines of the free-market principles of supply and demand: certain highly developed, time-intensive, and costly products are offered, and indeed aggressively advertised, and in the end purchased by those desiring the "product."[1] One can fairly say that currently the education market in the United States is a buyers' market, with stiff competition between the various and arguably too numerous sellers. Simultaneously, with a slowing economy, a tough employment market, and skyrocketing tuition rates, many if not most students and parents are increasingly operating in an unsurprisingly pragmatic way: as educated consumers seeking the best product for the lowest price. In short, most of them will choose those colleges or universities that offer the least expensive training or education combined with the best placement record for their graduates in well-paying jobs. This is the great moment for community colleges, distant learning programs, and state college and university systems that specialize in offering affordable programs of training and certification in specific skills and competencies. For good reasons, these colleges can promise to deliver what many buyers seek—advanced training and certification that positions them well, after graduation, to land a job, ideally a well-paying job.

Only a relatively small and distinguished group of institutions of higher learning are minimally affected by this trend on the education market, which the cartographers of American higher education usually divide into three major sections. The institutions I have in mind are, first and foremost, the top-tier American research universities, those that, according to the Carnegie Classification of Institutions of Higher Learning in the United States, are designated RU/VH—doctorate-granting research universities with very high research activity. About seventy of the roughly one hundred universities of this category have endowments that in 2012 exceeded $1 billion, with Harvard leading the list with more than $30 billion. There are three Catholic research universities that, according to this conventional cartography, belong fully to this section: the University of Notre Dame, Georgetown University, and Boston College. In matters of endowment far off but in matters of academic substance and research potential much closer to this section are The Catholic University of America, Marquette University, Fordham University, and St. Louis University.

Next to these top-tier research universities there is another set of in-

1. For an informative account of the present state of American undergraduate education—its history, its present crisis, and its opportunities—see Andrew Delbanco, *College: What It Was, Is, and Should Be* (Princeton, NJ: Princeton University Press, 2012).

stitutions of higher learning that are relatively unaffected by the present trend. This set is made up of the small and exclusive club of private liberal arts colleges with large endowments. These colleges can afford to be extremely selective in their admissions and are consequently able to make a viable promise that most if not all their graduates will be accepted by prestigious professional schools and PhD programs of the RU/VH universities. Many if not most of these colleges have a Protestant origin but long since have cut their ties to any visible form of Christianity. They are profoundly secular, remarkably wealthy, and extremely successful in placing their students in the elite research universities. Holy Cross in Worchester, Massachusetts, might be a typical example of the few Catholic colleges that belong to this section.

Finally, the category of institutions that are the most affected by the present trend in the education market: smaller and midsize Christian liberal arts colleges and universities, including most Catholic ones, that have comparatively small endowments and are consequently tuition driven and hence dependent on a stable and ideally increasing student enrollment. The numerous Catholic teaching universities—those with large undergraduate programs, some master's programs, and few small if any doctoral programs—belong to this section. Many of these Catholic universities have an explicit and strong Catholic profile and are deeply committed to the idea of the Catholic university. Franciscan University of Steubenville; Ave Maria University; the University of Dallas; the University of St. Thomas, St. Paul; and the University of St. Thomas, Houston, stand first and foremost among them. They find themselves often in a tight squeeze financially. To relieve the pressure by increasing tuition would make them less competitive and endanger the critical mass of student enrollment. Yet to release the pressure by making the education more affordable for students and thus hopefully increase the total enrollment might result in noncompetitive faculty salaries and other financial restraints that again would weaken the institution's competitiveness. The only way forward often seems to be an aggressive increase of the endowment by way of increasing the pool of wealthy donors. This also has its downside, for nowadays most of the large gifts are increasingly purpose bound. Therefore the college or teaching university might end up with a chair or program it neither wants nor needs but for which there is a donor available. If this strategy is followed, colleges could develop in rather haphazard ways depending on where donors want to "invest."

In their greatly instructive study *Catholic Higher Education: A Culture in Crisis*, Melanie M. Morey and John J. Piderit, SJ, identify four models of Catholic colleges and universities in the United States: Catholic Immersion Universities, Catholic Persuasion Universities, Catholic Diaspora Universities, and Catholic Cohort Universities.[2] The goal of Catholic Immersion Universities is "to attract committed Catholic students, to educate them more deeply about the Catholic tradition, and to both encourage and actively support their practice of the faith."[3] Catholic Persuasion Universities intend "to instill in all students, whether Catholic or not, a certain religious maturity in knowledge of the Catholic faith."[4] The goal of Catholic Diaspora Universities is "to orient students to the Catholic Church without requiring much knowledge or practice."[5] Catholic Cohort Universities, finally, intend "to graduate talented students with the potential to operate in important sectors of civil, business, and cultural society in the United States and in other countries from which some students come."[6] This heuristic of four distinctive models arises from a presupposed framework of culture (instead of an economic framework of supply and demand) in which the mission of Catholic colleges and universities takes shape in different ways. This heuristic is helpful because it captures another important aspect of the way Catholic colleges and universities respond to the context in which they find themselves. If I had to integrate Morey and Piderit's four models within the three sectors of the standard economic supply-demand map, I would suggest the following: although one may admittedly find instantiations of all four models in each of the three sectors, arguably by tendency, Catholic Cohort Universities are more often found in sectors 1 and 2, because their large endowments make it possible—and therefore according to the ruling economic logic mandatory—to become part of the non-Catholic cohorts of advanced research universities or elite col-

2. Melanie M. Morey and John J. Piderit, SJ, *Catholic Higher Education: A Culture in Crisis* (Oxford: Oxford University Press, 2006).

3. Ibid., 62.

4. Ibid., 63.

5. Ibid., 64.

6. Ibid., 65.

leges. Catholic Immersion Universities, Catholic Persuasion Universities, and Catholic Diaspora Universities most likely populate sector 3, where—depending on size, endowment, location, and primary constituency—these models provide ways for Catholic colleges and teaching universities to compete more successfully with each other and with proximate state university systems, Protestant colleges, and community colleges. The increasing economization and commodification of all aspects of American life make the models that arise from a heuristic of culture an unavoidable function of the market dynamic of supply and demand.

Next to the iron fist of the economic supply-demand logic, there is a further significant challenge worth mentioning. A push of often thirty to forty years of emancipation from identifiable ecclesial ties and expectations as well as central Catholic commitments has produced in not a few Catholic colleges and teaching universities an increasingly professionalized administrative staff, as well as specialized and guild-committed faculties that turn out to be increasingly estranged from the original mission and vision of the Catholic institutions they serve.[7] Add to this phenomenon the broader secularizing trend in the United States in the last ten years, and the temptation becomes overwhelming for not a few board of trustees members, administrators, and faculty members to regard the very remnants of Catholic commitments still present in their respective Catholic colleges or teaching universities to be the one single obstacle that stands between them and the presumptive increase of viability of their institution or, in some more advanced cases of estrangement, its overdue success as a rising star in the secularist sky of "polytechnic utiliversities."[8]

Catholic colleges and teaching universities that give in to this temptation to develop a self-understanding on exclusively economic terms will sort themselves out into two groups. A most likely smaller and wealthier first group will attempt to compete with the rich but completely secularized colleges that serve as feeder institutions for the

7. The most comprehensive and sobering study of this sad story remains James Tunstead Burtchaell, *The Dying of the Light: The Disengagement of Colleges and Universities from Their Christian Churches* (Grand Rapids, MI: Eerdmans, 1998). For his treatment of Catholic institutions of higher learning, see pp. 557–742.

8. See my article "Polytechnic Utiliversity," *First Things* 237 (November 2013): 47–52.

RU/VH universities. They will go for the expensive product that promises a greater professional yield for the buyer. A most likely larger second group will compete with the state university system and the best among the community colleges for those students who look for a more affordable product with a tangible practical yield of immediate post-graduation employment. Catholic colleges and teaching universities of this group consequently present themselves as private polytechnic utiliversities competing with the state- or community-funded versions. Both groups of Catholic colleges and teaching universities will be hospitable to Catholic campus ministry, will welcome all other Christian and also other religious traditions, and, as experience shows, tolerate or even celebrate the "brave new world" of practical sexual inquiry, experimentation, and self-definition among students and faculty. And, so long as enrollment warrants it, they will, of course, maintain a department of religion. In all of this they will not differ notably from the state-funded system of polytechnic utiliversities. They will, however, differ from the state-funded system in one small way: for obvious reasons of recruitment, they will maintain a vague but discernible Catholic image on their official websites. But for both groups of colleges and teaching universities, the interior hard-core structure of the institution, the diversification of degree programs, the ideological plurality of their faculty and student bodies, and the pragmatic bent of the curriculum will be completely disconnected from the Catholic or value-related veneer, not unlike certain postmodern architecture, where the aesthetic of the façade conceals a completely different interior structure of mere functionality.

I regard this development as eventually suicidal for the identity and vocation of each group of Catholic institutions of higher learning. The smaller and more ambitious first group of colleges will most likely never fully catch up with the secular liberal arts colleges graced with old money and superb connections. Rather, in attempting to close the gap, these colleges will probably lose what they have going for themselves, what makes them different from state universities and secular private colleges—precisely their Catholic identity and vocation that enable them to offer a coherent and integral liberal arts education. Similarly, colleges and teaching universities in the larger second group will never be able to offer degree programs as inexpensively as community colleges that cooperate with proximate state universities and their combined long-distance learning offerings, nor will they ever be able to offer the spectrum of programs in the sciences, engineering, and the like that large state universities can afford to offer. In the attempt of mimicking these institutions, the Catholic colleges and teaching universities will most likely not gain the competitive edge they seek; furthermore, in the process of the attempt, they will likely lose their unique identity and character—in short, the difference that makes them attractive in the first place. In both cases, the objective economic and social pressures are seen rather stoically as fate—you either accommodate to it willingly, you will be dragged along by it, or, worse, you will be crushed by it. A loss of nerve is often due to a loss of vision.[9] But the loss of vision often arises from a deeper problem, the tacit capitulation to secular reason. For only after this tacit capitulation has occurred does the economic pressure seem to turn into the issue of paramount importance and the submission to a purely economic and managerial model the only way of "survival." But such a survival strategy on purely economic terms will in the end only unleash a more rapid self-secularization. For the problem—much more pernicious than the pressing economic situation most Catholic colleges and teaching universities find themselves in—is the pervasive and invasive character of secular reason. And it is secular reason that breeds a particularly reductive understanding of academic freedom, an understanding that in turn eventually undermines the educational mission central to a Catholic university. Before considering the authentic academic freedom characteristic of a Catholic university in contrast to the reductive understanding of academic freedom that secular reason engenders, it is apposite to consider even if only briefly secular reason itself and its imperious claims.

9. For an informative and encouraging study that looks at six American colleges that have successfully fought to maintain or regain their vision, see Robert Benne, *Quality with Soul: How Six Premier Colleges and Universities Keep Faith with Their Religious Traditions* (Grand Rapids, MI: Eerdmans, 2001). The Catholic institution of higher learning on which Benne focuses is the University of Notre Dame. Consideration of the developments and events at the University of Notre Dame in the last fifteen years—i.e., between the time Benne composed his study and the present—might lead to a more qualified and less positive assessment than Benne was able to offer in 2001.

The Pernicious Problem: The Imperious Claims of Secular Reason

For many decades, a well-documented secularizing trend—first subtle, eventually increasingly overt—has been afoot in Christian institutions of higher education in America, including most Catholic colleges and universities. The contemporary battle cries of the agents of secularization are "diversity," "tolerance," "universal acceptance," "personal authenticity," and most recently "epistemic justice," but also "practical pay-off" along the lines of tangible professional skills and competencies that guarantee a well-paying job and hence advanced standing in the "goods life" of the American consumer culture.[10] Pope Emeritus Benedict XVI regarded these deeply entrenched attitudes as specific expressions of the widespread tyranny of relativism, and many Catholic colleges and teaching universities in America have long since capitulated to it. But there is a price to pay for this capitulation. In his 2009 talk prepared for the formerly papal university La Sapienza in Rome, Benedict XVI poignantly stated:

> The danger for the western world—to speak only of this—is that today, precisely because of the greatness of his knowledge and power, man will fail to face up to the question of the truth. This would mean at the same time that reason would ultimately bow to the pressure of interests and the attraction of utility, constrained to recognize this as the ultimate criterion. To put it from the point of view of the structure of the university: there is a danger that philosophy, no longer considering itself capable of its true task, will degenerate into positivism; and that theology, with its message addressed to reason, will be limited to the private sphere of a more or less numerous group. Yet if reason, out of concern for its alleged purity, becomes deaf to the great message that comes to it from Christian faith and wisdom, then it withers like a tree whose roots can no longer reach the waters that give it life. It loses the courage for truth and thus becomes not greater but smaller.[11]

10. For an incisive analysis and critique of the American pursuit of the "goods life," see "Manufacturing the Goods Life," in Brad S. Gregory, *The Unintended Reformation: How a Religious Revolution Secularized Society* (Cambridge, MA: Harvard University Press, 2012), chap. 6, 235–97.

11. For the full text of this speech, see the Vatican website, accessed August 20, 2017, http://www.vatican.va/holy_father/benedict_xvi/speeches/2008/january/documents/hf_ben-xvi_spe_20080117_la-sapienza_en.html.

What the pope emeritus indicts here is the unexamined negative framework of a "secular reason"—uncritically reductive and in the end unscientific because unhistorical and antihermeneutical—as the everyday default working paradigm for contemporary colleges and universities, including Catholic colleges and teaching universities in America.

Interestingly, Pope Emeritus Benedict's concern is echoed in unexpected and surprising ways by those of the postmodern avant-garde who have come to realize that "secular reason" is a figment unable to account for itself. Stanley Fish, currently the Floerscheimer Distinguished Visiting Professor of Law at Yeshiva University's Benjamin N. Cardozo School of Law in New York City, not long ago introduced and discussed a noteworthy book by University of San Diego Warren Distinguished Professor of Law Steven D. Smith, *The Disenchantment of Secular Discourse*.[12] In it, Smith attempts to break open from the inside what Charles Taylor once aptly called "the citadel of modern secular reason."[13] Fish observes that, according to Smith's persuasive line of argumentation, "there are no secular reasons ... of the kind that could justify a decision to take one course of action rather than another." Consider Fish's astute summary of Smith's argument:

> Secular reason can't do its own self-assigned job—of describing the world in ways that allow us to move forward in our projects—without importing, but not acknowledging, the very perspectives it pushes away in disdain. While secular discourse, in the form of statistical analyses, controlled experiments and rational decision-trees, can yield banks of data that can then be subdivided and refined in more ways than we can count, it cannot tell us what that data means or what to do with it. No matter how much information you pile up and how sophisticated are the analytical operations you perform, you will never get one millimeter closer to the moment when you can move from the piled-up information to some lesson or imperative it points to.[14]

12. Steven D. Smith, *The Disenchantment of Secular Discourse* (Cambridge, MA: Harvard University Press, 2010).

13. Charles Taylor, "A Philosophical Postscript: Engaging the Citadel of Secular Reason," in *Reason and the Reasons of Faith*, ed. Paul J. Griffiths and Reinhard Hütter (New York: T&T Clark, 2005), 339–53.

14. Stanley Fish, "Are There Secular Reasons?," *New York Times*, February 22, 2010, http://opinionator.blogs.nytimes.com/2010/02/22/are-there-secular-reasons?/.

This profound incapability to move from the amassment of facts to the consideration of the true, the good, and the beautiful, let alone to any substantive moral or spiritual orientation, is in fact just what one should expect from secular reason and colleges and universities committed to it. Secular reason and the ensuing strictly limited secular discourse have intentionally cut themselves off from the intellectual and moral sources that would allow them to acknowledge and advance the overarching teleology that gives intrinsic value to a liberal arts education and the unity of knowledge that a Catholic college and teaching university at its best is able to provide.[15]

The consequences of the consistent secularism that secular reason spreads are dire. Pope Emeritus Benedict did not exaggerate in his proposed speech for La Sapenzia University:

> If our culture seeks only to build itself on the basis of the circle of its own argumentation, on what convinces it at the time, and if—anxious to preserve its secularism—it detaches itself from its life-giving roots, then it will not become more reasonable or purer, but will fall apart and disintegrate.
>
> At the center of secular reason's imperious claim stands the reductive account of academic freedom and the unsubstantiated, but solidly received opinion that the very possibility of a supernatural revelation must be dismissed on *a priori* assumptions, assumptions that in turn cannot be warranted philosophically in the normative framework of secular reason itself.[16]

In sum, these are some of the untoward ideological and socioeconomic conditions that Catholic colleges and universities must struggle with in the scene of American higher education—the imperious but un-

15. For a profound as well as panoramic narrative providing the intellectual background for how secular reason and the ensuing strictly limited secular discourse have cut themselves off from the intellectual and moral resources that would allow them to acknowledge the overarching teleology that gives intrinsic value to a liberal arts education, see Thomas Pfau's magisterial study, *Minding the Modern: Human Agency, Intellectual Traditions, and Responsible Knowledge* (Notre Dame, IN: University of Notre Dame Press, 2013).

16. One modern thinker who has advanced a compelling analysis of this aporia at the heart of secular reason is John Henry Newman. See especially his *Fifteen Sermons Preached before the University of Oxford Between A.D. 1826 and 1843*, introduction by Mary Katherine Tillman (Notre Dame, IN: University of Notre Dame Press, 1997), and his *Essay in Aid of a Grammar of Assent*, introduction by Nicholas Lash (Notre Dame, IN: University of Notre Dame Press, 1979).

warrantable claims of secular reason, a reductive understanding of academic freedom, and a competitive buyers' market of higher education driven exclusively by a utilitarian and pragmatic logic. In this context, *Ex corde Ecclesiae* constitutes nothing less than a most prescient magisterial gift that enables Catholic universities in America to recuperate their constitutive identity—the idea of a Catholic university—and their mission, propelled by the complementary double center of the gift of revealed truth and the realization of authentic academic freedom.

Recuperating the Idea of a Catholic University

To recuperate the idea of a Catholic university, we must turn to the idea of a university as such, because in the West the idea of a university has emerged historically with and in the Catholic university. And therefore, arguably, the idea of a university should continue to be most perspicuously realized in a Catholic university. As Pope John Paul II stated beautifully in the opening line of his apostolic constitution *Ex corde Ecclesiae*, "*Born from the heart of the Church*, a Catholic University is located in that course of tradition which may be traced back to the very origin of the University as an institution."[17]

Two eminent Catholic academicians who have thought extensively about the nature of the university understood this point exceedingly well, namely, that the Catholic university—rightly understood and authentically instantiated—should be the paradigmatic realization of the idea of a university. Arguably one of the greatest Catholic thinkers of the nineteenth century, Blessed John Henry Cardinal Newman, and one eminent Catholic thinker of the twentieth century, the Dominican philosopher and theologian Benedict Ashley, held it as axiomatic that "university" is essentially related to "universe." Newman states in his still highly relevant *The Idea of a University*: "As to the range of University teaching, certainly the very name of University is inconsistent with restrictions of any kind.... A University should teach universal knowledge."[18] And Benedict Ashley, in his equally relevant *The Way*

17. *EcE*, 1.

18. John Henry Newman, *The Idea of a University*, ed. Charles Frederick Harrold (New York: Longmans, Green, 1947), 19, Discourse II, 1.

toward Wisdom, confirms: "The very term 'university' means many-looking-toward-one, and is related to the term 'universe,' the whole of reality."[19] Both Newman and Ashley identify three characteristics that are essential to the idea of a university, characteristics to which, I think, contemporary universities still have to measure up in order to deserve the denomination "university."

First, a university is an institution of teaching universal knowledge. While no single university must teach all extant academic disciplines, a university—differently from a polytechnicum and college—must *in principle* be open and aspire to teaching universal knowledge.

Second, the unity and interrelatedness of university disciplines reflect the unity and interrelatedness of all knowledge. The university lives from an underlying metaphysical principle—the convertibility of truth and being—such that no truth can contradict another truth and that all truths are inherently interconnected. Incidentally, the nominalist and now postmodern thesis of the radical incommensurability of the domains of discourse destroys the unity of truth and knowledge and with it the very idea of a university.

Third, the university is not an accidental, but a unity per se that carries its end or purpose in its constitutive practices of education and inquiry. In short, the de facto unity of a university is constituted by practices of education and inquiry and a curriculum that reflects tangibly the inherent interconnectedness of universal knowledge. The path of recuperating the idea of a Catholic university opens up the consequent path of recuperating authentic academic freedom.

Recuperating Authentic Academic Freedom

Like every other being in this world, natural or artificial, the university is a specific entity. This entity constitutes the highest species in the genus of school, for the university realizes the genus of school most extensively, intensively, and comprehensively. Simply to exist as a university is its first perfection. To realize its *telos* or end is its second perfection.

19. Benedict M. Ashley, OP, *The Way toward Wisdom: An Interdisciplinary and Intercultural Introduction to Metaphysics* (Notre Dame, IN: University of Notre Dame Press, 2006), 20.

Like any other being, a university realizes the *telos* or end of its essence by way of activities characteristic of its nature. The end of the university is acquiring and conveying universal knowledge. This entails, first, conveying old and new knowledge; second, acquiring new knowledge; and third, integrating knowledge and reflecting comprehensively and critically upon it. In short, the essence of a university is—as *Ex corde Ecclesiae* puts so succinctly—nothing but "the *gaudium de veritate*, so precious to Saint Augustine, which is that joy of searching for, discovering and communicating truth in every field of knowledge."[20]

Now, readers will likely expect me to say that academic freedom is the indispensable ambience *in* which the end of the university can be realized. Understood in this way, the point of academic freedom would be to facilitate the university's second perfection, that is, to facilitate the realization of the *telos* of its essence by way of activities characteristic of its nature. Now, this is the conventional wisdom that turns out to be—while not completely wrong—insufficient, to say the least. For the account of freedom that this understanding of academic freedom as facilitating ambience presupposes is exclusively the negative freedom of procedural liberalism, the freedom from interference. This notion of academic freedom is too formalistic, too two-dimensional, too ateleological, in short too unacademic, to be worthy of denoting academic freedom in its full and perfective sense, which characterizes the positive freedom for excellence. Academic freedom is not a facilitating ambience. Rather, exercising authentic academic freedom is nothing short of realizing the essence of the university. In this sense, academic freedom is constitutive of the idea of a university, because the knowledge characteristic of the university is essentially "free" knowledge (which "accidentally" can also turn out to be useful).

Authentic academic freedom receives its specific sense from the distinction between the *artes liberales*, the liberal or free disciplines, on the one hand, and on the other hand the *artes serviles*, the applied or useful arts or sciences. While the *artes serviles* may be part of a university, they are not essential to a university but are essential to what should properly be called a "polytechnicum," institutions like the Massachusetts Institute of Technology, the California Institute of Technology, Virginia

20. *EcE*, 1.

Polytechnic Institute and State University, and the like. Consider again John Henry Newman: "Knowledge, I say, is then especially liberal, or sufficient for itself, apart from every external and ulterior object, when and in so far as it is philosophical."[21] The freedom denoted in authentic academic freedom is the freedom that arises from the philosophical character of knowledge.

But what exactly is this philosophical character of knowledge? In his classic *Leisure, the Basis of Culture*—a book that I regard as an absolute "must read" for all faculty, administrators, and students in Catholic colleges and universities—the eminent Catholic philosopher Josef Pieper offers a helpful clarification. He states:

> Strictly speaking, a claim for academic freedom can only exist when the "academic" itself is realized in a "philosophical" way. And this is historically the reason: academic freedom has been lost, exactly to the extent that the philosophic character of academic study has been lost, or, to put it another way, to the extent that the totalitarian demands of the working world have conquered the realm of the university.[22]

If Pieper is right, and I have good reason to think he is, the greatest enemy of authentic academic freedom turns out to be also the greatest enemy of the university qua university: its total instrumentalization and its consequent transformation into a polytechnicum, under the label of "university." What undermines and eventually destroys authentic academic freedom also undermines and eventually destroys the university itself. It is not surprising that under the pressure of a comprehensive instrumentalization of all university disciplines in conformity with the totalizing logic of the world of work—namely, the by now globalized dynamic of production and consumption—authentic academic freedom devolves into the merely negative freedom from interference. This purely defensive freedom is meant to protect academicians from being turned into pure commodities, that is, from random replacement, from economic exploitation, and from politically and managerially manipulated intrusions into their classrooms and into the substance of their teaching and research. In a context of such instrumentaliza-

21. Newman, *Idea of a University*, 98, Discourse V, 5.

22. Josef Pieper, *Leisure, the Basis of Culture*, introduction by Roger Scruton, trans. Gerald Malsbary (South Bend, IN: St. Augustine's Press, 1998), 75.

tion and hence fluidification of academic work, academic freedom in its most minimal realization, negative freedom, is indeed indispensable: the freedom that protects inquiry and teaching from open and hedged attempts of manipulation and functionalization, attempts that aim at substituting the search for truth with the search for utility or, worse, at reducing truth itself to a function of utility.[23] As *Ex corde Ecclesiae* observes,

> Every Catholic University, as a university . . . guarantees its members academic freedom, so long as the rights of the individual person and of the community are preserved within the confines of the truth and the common good.[24]

Ex corde Ecclesiae implicitly differentiates here between, on the one hand, the inauthentic freedom of indifference that it rejects with reference to the truth and the common good and, on the other hand, the protective negative freedom from interference that can be exercised well only within the confines of the truth and the common good. Severed from the confines of the truth and the common good, the protective negative freedom from interference will always eventually degenerate into the all too familiar freedom of indifference, the root of which is nothing but the sovereignty of self-will beyond truth and falsehood, beyond good and evil.

Although academic freedom understood as negative freedom is not without its importance in the contemporary context of the commodification of higher learning, the frequent reduction of authentic academic freedom to the merely negative freedom of protection from extrinsic interference is detrimental, because the fight for and insistence upon this kind of negative academic freedom blocks sight not only of

23. For a defense and at the same time a strict limitation of academic freedom to the negative freedom of protection from arbitrary interference in the professional activity of professors, see Stanley Fish, *Versions of Academic Freedom: From Professionalism to Revolution*, Rice University Campbell Lectures (Chicago, IL: University of Chicago Press, 2014). Fish argues rightly against a utopian extension of academic freedom into some form of "legal protectorate" that would offer security to the professor outside of the area of his or her academic and scientific competency. He seems, however, to be unable to appreciate the nature of authentic academic freedom and the degree to which the minimalist negative freedom of professional protection from interference depends on the antecedent and encompassing authentic academic freedom.

24. *EcE*, 12; see also 29.

what authentic academic freedom is but also of the root problem that necessitates this self-protective measure, namely, the transmutation of all knowledge into a form of *technē* and of academicians into hired experts and clerks. Having replaced authentic academic freedom that arises from the *gaudium de veritate*, the joy of searching for and discovering truth, with the computational metrics of research output, the late modern research university has forgone the community of scholars and students, the *universitas magistrorum et scholarium*, and only recognizes stakeholders and staff that meet quite accidentally in the processes of knowledge production and knowledge consumption.

This problem at the root of the modern secular research university becomes obvious as soon as authentic academic freedom is recognized as nothing but the very realization of the essence or idea of a university. Differently put, authentic academic freedom exists only where inquiry and teaching are ordered to truth and where the community of academicians is reflexively aware of this teleological ordering of the practices of teaching and inquiry. Newman puts this crucial matter the following way:

> Truth is the object of knowledge of whatever kind; and when we inquire what is meant by Truth, I suppose it is right to answer that Truth means facts and their relations.... All that exists, as contemplated by the human mind, forms one large system or complex fact.[25]
>
> Viewed together, [the sciences] approximate to a representation or subjective reflection of the objective truth, as nearly as possible to the human mind.[26]

Being ordered to this end, the approximation to a representation of the objective truth as nearly as possible to the human mind, and pursuing this end through the means appropriate to each academic discipline in light of its specific subject matter by way of inquiry and teaching, is the realization of authentic academic freedom and concomitantly of the essence of the university. With reference to John Henry Newman, *Ex corde Ecclesiae* tacitly presupposes the notion of authentic academic freedom when it states:

25. Newman, *Idea of a University*, 40*ff.*, Discourse III, 2.
26. Newman, *Idea of a University*, 43, Discourse III, 2.

It is the honour and responsibility of a Catholic University to consecrate itself without reserve to *the cause of truth*. This is its way of serving at one and the same time both the dignity of man and the good of the Church, which has 'an intimate conviction that truth is (its) real ally ... and that knowledge and reason are sure ministers of faith.' Without in any way neglecting the acquisition of useful knowledge, a Catholic University is distinguished by its free search for the whole truth about nature, man, and God.[27]

This free search for the whole truth about nature, man, and God is nothing but the very realization of authentic academic freedom. What does such academic freedom look like in the various fields of inquiry and teaching?

In the *natural sciences*, authentic academic freedom is realized emphatically not in the all too eagerly looked for applicability. Rather, authentic academic freedom is realized paradigmatically in the philosophical reflexivity that enables scientists, first, to make explicit the antecedent philosophical beliefs and moral commitments they bring to their inquiries and teaching and, second, to maintain the critical distinction between, on the one hand, historically successive models and paradigms and, on the other hand, a transcending truth toward which all inquiry and the succession of paradigms and models are teleologically ordered. It is the staunch and persistent realization of authentic academic freedom that protects natural scientists from reducing themselves to mere laboratory technicians and to executioners of the research agendas dictated by the biotechnological and the military-industrial complexes.

In the *technological* and otherwise applied sciences, authentic academic freedom is realized in the reflexive awareness and thematization in the practice of inquiry and teaching of these sciences that every applied science qua applied science depends on antecedent moral commitments and a concomitant teleology of the common good and of human flourishing in order to make sense as an applied science in the first place. It is not essential to a polytechnicum but rather to a university and the concomitant realization of authentic academic freedom that these antecedent commitments and the concomitant teleology of the common good be reflected in the context of teaching these applied sciences. Ac-

27. *EcE*, 4.

cording to *Ex corde Ecclesiae*, "its Christian inspiration" enables a Catholic university "to include the moral, spiritual and religious dimension in its research, and to evaluate the attainments of science and technology in the perspective of the totality of the human person."[28]

Unsurprisingly, therefore, in humanistic studies, authentic academic freedom is realized paradigmatically insofar as the question of being human is thematized and the antecedent ontological and moral commitments are made explicit that drive literary, historical, and artistic inquiry and teaching. Nota bene: All humanistic studies are ultimately forms of moral philosophy—that is, morally committed inquiries into what it means to be human[29]—and such inquiry must feed back into the fundamental orientation of the technical and other applied sciences. *Ex corde Ecclesiae* is quite explicit about this:

> Because knowledge is meant to serve the human person, research in a Catholic University is always carried out with a concern for the *ethical* and *moral implications* both of its methods and of its discoveries. This concern, while it must be present in all research, is particularly important in the areas of science and technology. "It is essential that we be convinced of the priority of the ethical over the technical, of the primacy of the person over things, of the superiority of the spirit over matter. The cause of the human person will only be served if knowledge is joined to conscience. Men and women of science will truly aid humanity only if they preserve 'the sense of the transcendence of the human person over the world and of God over the human person.'"[30]

In philosophy, authentic academic freedom is realized paradigmatically insofar as it is here that the nature of the "academic" and hence the nature of the university is explicitly thematized and extensively reflected. Newman puts the matter again succinctly:

> The comprehension of the bearings of one science upon another, and the use of each to each, and the location and limitation and adjustment and due appreciation of them all, one with another, this belongs, I conceive, to a sort of science distinct from all of them, and in some sense a science of scienc-

28. *EcE*, 7.

29. For a paradigmatic instantiation of what it means for humanistic studies to embark upon morally committed inquiries into what it means to be human, see Pfau, *Minding the Modern*.

30. *EcE*, 18.

es, which is my own conception of what is meant by Philosophy, in the true sense of the word, and of a philosophical habit of mind.[31]

If we spell out the implications of Newman's statement, it becomes plain that every university discipline must be philosophical in order to be academic and thus to realize authentic academic freedom. Unsurprisingly, it is philosophy in the tradition initiated by Plato, continued by Aristotle, deepened by Augustine and Aquinas, and renewed by Hegel and Husserl, let alone by the noteworthy neo-Aristotelian, neo-Thomist, and personalist efforts of the twentieth century. In short, it is nothing but the expansive tradition of philosophy in the perennial sense that is the genuine guardian of authentic academic freedom. In a Catholic university, philosophy realizes its authentic academic freedom paradigmatically in the integration of knowledge, in reflecting upon the unity of knowledge, and in the concomitant realization of the openness of the human intellect to transcendence—a realization realized best in the dialogue between reason and faith. *Ex corde Ecclesiae* observes:

> In promoting this integration of knowledge, a specific part of a Catholic University's task is to promote *dialogue between faith and reason*, so that it can be seen more profoundly how faith and reason bear harmonious witness to the unity of all truth. While each academic discipline retains its own integrity and has its own methods, this dialogue demonstrates that "methodical research within every branch of learning, when carried out in a truly scientific manner and in accord with moral norms, can never truly conflict with faith. For the things of the earth and the concerns of faith derive from the same God." A vital interaction of two distinct levels of coming to know the one truth leads to a greater love for truth itself, and contributes to a more comprehensive understanding of the meaning of human life and of the purpose of God's creation.[32]

It is impossible to clap with one hand. Likewise, such a dialogue between faith and reason is impossible without the genuine and substantive participation of Catholic theology. Hence we must, last but not least, turn to Catholic theology.

Authentic academic freedom is realized paradigmatically in Catholic theology thus: the transcendent truth, truth itself—which is *formally* the end and goal of all the other academic disciplines—is *materially* re-

31. Newman, *Idea of a University*, 46, Discourse III, 4.

32. *EcE*, 17.

ceived by divine faith and articulated, interpreted, clarified, specified, and defended in the labors of the *intellectus fidei*, called Catholic theology. Only the revealed truth in its fullness embraced in an ever deepening effort of the *intellectus fidei* sets Catholic theology fully free—free from error, free from being co-opted by the spirit of the age and by the idol of pure positivist or historicist *Wissenschaftlichkeit*, free for contemplation of the revealed truth, free for inquiry into the revealed truth, and free for teaching the revealed truth.

I claimed above rather boldly that authentic academic freedom and concomitantly the essence of a university are paradigmatically realized in a Catholic university. How can I make good on such a bold claim? Newman and Ashley understood perfectly well that an authentic Catholic university is most fundamentally committed to the catholicity of truth, which means that all university disciplines share the common *telos* of truth. As *Ex corde Ecclesiae* observes,

> By means of a kind of universal humanism a Catholic University is completely dedicated to the research of all aspects of truth in their essential connection with the supreme Truth, who is God.[33]

Authentic academic freedom realizes the catholicity of truth in a comprehensive and integral curriculum that reflects the interior coherence of a potentially universal knowledge and that thematizes the philosophical, academic aspect of each discipline. Unsurprisingly, authentic academic freedom and the catholicity of truth depend on each other: The catholicity of truth gives full scope to academic freedom, and academic freedom realizes this scope as the freedom for truth. It is approximated carefully by hypothesis, experiment, and model in the natural sciences, as it discloses itself phenomenologically in humanistic studies, as it is honed in the process of aporetics and dialectics in philosophy in its perennial sense, as it is discovered in the free play of mathematics, and as it is contemplated in Catholic theology as received from God directly by way of revelation, incarnation, and inspiration. The catholicity of truth and the search to which it gives rise is ordered to the final end toward which the human intellect itself is directed, the immediate vision of "the supreme Truth, who is God."[34]

33. *EcE*, 4.
34. *EcE*, 4.

After having recuperated the broad contours of the idea of a Catholic university and established the nature of authentic academic freedom in distinction from the merely negative academic freedom from interference and the inauthentic freedom of indifference, it is apposite to address what is at the same time the stumbling block and offense for secular reason and the core of the identity of a Catholic university—the revealed truth of the *depositum fidei.*

Revealed Truth: The Heart of a Catholic University and a Stumbling Block and Offense for Secular Reason

Ex corde Ecclesiae states: "A Catholic University's privileged task is 'to unite existentially by intellectual effort two orders of reality that too frequently tend to be placed in opposition as though they were antithetical: the search for truth, and the certainty of already knowing the fount of truth.'"[35] The university discipline for which "the certainty of already knowing the fount of truth" is an essential property is, of course, Catholic theology. And one way of characterizing the unique position of Catholic theology in relation to all other university disciplines is the contrast between the possession of ultimate truth versus the search for ultimate truth: Catholic theology possesses already the truth as revealed, while all the other disciplines find themselves in an ever deepening search for it. This characterization is correct so long as one understands that the relationship of revealed truth to Catholic theology is emphatically not one of a positivist *datum*, the sheer givenness of facticity that would grant theology the rights of ownership, analogous to those we hold over commodities of our own. On the contrary, the relationship of revealed truth to Catholic theology is that of a *donum*, a gift that puts theology into the position of recipient. Therefore the relationship of Catholic theology to revealed truth is emphatically not the critical conceptual *dominium* that a misplaced *Wissenschaftlichkeit* exercises over revealed truth, but rather one of intellectual stewardship (*procuratio*) in relationship to the gift of revealed truth. Revealed truth is received in divine faith, which itself is a gift of grace, a *donum*, and

35. *EcE*, 1.

emphatically neither an empirical *datum* to be simply acknowledged as a fact nor an epistemic *dominium* over God.

Furthermore, revealed truth is simultaneously given and transcendent. As transcendent, revealed truth surpasses the confines of our knowledge, and as revealed, it is received according to the mode of the human knower. Revealed truth as revealed is essentially testimony about God received from God. As given in communication, it necessarily takes propositional form, whether as narrative or as argument. Furthermore, revealed truth is not had without the instrumental causality of ideational, discursive, magisterial/doctrinal, and liturgical/sacramental mediation and specification. Catholic theology depends directly on three sources by way of which it receives these specifications of revealed truth: the Holy Scriptures and sacred tradition as received, interpreted, and specified by the Church's Magisterium. These three form an interdependent unit whose parts work together under the inspiration of the Holy Spirit. In the Dogmatic Constitution on Divine Revelation, *Dei Verbum*, the Council Fathers of the Second Vatican Council put it thus: "In the supremely wise arrangement of God, sacred Tradition, sacred Scripture, and the Magisterium of the Church are so connected and associated that one of them cannot stand without the others."[36]

Revealed truth is of a kind that is always first and foremost suffered, undergone, and as such actively received. Revealed truth is testimony that is always qua testimony propositional. Yet revealed truth remains at the same time transcendent truth; its propositionality does not reduce its transcendence to the sheer facticity of conveyed information, and it does not reduce the spirit to the letter but rather conveys the spirit by way of the letter and transcendence by way of propositionality. The propositionality characteristic of inspired testimony is the very conduit of the transcendence of revealed truth. Revealed truth has its acme and center in the incarnate Logos, the Word of God made flesh. Analogous to the hypostatic union of the human and divine natures in the person of the Logos, the Son of God, where the human nature of Christ has a specific created historical concreteness, also divine truth qua revealed truth does have a distinct propositional concreteness as it is received by and into the faith of the Church, a created concreteness that is apposite

36. Vatican II, dogmatic constitution *Dei verbum* 10, November 18, 1965. *Acta Apostolicae Sedis* 58 (1966): 817–30.

to the way knowledge is received in the human knower. Yet at the same time, revealed truth has an inexhaustible depth of surpassing transcendence irreducible to the empiricist *datum* of mere historical facticity and impervious to the proud epistemic *dominium* of secular reason and its imperious claims.

Recuperating Authentic Academic Freedom in Catholic Theology

In Catholic theology, authentic academic freedom cannot be realized, in the flight from the testimonial propositionality of revealed truth into an essentially transpropositional, apophatic religious transcendence or into a primordial and essentially prepropositional religious subjectivity. Nor, for that matter, can authentic academic freedom in Catholic theology be realized in the flight from magisterial authority. Rather, authentic academic freedom in Catholic theology is realized precisely in the fidelity to the testimonial propositionality of revealed truth as conveyed by sacred Scripture and sacred tradition, and as specified by the Magisterium of the Church. The flight of Catholic theology into a purely negative academic freedom from interference where the Magisterium of the Church—or, more fundamentally, even the very testimonial propositionality of revealed truth—is taken to be an interference, into a positivist or historicist *Wissenschaftlichkeit* that is incongruous with the subject matter of Catholic theology, simply amounts to the abandonment of authentic academic freedom and hence to the self-abolition of Catholic theology as a properly *academic* university discipline. *Ex corde Ecclesiae* expresses the matter succinctly. It is worth quoting in full:

> The Church, accepting "the legitimate autonomy of human culture and especially of the sciences," recognizes the academic freedom of scholars in each discipline in accordance with its own principles and proper methods, and within the confines of the truth and the common good. Theology has its legitimate place in the University alongside other disciplines. It has proper principles and methods which define it as a branch of knowledge. Theologians enjoy this same freedom so long as they are faithful to these principles and methods. Bishops should encourage the creative work of theologians.

They serve the Church through research done in a way that respects theological method. They seek to understand better, further develop and more effectively communicate the meaning of Christian Revelation as transmitted in Scripture and Tradition and in the Church's Magisterium. They also investigate the ways in which theology can shed light on specific questions raised by contemporary culture. At the same time, since theology seeks an understanding of revealed truth whose authentic interpretation is entrusted to the Bishops of the Church, it is intrinsic to the principles and methods of their research and teaching in their academic discipline that theologians respect the authority of the Bishops, and assent to Catholic doctrine according to the degree of authority with which it is taught. Because of their interrelated roles, dialogue between Bishops and theologians is essential; this is especially true today, when the results of research are so quickly and so widely communicated through the media.[37]

What is true for the integral part is also true for the whole. Therefore what is true for Catholic theology is also true for the Catholic university. A Catholic university is academic in the proper sense of the word insofar as it realizes that its relationship to the supreme truth as mediated by the Church is essential to its institutional identity and that therefore, to quote *Ex corde Ecclesiae*, "the *institutional* fidelity of the University to the Christian message includes a recognition of and adherence to the teaching authority of the Church in matters of faith and morals."[38] In short, the realization of academic freedom in Catholic theology as well as in the institutional identity of the Catholic university stands and falls with the proper reception of and fidelity to revealed truth.

Recuperating Authentic Academic Freedom in Relation to Revealed Truth in Academic Disciplines Other Than Catholic Theology

The relationship of revealed truth to authentic academic freedom realized in academic disciplines other than Catholic theology is governed by the fundamental principle of the catholicity of truth, namely, that truth cannot contradict truth. When things are in good order in a

37. *EcE*, 29.
38. *EcE*, 27.

Catholic university, revealed truth obviously informs Catholic theology formally and materially; it informs the liturgical life as well as the core curriculum; it informs existentially all academicians by way of what is called the "formation of conscience"; it informs critically by way of Catholic theology the moral suppositions antecedent to and consequent upon the humanistic studies and the applied sciences. In this way, through a truly *academic* Catholic theology, revealed truth protects, secures, and strengthens the exercise of authentic academic freedom in other university disciplines. In short, when things are in good order in a Catholic university, revealed truth—as believed, taught, liturgically celebrated, and lived—informs all operations of the university. In the words of *Ex corde Ecclesiae*:

> In a Catholic University … Catholic ideals, attitudes and principles penetrate and inform university activities in accordance with the proper nature and autonomy of these activities. In a word, being both a University and Catholic, it must be both a community of scholars representing various branches of human knowledge, and an academic institution in which Catholicism is vitally present and operative.[39]

Needless to say, Catholic theology and philosophy (in its perennial sense) play a central role in the curriculum as well as in the intellectual life of such a university. For it is in the dialogue between these two paradigmatically academic disciplines that the catholicity of truth is reflected upon explicitly and the nature of authentic academic freedom articulated and defended. *Ex corde Ecclesiae* states:

> Aided by the specific contributions of philosophy and theology, university scholars will be engaged in a constant effort to determine the relative place and meaning of each of the various disciplines within the context of a vision of the human person and the world that is enlightened by the Gospel, and therefore by a faith in Christ, the *Logos*, as the centre of creation and of human history.[40]

It is also needless to say that if a Catholic university were to banish Catholic theology and philosophy from its core curriculum and even from the university itself, it would thereby forego its commitment to the

39. *EcE*, 14.
40. *EcE*, 16.

catholicity of truth; indeed, it would simply decapitate itself. Unsurprisingly, therefore, *Ex corde Ecclesiae* recommends: "Because of its specific importance among the academic disciplines, every Catholic university should have a faculty, or at least a chair, of theology."[41]

Conflict between revealed truth and authentic academic freedom may arise from the failure of disciplines other than Catholic theology to realize their respective, properly academic nature. Recall that "academic" denotes also a critical methodological awareness of the nature, integrity, and limitations of a discipline and an awareness of the limitations of knowledge respective to the disciplinary object of study in any given university discipline. Such a failure to realize the properly academic nature of a particular discipline might consist in indifference to the catholicity of truth, in the confusion of science with scientism, in the replacement of philosophy in its perennial sense with the modus of ideology characteristic of not a few things that presently go under the label of "philosophy," or in the reduction of humanistic studies to historicism, to genealogy, or to a branch of neuroscience. This conflict can be exacerbated by Catholic theology itself when it abandons its respective, properly academic nature, which includes essentially fidelity to the revealed truth. At the very moment when Catholic theology reduces itself to Christian religious studies—that is, when it embraces and internalizes the unfitting and hence unacademic norm of positivist or historicist *Wissenschaftlichkeit*—it foregoes fidelity to the revealed truth and concomitantly authentic academic freedom.

Received, interpreted, and defended well by Catholic theology, revealed truth in virtue of its transcendence and in virtue of its testimonial propositionality opens up the horizon of the catholicity of truth and thereby encourages other university disciplines to realize their properly academic nature and thereby their authentic academic freedom. Reciprocally, insofar as the other university disciplines realize their properly academic nature and thereby contribute to the catholicity of truth, they encourage Catholic theology to search ever more deeply for the revealed truth and increasingly unfold its surpassing riches. By being maximally academic and by realizing thereby authentic academic freedom and thus giving witness to the catholicity of truth, the *universitas scien-*

41. *EcE*, 19.

tiarum assists Catholic theology in realizing its own authentic academic freedom. Consider again *Ex corde Ecclesiae ipsa voce*:

> In the world today, characterized by such rapid developments in science and technology, the tasks of a Catholic University assume an ever greater importance and urgency. Scientific and technological discoveries create an enormous economic and industrial growth, but they also inescapably require the correspondingly necessary *search for meaning* in order to guarantee that the new discoveries be used for the authentic good of individuals and of human society as a whole. If it is the responsibility of every University to search for such meaning, a Catholic University is called in a particular way to respond to this need: its Christian inspiration enables it to include the moral, spiritual and religious dimension in its research, and to evaluate the attainments of science and technology in the perspective of the totality of the human person. In this context, Catholic Universities are called to a continuous renewal, both as "Universities" and as "Catholic." For, "What is at stake is the *very meaning of scientific and technological research, of social life and of culture*, but, on an even more profound level, what is at stake is *the very meaning of the human person*." Such renewal requires a clear awareness that, by its Catholic character, a University is made more capable of conducting an *impartial* search for truth, a search that is neither subordinated to nor conditioned by particular interests of any kind.[42]

Conclusion

In *Ex corde Ecclesiae*, Catholic universities have a great gift that secular universities lack. Compared to Catholic universities, secular universities, especially advanced research universities, are like orphaned children who do not know where they come from nor where they are going. And when upwardly mobile Catholic universities eager to catch up with the leading secular research universities eventually leave behind their institutional identity as Catholic university, they will all too soon begin to suffer from the same condition that ails the secular research universities—the absence of a proper unifying teleology and hence the absence of authentic academic freedom. Such merely nominal Catholic

42. *EcE*, 7 and 8.

colleges and universities will inevitably fall prey to the imperious claims of secular reason and the concomitant reductive understanding of academic freedom as a merely negative freedom or, worse, as a freedom of indifference. Catholic universities mindful of their Catholic identity, of which the catholicity of truth is an integral component, are protected from giving in to the mimetic desire, because Catholic universities receive the gift of accountability from the revealed truth by way of the Catholic Church. They are called by the Church to nothing less than the exercise of authentic academic freedom. In short, the Catholic university is called to live out a truth that is as demanding as it is beautiful, namely, that fidelity to the revealed truth does not contradict but rather perfects authentic academic freedom. It is only appropriate to leave the last word to *Ex corde Ecclesiae*:

> It is the honour and responsibility of a Catholic University to consecrate itself without reserve to *the cause of truth*. This is its way of serving at one and the same time both the dignity of man and the good of the Church, which has "an intimate conviction that truth is (its) real ally . . . and that knowledge and reason are sure ministers to faith." Without in any way neglecting the acquisition of useful knowledge, a Catholic University is distinguished by its free search for the whole truth about nature, man and God. The present age is in urgent need of this kind of disinterested service, namely of *proclaiming the meaning of truth*, that fundamental value without which freedom, justice and human dignity are extinguished. By means of a kind of universal humanism a Catholic University is completely dedicated to the research of all aspects of truth in their essential connection with the supreme Truth, who is God. It does this without fear but rather with enthusiasm, dedicating itself to every path of knowledge, aware of being preceded by him who is "the Way, the Truth, and the Life," the *Logos*, whose Spirit of intelligence and love enables the human person with his or her own intelligence to find the ultimate reality of which he is the source and end and who alone is capable of giving fully that Wisdom without which the future of the world would be in danger.[43]

43. *EcE*, 4.

[4]

Academic Freedom, Divine Revelation, and Catholic Universities

Terrence W. Tilley

When some of my colleagues learned that I was invited to the campus of Franciscan University to speak at the Fidelity and Freedom symposia, they were surprised. After being a consultant to the United States Conference of Catholic Bishops subcommittee on *mandatum*, I published an essay, "The Misunderstood *Mandatum*," and characterized *mandatum* as "a bad idea whose time had come." Why would "*mandatum*-friendly" Franciscan University invite me? My own theological stance can surely be characterized as "progressive"; others would have less friendly characterizations, like Thomas Weinandy, who wrote an article asserting that one of my publications was guilty of "doctrinal ambiguity and error" (a view that I dispute, of course).[1] My colleagues seem puzzled: how could I fit at Franciscan University in a discussion focused on academic freedom and revealed truth?

But what I would not "fit" is *their* idea of "your mold." We live in and live out a dynamic Catholic tradition.[2] To do so we must—as Cardinal

1. Thomas G. Weinandy, OFM, Cap., "Terrence Tilley's Christological Impasses: The Demise of the Doctrine of the Incarnation," *Fellowship of Catholic Scholars Quarterly* 32, no. 3 (Fall 2009): 10; my response was published on the National Catholic Reporter website, December 5, 2009, http://ncronline.org/blogs/ncr-today/exchange-between-terrence-tilley-and-fr-thomas-weinandy.

2. This tradition is more dynamic than most people seem to think. See my *Inventing Catholic Tradition* (Maryknoll, NY: Orbis Books, 2000), and John Thiel, *Senses of Tradition:*

Dulles did—hear and read each other's work carefully, interpret it charitably, report it accurately, argue thoughtfully, and disagree respectfully (when we disagree), as we all serve God's truth. To do less than this with and for each other is to refuse to keep faith with that tradition as we struggle to incarnate it in the present.

As part of this exploration, I offer three reflections. First, how can we understand academic freedom?[3] Second, how can we understand divine revelation? Third, given these understandings, what does this say about how we should live in and live out the idea of a Catholic university? Whether or not you find these reflections persuasive, I hope that they will serve to stimulate your thinking and to advance the discussion of these vital topics.

Academic Freedom

In the United States, we tend to associate academic freedom[4] with the American Association of University Professors. The AAUP claims that "institutions of higher education are conducted for the common good and not to further the interest of either the individual teacher or the institution as a whole. The common good depends upon the free search for truth and its free exposition."[5] This principle surely deserves

---

Continuity and Development in Catholic Faith (New York: Oxford University Press, 2000), for discussions of this point.

3. *Ex corde Ecclesiae* (*EcE*) refers to academic freedom four times: 12, 29, 37, and note 15. What I propose in this section and in the final part of this essay is intended to flesh out this concept (left rather undeveloped in *EcE*).

4. I am indebted to James L. Heft, SM, for discussions on this topic. Also see his "Academic Freedom and the Catholic Community," in *Theology and the University: The Annual Publication of the College Theology Society 35 (1987)*, ed. John Apczynski (Lanham, MD: University Press of America, 1990), 207–36; and "Academic Freedom and the Catholic University," a talk given at the University of Notre Dame, March 8, 2006. Thanks to Fr. Heft, Dr. Maureen Tilley, and Dr. J. Patrick Hornbeck II for comments on an earlier version of this talk. They, of course, are not responsible for my reflections.

5. "Protecting Academic Freedom," American Association of University Professors, accessed August 21, 2017, http://www.aaup.org/issues/academic-freedom. Also see *EcE* 4; National Conference of Catholic Bishops, "The Application of *Ex corde Ecclesiae* for the United States," *Origins* 29, no. 25 (December 1, 1999): 402–9. See also Committee on Catholic Education, United States Conference of Catholic Bishops, *Catholic Mission and Culture in Colleges and Universities: Defining Documents: 1965–2014* (Washington, DC: USCCB,

our endorsement. Consideration of "the common good" has so terribly diminished in public discourse in the United States that *advocacy* for the common good has become a distinguishing characteristic of specifically Catholic social thought. The search for truth is certainly a Catholic commitment. In the AAUP's 1970 comments on their key 1940 statement, they also note that members of the academic profession have "responsibilities to institutions and students," among others.[6] Linking rights and responsibilities, not merely asserting rights, is also characteristic of Catholic social thought. How could one object to such principles?

One might object to them by how they are fleshed out. First, the central AAUP principles apply only to "teachers" and "researchers." Students are not *subjects* of academic freedom in the AAUP statement, a glaring omission.[7] Second, while all in the academy—including those of us who work in explicitly denominational institutions—should be appreciative of the protections afforded by peer review and due process promoted by AAUP, the notion of "freedom" inscribed in these documents is almost purely procedural. Is that notion of freedom sufficiently robust for Catholics to wholeheartedly support it? Third, the AAUP more recently stated, "A college or university is *a marketplace of ideas*, and it cannot fulfill its purposes of transmitting, evaluating, and extending knowledge if it requires conformity with *any orthodoxy of content and methods*."[8] The image of a university as a "market" is rooted in the notion that the fittest ideas will survive in a free competition—a kind of intellectual Darwinism. But no marketplace is entirely free, and stretch-

2014), 216–34, esp. article 2. Also available at the USCCB website, accessed August 21, 2017, http://www.usccb.org/beliefs-and-teachings/how-we-teach/catholic-education/higher-education/the-application-for-ex-corde-ecclesiae-for-the-united-states.cfm.

6. AAUP, "1940 Statement of Principles on Academic Freedom and Tenure," accessed October 28, 2014, http://www.aaup.org/report/1940-statement-principles-academic-freedom-and-tenure.

7. In "Academic Freedom and Outside Speakers" (2007), the AAUP mentioned the students' "liberty to learn," accessed October 30, 2014, http://www.aaup.org/report/academic-freedom-and-outside-speakers. Although the AAUP focus is on the faculty, they have more recently begun to give attention to students as subjects of academic freedom, but apparently only as self-funding consumers in a marketplace of ideas.

8. AAUP, "Recommended Institutional Regulations on Academic Freedom and Tenure" (2013 version of recommendations first developed in 1957), accessed October 28, 2014, http://www.aaup.org/report/recommended-institutional-regulations-academic-freedom-and-tenure (emphasis added).

ing "the survival of the fittest" to cover ideas is rather implausible. Can Catholics endorse such a consumerist notion of the search for truth valorized by the AAUP's image of the university as a market? And can't some ideas—for example, "hate speech"—be precluded from academia, as they can be and sometimes are terribly harmful in the time before they eventually wither in the face of "fitter" ideas? Although the marketplace of ideas may well "weed out" bad science, such as the idea of "cold fusion," bad ideas in the social sciences and humanities, and especially in ethics, may "live long and prosper," potentially doing terrible damage to generations of students. Such a Darwinian approach is, at best, inadequate.[9]

What this means is that the procedural version of academic freedom is *necessary* for all colleges and universities to thrive, but *not sufficient*. Catholic colleges and universities cannot *be* institutions of higher learning without procedural safeguards such as those of the AAUP. Yet to serve the common good, there needs to be at least a minimal conception of what the common good is. Now, politically and socially we debate many constituents of what constitutes "the common good," but "serving the common good" is more than offering a consumerist marketplace for ideas judged only by how many consumers buy them. How can we figure out what that "more" is? Whatever it is, it will be *substantial*, not merely *procedural*.[10]

A step in that direction can be seen in the AAUP Principles, which state that academic freedom entitles teachers "to freedom in the classroom in discussing *their subject*, but they should be careful not to introduce into their teaching controversial matter which has no relation to *their subject*."[11] So if they abandon their subject, the concept of academic freedom cannot apply to them—certainly in the classroom, but I would argue in their research as well.[12]

9. There are also some views with no rational support. Call these "green cheese" ideas: it is irrational to propose and argue for the claim that the moon is made of green cheese. Academic freedom does not extend to advocating rationally indefensible ideas as worthy of being held by a reasonable person. Even in the marketplace of ideas, some proposals should be left out as simply not worthy of anyone buying them.

10. According to *EcE* 12, a Catholic university "possesses that institutional autonomy necessary to perform its functions effectively and guarantees its members academic freedom, so long as the rights of the individual person and of the community are preserved within the confines of the truth and the common good." Also see 29, 37, and norms 4 and 5.

11. AAUP, "1940 Statement of Principles"; emphasis added.

12. "Academic freedom" is not the same thing as "freedom of speech." The former is a

The academic freedom to inquire and to decide among contested proposals presumes that the subject or realm of knowledge is under inquiry. Far more claims made in the particular realm are *not* under inquiry in doing research. Just as sailors at sea cannot replace all of the parts of a ship at one time, but must stand upon the whole to replace a plank, so scholars presume a whole set of claims and values as they debate one particular aspect of that nexus.[13] For example, in evaluating claims about "dark matter," physicists presume a huge structure of theoretical physics; in exploring evolution, biologists accept an overarching scheme in order to bring clarity to particular controverted areas in the scheme; in debating the morality of contraception, Catholic theologians presume a huge structure of theology; in analyzing St. Augustine's attitudes toward women, historians presume a body of reliable texts and much interpretive work.[14] If some abandon the structure of physics, they abandon physics as a subject; if some abandon evolution, they abandon biology as a discipline; if some abandon the structure of theology, they abandon theology as a discipline; if some try to interpret Augustine with no reference to historical interpretation, they are abandoning history as a discipline. Academic freedom to explore and assert a particular claim requires taking for granted—presuming—the claims of the discipline.

Academic freedom, then, is freedom to seek truth in pursuing a subject. But this freedom presumes "the subject" that is pursued. If one abandons the subject, one abandons the academic freedom associated

---

right relative to research and teaching; the latter is a broader political right independent of academic freedom.

13. Philosophers call this point "Neurath's Boat." See W. V. O. Quine, *Word and Object* (Cambridge: Massachusetts Institute of Technology Press, 2013), 3: "We are like sailors who on the open sea must reconstruct their ship but are never able to start afresh from the bottom. Where a beam is taken away a new one must at once be put there, and for this the rest of the ship is used as support. In this way . . . the ship can be shaped entirely anew, but only by gradual reconstruction."

14. Unfortunately, over the last half century or so, we have lost the ability to use "theological notes." Such glosses were used to show the status of doctrines. Some are *de fide divina*, or to controvert is to controvert the heart of the faith; *any* disputes in this area are weighty and demanding. Others are as low as *probable*; these are certainly debatable. The form and content of the notes are a matter of debate, but investigating the doctrine that Jesus Christ was truly human and truly divine is certainly more profound than denying the reality of limbo or purgatory, or affirming some moral liceity for sexual congress not open to reproduction undertaken in a morally good relationship.

with the subject one has abandoned. Within the subject, no formula or issue is beyond question. But when questioning one issue or formula, as in repairing one part of the ship, one must stand on the ship as a whole and take the whole of the body of work "for granted." Without the subject as a whole discipline, there is no academic freedom.

The next step is to see how academic freedom can serve the common good in a Catholic university where theologians and other scholars work to explicate and illuminate God's creation and revelation. To move to that question first requires an understanding of divine revelation.

Divine Revelation or "Revealed Truth"

In this section, I offer four reflections on revelation. First, what is revelation? Fundamentally, it is God's self-manifestation. In his introduction to the English translation of the Dogmatic Constitution on Divine Revelation of the Second Vatican Council, R. A. F. McKenzie, SJ, lays out elements of a doctrine of revelation. Revelation is a "manifestation by God—primarily of Himself; secondarily of His will and intentions." That manifestation is a communication that is "part of a larger pattern ... destined ultimately for the good of all." This communication is public, not private, and "has to be made known to others by the testimony of its recipient. Passed on orally, it *becomes* tradition; recorded in writing, it *becomes* Scripture." Hence Scripture and tradition *contain* revelation, but neither Scripture nor tradition simply *is* divine revelation. McKenzie sees that the relationship between divine revelation on the one hand, and Scripture and tradition on the other, is not to be conceived as between a whole and its parts, but as Scripture and tradition in some way sacramentally bearing revelation.[15]

15. R. A. F. McKenzie, SJ, "Revelation," in *Documents of Vatican II*, ed. Walter M. Abbott, SJ, and Joseph Gallagher (New York: Guild Press, America Press, Association Press, 1966), 106, emphasis added. McKenzie also comments on the particularity of revelation—that it occurs at specific times and places to or for specific people. As a way of claiming that revelation is not some universally diffused background noise to which humans may or may not listen, this claim is unexceptionable. Yet it can be misleading in that it may open the door for the disputes about the "bearers" of revelation too quickly. Questions such as "Is this person, text, tradition, practice revelatory?" are questions for appraisal. They come only after (at least logically) one has come to at least tentative answers to questions about what revelation is and how it functions.

Avery Dulles, SJ, defined revelation as "the self-manifestation of God through a form of communication that could be termed, at least in a broad sense, symbolic" (266).[16] In his analysis of the Vatican II's understanding of revelation, he noted that the Council "clearly taught that the Holy Spirit is active in continuing to communicate the revelation already given … Granted that God addresses the Church through the Scriptures and the sacraments, does God not speak also through creation and through secular history?" (234–35). Revelation is God's "word," but not a communication narrowly limited to the formal structures, not limited to the history or texts of Judaism and Christianity, and not fully contained in particular events and people of the past. McKenzie's comments and Dulles's theological claims articulate a contemporary, orthodox Catholic account of revelation.

Second, how can we understand revelation? Here Cardinal Dulles has much to offer. He rejected claims that revelation can be construed as the delivery of immutable divine propositions into the hands or ears of ancient writers (objectivism) or as the influence of a purely internal light or feeling or focal awareness on the part of individuals (subjectivism). As he put it, God does not insert "prefabricated propositions … into the human mind" (267). Dulles also distinguishes "virtual" revelation from "actual" revelation. Virtual revelation is God's self-manifestation ontologically prior to its being accepted. Acceptance in faith makes virtual revelation actual.[17]

Dulles finds that revelation both shapes and is shaped by faith. He wrote:

16. Avery Dulles, SJ, *Models of Revelation*, 2nd ed. (Maryknoll, NY: Orbis Books, 1992), 266. Subsequent references to this book will be given parenthetically in the text of this section that develops work on Dulles's theology presented in *Inventing Catholic Tradition*, 170–77. Lest it be thought that Dulles's position is, in some sense, purely "symbolist" or "merely symbolic," Dulles affirms that God's symbolic communication should be understood as a sacramental symbol; such symbols "contain and mediate the reality they signify" (267). In this, Dulles is an epistemic realist: "symbols give rise to true affirmations about what is antecedently real" (267).

17. Cf. Joseph Ratzinger: "For revelation always and only becomes a reality where there is faith," as in "The Question of the Concept of Tradition: A Provisional Response," in *God's Word: Scripture—Tradition—Office*, trans. H. Taylor (San Francisco: Ignatius Press, 2008 [1965]), 52.

On the one hand, revelation precedes faith inasmuch as, before anyone can believe there must be symbols wherein God expresses what he is, and wills to be, for the world. These symbols, before their meaning is understood and accepted, are virtual revelation. When believers accept revelation, they allow their minds to be determined by the meaning they find in the symbols. Thus revelation shapes their faith.

On the other hand, faith exists before revelation inasmuch as the symbols do not yield their meaning except to religious inquirers or believers who are actively committed to the search for truth. The quest itself involves a kind of implicit faith—a confidence that the search is not a futile one and that God's revelation, if it exists, can be recognized. When the search has succeeded, faith actively receives revelation and provides it, so to speak, with a dwelling place in the mind. Since revelation cannot exist as such outside a created mind, revelation may be said to presuppose faith. (279–80)

Without such acceptance in faith, revelation is real but only virtual, and thus inaccessible to those who have not accepted it.

Dulles finds that revelatory symbols display human responses to the divine initiative. The claim that, in some way, humans create their own symbols arbitrarily and then dub them with the honorific "revelation" is anathema. For Dulles, true symbols must be reflective of the real, and specifically the real manifestation of God in "the interplay of nature and history" (266). Nonetheless, no "clear dichotomy can be drawn between the symbolic and the nonsymbolic" (132). Dulles distinguishes "the figures of speech and the literary imagery" that are based on the fundamental symbols "out of which they emerge" (267). Whether the fundamental symbols are "bases" for reflections or "distillations" of what is received is arguable. Clearly, they "are not pure creations of the human imagination. The basic symbols of Christian revelation … are the persons, events, and other realities whereby God brings into existence the community of faith we call the Christian Church" (266).[18] For Dulles,

18. Dulles's assertion that revelatory symbols are not pure human creations is not surprising. No human linguistic constructions are so pure. Each construction grows out of previous practices and beliefs. Just as there is no pure "given" available to us as human knowers, as in the much-discussed "myth of the given," neither is there a pure "taken" in human knowing as if knowing were pure construction. If virtual revelation is a pure given, it is not available to us. For discussion of the "myth of the given," see Wilfred Sellars, "Empiricism and the Philosophy of Mind," in *Minnesota Studies in the Philosophy of*

revelation "is always mediated through symbol" (131) and produced in particular historical contexts.[19]

Symbols carry meaning. They get their meaning from a web of meanings, a semiotic system. If revelation is always mediated through symbols, then actual revelation must be expressed in symbols that acquire their meaning in a semiotic system. Although events, texts, people, or things may be virtually (potentially) revelatory, there is no way to identify or recognize them except in the response of faith as symbols—which transforms those objects into actual revelation. Dulles also claims that there are "real symbols" out of which the "figures of speech and literary imagery" of religious symbolism emerge" (266). These are not virtual, but actual symbols expressing revelation. Part of theological work—which assumes in its discipline *that* there is divine revelation—is to explore *what* symbols are actively revelatory and central to the tradition: we need to discern which symbols and figures are effective. Questions about which symbols we should use to express faith effectively are dealt with in the discipline of theology, the discipline St. Anselm called "faith seeking understanding."

Dulles recognizes that the symbols we use to express and understand divine revelation are "given in a specific history" and mediated through Scripture "read in the light of living and ongoing tradition" (268). God's self-manifestation through and in symbolic communication "has cognitive value that can be expressed, to some extent in true propositions" (268).

But as symbols get meaning from the semiotic systems that "house" them, so propositions get their meaning from the sentences we use to express them in natural human languages. If propositions exist (and there is some debate about that among philosophers), they can only be expressed in human languages. Human languages are not immutable. The meaning of sentences can and does shift as the language shifts—historical theologians, for example, generally accept that the meaning

Science, vol. 1, ed. H. Feigl and M. Scriven (Minneapolis: University of Minnesota Press, 1956), 253–329.

19. Dulles does not mean that theologians progressively elucidate the faith in the problematic way that would affirm we got it better today than Aquinas did in the thirteenth century. Dulles's approach of "historical situationism" is explored especially in "Tradition as a Theological Source," in *The Craft of Theology* (New York: Crossroad, 1996), 87–104.

of "person" in contemporary English is different from the meaning of *prosōpon* in ancient Greek or even *persona* in ancient Latin, so "There are two natures in one person, Jesus Christ" in contemporary English may not (and I think cannot) convey exactly what the ancient creeds did. Theologians explore whether sentences that do not share "cognate" terms like "person" and "persona" may better express Christological doctrine today.

Third, it is clear for Dulles that revelation is not an epistemic foundation for faith independent of faith. Revelation, in Dulles's view, cannot function as a source or norm of faith independent of *the response(s) of faith.* Actual revelation is not prior to faith but is the correlate of faith. Because "virtual revelation" is not available to us without faith, revelation cannot function as a foundation for Christian faith and practice, but as the correlate of faith within a tradition of the practice of faith.[20] Thus we cannot directly examine God's "virtual revelation" or use "virtual revelation" to warrant our claims. We can only utilize actual revelation, the correlate of faith, and examine revelatory symbols that express divine revelation in the concrete.

The question is *not* whether God reveals—Catholic theology as a discipline presumes that it is not up for question in the discipline of Catholic theology. Rather, theologians must ask, "Which responses to God serve well to express God's self-manifestation for us?"

Fourth, if Dulles's account of revelation as historically contextualized symbolic mediation is an adequate account of revelation as promulgated by Vatican II on revelation, what follows? Three implications seem to me important in this area.

1. The exploration of the symbols and sentences that express the truth that God has revealed is a work proper to theologians. Theological disciplines explore how to communicate what God is revealing.

An analogous approach is found in the *Essay on Development* by John Henry Newman. For Newman, the idea of Christianity *appears*

20. Dulles writes, "God, as encompassing cause, produces both the symbols that speak to faith and the faith that discerns the symbols" (280). I would say that God is the primary cause; humans responding to God are secondary causes. For a brief account of the history of the use of revelation as a foundational category in Catholic theology, see Francis Schüssler Fiorenza, *Foundational Theology: Jesus and the Church* (New York: Crossroad, 1985), 256–59, 266–67. His alternative hermeneutical approach is summarized at 285–311.

in a succession of historical events, but is not *reducible to* them. Divine faith *is* what it is. The events *show* what it is. Newman distinguished what *constitutes* faith (an ontological claim: it is a divine gift, as is Dulles's "revelation") from how we *recognize* which claims express the faith (an epistemological claim akin to Dulles's understanding of the symbols of faith). Newman is clear that the idea of Christianity never changes essentially. What clearly develops is the expression of that idea: "these expressions [creeds and dogmas] are never equivalent to" the idea. Nonetheless, these expressions "live in the one idea which they are designed to express, and which alone is substantive ... Catholic dogmas are, after all, but symbols of a divine fact, which, far from being compassed by those very propositions, would not be exhausted, not fathomed, by a thousand."[21] The historical events that constitute change in the expressions of the faith thus do not determine what the faith is, but express and show the faith.

It is difficult to overstate the importance of the distinction of what a thing *is* and what *expresses* and *shows* it. This is not at all the same distinction as the classic philosophical distinction between "appearances" and "reality." The faith is a divine gift that is lived in and lived out. The life of faith is a life lived under the guidance of a Christian vision. The articulation of that vision and the practice of the faith vary from time to time and place to place. None of those expressions and other practices is sufficient to express fully and completely the true gift of God. They are expressions of that gift. These expressions are necessary if the gift of faith is to be communicated and known; without them, the faith cannot be known or communicated "in this world." The faith, then, is not reducible to any one articulation or any one pattern of practice (though some expressions and practices are incompatible with authentic expressions; hence Newman's notes on what constitutes an authentic development). The idea of Christianity never changes, but its expressions do. In short, theologians can properly dispute about how God acts in self-manifestation and whether particular human responses are revelatory—disputes about particular claims that merit academic freedom in the overarching discipline of Catholic theology.

21. John Henry Newman, *An Essay on the Development of Christian Doctrine*, 2nd ed. (London: James Toovey, 1846), 56–57; Newman is here quoting from his *University Sermons*. See my discussion in *Inventing Catholic Tradition*, 111*ff.*

2. Such explorations require that theologians distinguish between what *makes* a claim true, how we *recognize* the truth of claims, and how we *appraise* claims. What makes a revelatory symbol true is that it expresses the self-manifestation of God. We recognize a revelatory symbol because it is reliably produced and received as properly expressing God's self-revelation in and for a community of faith.[22] But there are disputes over whether a symbol has been reliably produced, for example, the dispute over the symbols *homoousios* and *homoiousios* before the Council of Nicea in 325: both "Arians" and "Athanasians" claimed their favorite was reliably produced. But the council finally appraised and adjudicated *homoousios*, one in being, not *homoiousios*, similar in being, as the proper symbol for speaking of the Son's relationship with the Father—an authoritative appraisal or adjudication that was not universally accepted at that time, but became widely received throughout Christianity. But once we recognize that (1) what constitutes revelation differs from (2) how we recognize revelatory symbols, we still need to (3) appraise those symbols or sentences in the context of mutable human languages, and we can see that debates about the formulations of revelation in doctrinal proposals and counterproposals are proper subjects of truly free and faithful academic inquiry in Catholic theology.

To be clear, when those symbols or sentences pertain to matters essential to the faith, the Magisterium properly comes into play. Theologians may and must appraise symbols. Such appraisals may be diverse. The bishops (themselves theologians, as at Nicea, or in response to sophisticated theological disputations, as at the Council of Trent in 1545–63) have the responsibility of adjudicating theological appraisals. Episcopal adjudication is different from theological appraisal; bishops can certainly do both. However, people functioning as bishops or theo-

22. Different faith traditions can and do produce different but reliably produced (in that tradition) claims. For instance, some Christians may reliably claim that revelation is found in the Bible, while some Muslims may reliably claim that God's revelation given to Mohammed is inscribed in the Qur'an. Some scientists may even find the revelations of scientific practice to be just that—revelatory. But if multiple reliably produced (or apparently reliably produced) claims about symbols of divine revelation are "on the table," and they are in conflict, then the question is how we *appraise* them in the context of religious diversity. That issue is not on the table here, but I developed an "appraisal account of truth" to address this issue in various publications, e.g., *Inventing Catholic Tradition*, 156–70, and *Faith: What It Is and What It Isn't* (Maryknoll, NY: Orbis Books, 2010), 102–27.

logians need to be clear on the force of their statements. On the account here, appraisal and adjudication properly have different forces, are issued by people with different status in the church, and have or should have different effects. Confusing theological appraisals (proposals) with definitive teaching is harmful to the expression and the life of faith.

3. As in other investigations noted in my discussion of academic freedom earlier, inquiring about whether a particular symbol, sentence, or proposal reflects God's revelation presumes the reliability of the rest of the body of proposals that constitute the faith. One can question whether God reveals only if one steps out of the barque of theology and into the ship of philosophy. In theology, one can investigate any particular symbol or sentence for its adequacy to communicate now what God reveals. I would take this as implied by Dulles when he wrote, "Revelation, rather than being presupposed as fully known from the start, is progressively elucidated as theology carries out its task" (283).[23] Theologians, then, are not faithful to the past by repeating past formulas. Fidelity to our whole tradition may require new particular forms in the present, for neither the cultural context nor the meanings of our sentences today are sure to be identical to those of the past. Faithful theologians qua theologians do not dispute *that* God reveals, but may propose new symbols and sentences that *express* that revelation. And to serve the common good of the church, theologians whose job is to understand the faith require academic freedom, even when theologians argue for significant—and perhaps startling—changes in one or two planks of the vessel of faith while they necessarily presume the faith as a whole.

The Catholic University

If my earlier comments regarding academic freedom are accurate, then a Catholic university can be neither a mere marketplace of ideas nor a closed circle that admits only those who are "in conformity with an orthodoxy of content and methods," as argued above. The former neglects the necessary commitment of scholars to substantial components of disciplines necessary for true academic freedom and espouses

23. See note 19 above.

a procedural account of freedom. The latter fails to allow for the necessary freedom of exploration required for properly doing any form of academic investigation, especially a theological one. So, what is left for a Catholic university?[24]

Here, our reflection on Cardinal Dulles's account of revelation and the work of theologians as well as a decade-old conversation between Archbishop Daniel Pilarczyk, co-chair of the National Conference of Catholic Bishops Subcommittee on *mandatum* and the religious studies department of the University of Dayton, provide a template for answering this question.[25] The conversation established that basic competency requires Catholic theologians—and others—to present Catholic teaching as Catholic teaching, that is, to inform the students about what the Church does teach. Catholic theologians should also present the arguments for that position. Archbishop Pilarczyk also agreed that Catholic theologians may present other positions and the arguments for them that are not in accord with current magisterial teaching. Catholic theologians may even indicate that they accept dissident positions on particular issues on the basis of "better" arguments. But neither Catholic theologians—nor any other faculty—can advocate that the students accept the professor's position as the students' own rather than the position of the official ecclesial Magisterium. In other words, the student must have the freedom to take her or his own position based on a judg-

24. To be blunt, *EcE*, for all its strengths, has been less than helpful at some points. For example, the recommendation that a majority of faculty should be Catholic may seem impractical for many universities, and also may run afoul of US labor law. I argued that point regarding the *mandatum* in "The 'Academic *Mandatum*' and Hiring and Retention in the Universities and Colleges," a report submitted to the Ad Hoc Committee on the *Mandatum* of the NCCB, November 11, 2000; revised October 21, 2001. If a religious affiliation or credential were not a Bonafide Occupational Requirement (BFOQ) required of all members of a unit of the university, it is not a BFOQ under US labor law. *Mandatum* may be a BFOQ for a department or unit composed exclusively of Roman Catholic theologians, but *mandatum* does not and cannot ensure conformity with current magisterial teaching among the professoriate. A few Catholic institutions hire only Roman Catholics for their theology departments, but most do not; for the majority, a *mandatum* requirement is dubiously legal. Whether a *mandatum* requirement is wise or effective is another question.

25. See James L. Heft, SM, "The Meaning of the *Mandatum*: A Report on the Dialogue Between One Archdiocese and a Catholic University Faculty of Theology," *Catholic Education: A Journal of Inquiry and Practice* 6, no. 4 (July 2003): 491–97; my understanding of this section of our dialogue (I was the Religious Studies Department chair at the University of Dayton at the time of the dialogue) goes beyond Heft's report, esp. at 496.

ment informed by fair and balanced presentation of current positions and the arguments for and against them.[26]

I would claim that this pattern can apply throughout the university. The student has the freedom to accept or reject various positions. That freedom is positive and negative. It is positive in that students must be enabled to understand the discipline, and that there are varied ideas and arguments for and against particular proposals within the discipline; they must be supported in their own search for truth about particular issues; and they should be shown the likely implications of accepting particular proposals in theory and in practice. It is negative in that the students must be free from being coerced or intimidated, whether in theology or physics.[27]

Given the variety of Roman Catholic colleges and universities around the country and around the world, a "one-size-fits-all" approach seems unwarranted. But the application of *Ex corde Ecclesiae* for the United States articulates a helpful general principle for maintaining the Catholic identity of the Catholic university. The *Application* states:

The responsibility for safeguarding and strengthening the Catholic identity of the university rests primarily with the university itself. All the members of the university community are called to participate in this important task in accordance with their specific roles: the sponsoring religious community, the board of trustees, the administration and staff, the faculty, and the students ... Men and women of religious faiths other than Catholic, on the board of trustees, on the faculty, and in other positions, can make a valuable contribution to the university. Their presence affords the opportunity for all

26. Here the notion of "theological notes," which has seemingly fallen into disuse, is helpful and has relevance. Both teacher and student should be aware, at least implicitly, of the status of the proposal under discussion so as to set burdens of proof correctly. An argument against a truly central and traditional doctrine has a high burden of proof to bear—perhaps something like "certain beyond a reasonable doubt." An argument against a traditional theological opinion (such as the post-Tridentine opinion that there are "two sources of revelation," a position attributed to the Council of Trent but not found in the documents) has (and had, at Vatican II) a much lighter burden of proof. An argument about current theological opinion may have a burden of proof that is equal for all sides. Determining where the burden of proof lies and what burden must be met can be clarified if one understands the "theological note" attached to the proposal or appraisal under dispute.

27. This does not entail a freedom to act on those proposals that they come to accept as a result of their reflection—exploring that issue requires far more discussion than this essay allows.

to learn and benefit from each other. The university should welcome them as *full partners in the campus community.*[28]

How can our universities put this principle into practice?

My friend and sometime colleague James L. Heft, SM, the director of the Institute for Advanced Catholic Studies now housed at the University of Southern California, has spoken frequently of an open circle as a useful image for the Catholic university. People of all faiths and of no faith, from every relevant discipline, are invited into the open circle of the Catholic university. The circle presumes (not without discussion, debate, criticism, and even disagreement) that an open and broad tradition, the Catholic intellectual tradition, centers the circle, however diverse the positions that members take may be.[29] The open circle is a polyphony of diverse voices, always in danger of becoming a cacophony of the laissez-faire market-place of ideas or a monotony of repetitive orthodox statements.

Centering on a Catholic intellectual tradition may ameliorate those possibilities. The Catholic intellectual tradition accepts some fundamental principles, such as those articulated in *Ex corde Ecclesiae* §15: "In a Catholic University, research necessarily includes (*a*) the search for an *integration of knowledge*, (*b*) a *dialogue between faith and reason*, (*c*) an *ethical concern*, and (*d*) a theological perspective." Not every member of the university community needs to accept these principles, but there should be an acknowledgment that such principles center the circle as a whole. Each community member contributes in a distinctive way to the work of the circle, even if those principles do not center on her or his teaching or research program. To discuss the full ramifications of this view would take far more time than we have here, but one is clear: a Catholic university as an open circle has a place for the discipline of theology and for practitioners of that discipline to have unfettered academic freedom as they work in teaching and research in the discipline, because our common good in the university is centered in understanding God's creation and self-manifestation.

28. "Application of *Ex corde Ecclesiae* for the United States," Norms, Article 4, §1, emphasis added. An explanatory reference to the text of *Ex corde Ecclesiae* is elided from the quotation.

29. I proffer a grammar for this tradition in *Inventing Catholic Tradition*, chapter 5. Others will have other accounts of the Catholic intellectual tradition; the very concept itself is thus an open—and controverted—one in Catholic academia.

Heft also argues that it is more important that the Catholic university not merely hire Catholics with doctorates who can teach, but Catholic *scholars*. What are Catholic scholars? Heft described them in the following way:

> Catholic scholars, indeed religious scholars, approach their disciplines with certain presuppositions: that the more deeply one gets into what it means to be human, the more inescapable are religious questions; that the more deeply one gets into any area of scholarship, the more likely one finds it necessary to make connections with other areas of knowledge; that the more intellectually vibrant a religious tradition is, the more it will learn from and influence the larger culture in which it is located; and that the incarnation, for Christian scholars, is a theological focal point for all these suppositions.[30]

If this is correct—and I think it mostly is—then hiring for mission is crucial for a Catholic university. But to do that requires articulating a college's or university's distinctive mission, not merely its "brand," and our various institutions will have and should have a variety of missions. In general, however, a key is hiring and developing faculty and staff who are willing to join the open circle by being, at minimum, somewhat sympathetic to the college's or university's mission, including the commitments appropriate to the Catholic intellectual tradition.

Conclusion

If my reflections are on track, then there is or should be a harmony between the practices of academic freedom and the exploration of God's self-revelation in a Catholic university that has a place for theology and valorizes the Catholic intellectual tradition. How this harmony is to be orchestrated will vary, of course, depending on the distinctive missions of the institutions.

Our various Catholic colleges and universities also form an open circle of diversity, but it is a circle of conviction. "Conviction of what?" you ask. The answer can be found in *Ex corde Ecclesiae* §17, which quotes

30. Heft, "Academic Freedom and the Catholic University," typescript, 5. In *Inventing Catholic Tradition*, chapter 5, I claim that the Incarnation and an analogical imagination are central to the Catholic intellectual tradition.

from *Gaudium et Spes* §36. Here's what the Second Vatican Council said in *Gaudium et Spes* on this matter:

> if methodological investigation within every branch of learning is carried out in a genuinely scientific manner and in accord with moral norms, it never truly conflicts with faith. For earthly matters and the concerns of faith derive from the same God. Indeed, whoever labors to penetrate the secrets of reality with a humble and steady mind, is, even unawares, being led by the hand of God, who holds all things in existence and gives them their identity.[31]

However rocky and difficult the proximate work may be, the conviction that unites us is that God has created a diversely awesome universe, including quarks, mosquitos, dolphins, and human societies and that God calls us to many diverse ways to understand its graced beauty. This commitment grounds our hope that ultimately whatever cacophony of discord appears in our shared work now will resolve into an amazing, almost unbearable, chorus of polyphonic hymnody. This commitment to understanding God's creation and self-manifestation shows the necessity of freedom to explore and perhaps dispute even the symbols and sentences that express the revealed truth of God's self-manifestation. This commitment grounds the academic freedom in a Catholic college or university. Or at least *I* think it does, for this commitment articulates what I see as our common good—to glorify God in our shared work, a God who manifests God's infinite goodness in all creation—and all of that good creation is open to our exploration in a Catholic university.

31. Vatican II, pastoral constitution *Gaudium et Spes*, December 7, 1965: *Acta Apostolicae Sedis* 58 (1966): 1025–115. English translation from Abbott and Gallagher, *Documents of Vatican II*, 234.

[5]

The Dialogue between Faith and Reason in a Catholic University

Susan K. Wood, SCL

The relationship between faith and reason in the context of a Catholic university bears on the proper relationship between secular learning and Christian commitment and thought, as well as on the relationship of a Catholic university precisely as a university and the Church. We ask, what does Athens have to do with Jerusalem?[1] How does Athens enrich Jerusalem? What does Jerusalem bring to Athens?

I propose that Catholic universities are places where the Church does its thinking,[2] that faith is enriched by its encounter with nontheological disciplines, that the Catholic university has a sacramental character, and that within this sacramental structure the university's primary activity is witnessing. Good thinking requires that theology and the Church look beyond themselves to other areas of knowledge. Theology needs this if it is to offer an integrative vision of creation, anthropology, and history. The Church requires this if it is to engage in mission

1. Tertullian, *Prescription against Heretics*, VII.

2. Bishop Spalding stated at the Third Plenary Council of Baltimore, "the ecclesiastical seminary is not a school of intellectual culture, either here in America or elsewhere, and to imagine that it can become an instrument of intellectual culture is to cherish a delusion." Cited by John Tracy Ellis, "American Catholics and the Intellectual Life," *Thought* (Autumn 1955): 351–88, at 371. Spalding maintained that a seminary was rightly a training school for a profession, even if that profession might be expected to have more than an ordinary kinship for intellectual pursuits.

beyond itself as opposed to mere self-maintenance. Bernard Lonergan urged theologians to seek integration with the other human sciences so that the Church might "remove from its action the widespread impression of complacent irrelevance and futility."[3] If the Church is to be truly Catholic, it need not only be open to all truth, but also engaged with all truth so that it may be a leaven within society.

In support of this position, we need only to think of the contributions of Thomas Aquinas, whose work originated not in a seminary or a monastery, but at the University of Paris, where he engaged with the new world represented by Aristotelian philosophy and Arabic science. We might also remember that Thomas was suspect in his own time for doing this. At his time in history, the medieval university still had close connections with the Church through charters from the Church. It was a clerical institution, and the intellectuals of the period with few exceptions were clerics. Of four faculties—theology, arts, medicine, and law—theology was queen. In the world of Thomas Aquinas, secular learning enriched theology at the same time that universities were largely ecclesiastical institutions.

Today, universities are not the only place where the Church's thinking occurs, but they are privileged places because of the confluence of the various elements that comprise culture, in both its historical and contemporary dimension, found within the university. Within the modern university, science, history, literary and artistic expressions of human experience, theological reflection, and professional study intersect. This rich confluence contributes to faith.

Faith is richer for the encounter with the secularity of the world as encountered in the nontheological disciplines. Of course, faith also adds a depth to secular knowledge by providing, among other things, a *telos* and a unitive worldview. Nevertheless, from the thesis that Catholic universities are places where the Church does its thinking, my emphasis is on how the university enriches the Church's understanding of the faith. Anselm defined theology as *fides quaerens intellectum*, that is, as faith seeking understanding. This does not mean that understanding replaces faith any more than the secular disciplines of a Catholic uni-

3. Cited by Joseph Komonchak in "Mission and Identity in Catholic Universities," in *Theological Education in the Catholic Tradition*, ed. Patrick W. Carey and Earl C. Muller, SJ (New York: Crossroad, 1997), 34–48, at 47.

versity obviate the need or desire for a theology department. Anselm's definition, however, does mean that faith uses reason to deepen and to know itself. I would add that this understanding of faith is itself broadened through encounter with the nontheological disciplines.

Typologies of the Relationship between Faith and Reason

Cardinal Avery Dulles, famous for his use of typologies, supplies a typology for the relationship between faith and reason. He comments that theologians may be divided into three main categories: those who see faith and reason as antagonistic, those who see them as pertaining to two separate spheres, and those who opt for a harmony between the two, some regarding faith as a higher form of knowledge and others looking upon faith as needing to be perfected by reason.[4] The truism often articulated by Catholics is that reason and faith, rightly understood and interpreted, cannot contradict one another because God as the author of both cannot deny himself. Nor can the truth of faith contradict the truth of science.[5]

But what faith and which reason, we may ask. Dulles hastens to acknowledge that the equivocal use of the notion of faith makes it difficult to categorize its relationship with reason. It can variously mean, for example, assent to doctrine, a unitive experience, a heartfelt trust in Christ, or a commitment to a certain style of action.[6] Similarly, the notion of reason may designate several different operations: a contemplative or intuitive reason, a discursive reason whether inductive or deductive, explicit reason, or implicit or tacit reason. This is further complicated by whether reason is understood as a power belonging to nature in a pure state, as a capacity of fallen nature, or as a faculty illuminated and elevated by grace.

Reason is an attribute of humanity and the basis of language, freedom

4. Avery Dulles, SJ, *The Assurance of Things Hoped For: A Theology of Christian Faith* (New York: Oxford University Press, 1994), 207.

5. Vatican II, pastoral constitution *Gaudium et Spes* 36, December 7, 1965: *Acta Apostolicae Sedis* (*AAS*) 58 (1966): 1025–115; *Catechism of the Catholic Church* (CCC), §159; *EcE*, 17.

6. Dulles, *Assurance of Things Hoped For*, 207.

creativity, the search for knowledge, the experience of art, and the actualization of moral commands. Without reason, participation in community is not possible.[7] As Paul Tillich states, "only a being who has the structure of reason is able to be ultimately concerned, to distinguish ultimate and preliminary concerns, to understand the unconditional commands of the ethical imperative, and to be aware of the presence of the holy."[8]

Faith is not the opposite of reason. Both extremes, fideism and extreme rationalism, have incurred ecclesiastical censures. Fideism, in the context of the nineteenth-century controversies, was the position that would not admit that one could prove with natural reason the preambles of faith, or the existence and authority of God.[9] Consequently, fideism also included the position that faith precedes reason and denied that reason leads a person to faith. Today, it is important to recognize that these nineteenth-century discussions of the relationship between faith and reason took place within a propositional model of revelation where faith was considered to be intellectual assent to the divine decrees revealed by God. The alternative to rational, objective criteria for faith was the subjective, interior experience of illumination. The whole tenor of the discussion was colored first by the limited notion of revelation predominant in the theology of the neo-Scholastics, and second by a correlatively restrictive notion of faith.

At Vatican II, the Constitution on Divine Revelation, *Dei Verbum*,[10] did not negate the previous council's pronouncements on the relation between faith, reason, and revelation, but cast them in a somewhat different light. Chapter 1 begins with God's revealing activity described in the context of salvation history. René Latourelle points out that *Dei Verbum* emphasizes the personal and theocentric character of revela-

7. Paul Tillich, *Dynamics of Faith* (New York: Harper & Row, 1957), 75.

8. Ibid., 76.

9. See, e.g., the *Theses on Faith and Reason against Fideism* subscribed to by Louis-Eugene Bautain by order of his bishop, November 18, 1835 (DH 2751–56), and the propositions the Commission of the Index presented to Augustine Bonnetty in 1855 (DH 2765–68). The First Vatican Council, in the dogmatic constitution *Dei Filius* "On the Catholic Faith" (April 24, 1870), treated the assent of faith (DH 3008–14, 3031–36) and the relationship between faith and reason (DH 3014–20, 3041–43). Canon 3 (DH 3033) explicitly condemns fideism. Rationalism is condemned in DH 3031.

10. Vatican II, dogmatic constitution *Dei verbum*, November 18, 1965: *AAS* 58 (1966): 817–30.

tion.[11] Where Vatican I states that it pleased God to reveal "the eternal decrees of his will," Vatican II states that God reveals the *sacramentum* of his will (*DV* 2).[12] Thus, rather than a legalistic and propositional notion of revelation, Vatican II presents a sacramental view. This sacramental view, wherein the hidden is made manifest by sign, encompasses the mystery of Christ. That which is revealed, the sign, does not exhaust that which is signified, the Christ, who is at once the mediator and the fullness of revelation. The word that is uttered is not merely the word of an eternal decree, but the Word, the Son of God. This personalistic view of revelation identifies revelation as a dialogue, the text using the words *alloquitur* and *conversatur* (*DV* 2).

As the notion of revelation expands, so does the notion of faith. A personalistic concept of revelation results in a dialogical address/response dynamic of faith. Not merely a "full submission of intellect and will assent to God as he reveals," "the obedience of faith" becomes also a "total and free commitment to God" (*DV* 5). Assent of intellect and will corresponds to the more propositional concept of revelation that prevailed at Vatican I. Even though the text in Vatican II's *Dei Verbum* places Vatican I's emphasis on the assent of faith by intellect and will in the broader context of total self-commitment, it does not develop this personal aspect of faith in any detail, nor does it develop the dialogical character of faith. A more adequate treatment of faith is given in the *Catechism of the Catholic Church*, where faith is situated within the personalistic context of invitation and response:

> *By his Revelation*, "the invisible God, from the fullness of his love, addresses men as his friends, and moves among them, in order to invite and receive them into his own company." The adequate response to this invitation is faith.[13]
>
> *By faith*, man completely submits his intellect and his will to God. With his whole being man gives his assent to God the revealer. Sacred Scripture calls this human response to God, the author of revelation, "the obedience of faith."[14]

11. René Latourelle, "Le Christ, signe de la révélation selon la constitution '*Dei Verbum*,'" in *Le Christ et l'Eglise signes du salut* (Montreal: Bellarmin, 1971), 71–97.

12. This is generally translated in English as "the hidden purpose of his will."

13. *CCC*, §142.

14. *CCC*, §143.

The text then draws on a personal typology of faith presenting Abraham and Mary as models of faith. It encompasses the complexity of faith as both personal adherence to God and assent to the truth of revelation in the statement "Faith is first of all a personal adherence of man to God. At the same time, and inseparably, it is a *free assent to the whole truth that God has revealed.*"[15]

The change in emphasis from Vatican I to Vatican II changes the manner in which the "signs" of what is revealed are to be interpreted, and this in turn places the role of "rational proof" in a different context. In Vatican I, the "signs," which offered rational proof of the existence and authority of God (i.e., the preambles of faith), were the miracles performed by Jesus. In Vatican II, however, all the individual miracles are set within the one decisive divine miracle that Jesus Christ exists.[16] Even though Vatican II does not negate Vatican I—because the sixth paragraph of chapter I of *Dei Verbum* reiterates that God manifests and communicates not only himself but also "the eternal decrees of his will" and states that "God, the first principle and last end of all things, can be known with certainty from the created world, by the natural light of human reason"—the position of these statements in the last paragraph of the chapter prioritizes the revelatory action of God. We can come to knowledge of God's existence through reason only because those created realities grounding the basis of our rational proof are themselves manifestations of the God who creates and conserves all things by his Word (cf. Jn 1:3) and provides evidence of himself in created realities (cf. Rom 1:19–30) (*DV* 3). Thus, even though reason may precede faith, revelation supplies the criteria of reason. This negates the possibility that reason operates independently of grace, for, in addition to the subjective assistance that prevenient grace provides the person who seeks the preambles of faith, the fact that all created reality is founded in Christ because it proceeds from God's creative Word places both faith and reason in a dependence on the revelation of God, whether this be the manifestation of his power in creation, the revelation of the eternal decrees

15. *CCC*, §150. The preceding analysis of faith and revelation is partially taken from Susan K. Wood, *One Baptism: Ecumenical Dimensions of the Doctrine of Baptism* (Collegeville, MN: Liturgical Press, 2009), 156–58.

16. Joseph Ratzinger, "Chapter I: Revelation Itself," in *Commentary on the Documents of Vatican II*, ed. Herbert Vorgrimler (New York: Herder & Herder, 1968), 176.

of his will, or the Incarnation of God's Son. Consequently, rather than set faith and reason against each other, it is more correct to examine their mutual interdependence.

Thus we must reject Dulles's first typology, the antagonism of faith and reason, especially if one is chosen at the exclusion of the other. Likewise, they cannot simply exist in separate spheres, never intersecting with one another, for reason itself judges whether there are sufficient grounds for revelation to be accepted as true, that is, as credible and worthy of belief.[17]

As for Dulles's third typology, I would not say, as some suggest, that faith is "perfected" by reason, but I do hold that faith, defined as the acceptance of revelation in whatever modality it is received, is not articulated, reflected upon, interpreted, or communicated apart from reason. Faith is not primarily epistemic—that is, a source of knowledge—but it is more basically a love for God and a volitional impulse to do as God wills. In this sense, faith is a first-order primary experience while articulated, reflected, and communicated faith represent a second-order experience necessitating reason. This relationship is analogous to how liturgical worship is primary theology, and subsequent reflection upon that experience is a second-order activity, what Aidan Kavanagh calls secondary theology.[18] Primary theology is prayer and contemplation as distinguished from secondary theological reasoning. Systematic theology forms propositions about the encounter between God and the world enacted within liturgical rites. Similarly, faith is the acceptance by intellect and will that responds in love, trust, and fidelity to God's self-communication in revelation. Neither self-reflection on that experience nor communication of that encounter occurs apart from reason.

Paul Tillich provides yet another interpretation of the interrelationship between faith and reason that integrates the two. For him, reason is the presupposition of faith, and faith is the fulfillment of reason.[19] Tillich describes the interrelationship of the two, saying, "faith is the act in which reason reaches ecstatically beyond itself."[20] Reason is finite,

17. Dulles, *Assurance of Things Hoped For*, 208.

18. Aidan Kavanagh, *On Liturgical Theology* (Collegeville, MN: Liturgical Press, 1992), 73–95.

19. Tillich, *Dynamics of Faith*, 77.

20. Ibid., 76.

but the human person experiences being grasped by what Tillich calls an "ultimate concern" and driven beyond himself or herself. A person's awareness of his or her potential infinity, this awareness appearing as ultimate concern, appears to a person as faith. Tillich says that the ecstatic experience of an ultimate concern does not destroy the structure of reason because this experience of being driven beyond oneself, what he calls "ecstasy," is "fulfilled, not denied, rationality."[21] He acknowledges that a state of estrangement from a person's true nature can lead to distorted reason and idolatrous faith but finds the solution in a revelatory experience. He defines revelation as "the experience in which an ultimate concern grasps the human mind and creates a community in which this concern expresses itself in symbols of action, imagination, and thought."[22] He says that Christianity claims to be based on this revelation. The community created by the revelation is the Church.

Tillich's analysis, more akin to a phenomenology of faith and reason than the metaphysical analysis of neo-Scholasticism, is nevertheless easily translated into the compatibility of faith and reason outlined above, faith representing the transcendent dimension of human volitional impulse toward union with God and reason, representing finite nature capable of being transformed by grace. Tillich's identification of the Church as the community created by revelation points to the communal character of faith as contrasted with more individualistic notions of faith.

Faith and Reason: Code Words for a Network of Relationships

When considered more broadly, "faith" and "reason" become code words for a whole network of relationships. Dulles observes that when Thomists contrast the two terms, they are particularly interested in the relation between the natural and the supernatural, "reason" being a cipher for natural knowledge and "faith" for supernatural knowledge.[23] Once we accept this shorthand, the relationship between faith and rea-

21. Ibid.

22. Ibid., 78.

23. Dulles, *Assurance of Things Hoped For*, 207.

son becomes analogous to the relationship between nature and grace, or church and world, or the sacred and the secular. These relationships are suggestive for a Catholic university interacting with secular disciplines and for the Church's mission in the world.

Integration of Faith and Reason in Catholic Universities

The search for the complementarity between reason and faith in the university is not new. John Tracy Ellis delivered a paper, "American Catholics and the Intellectual Life," in 1955, which became a catalyst for self-criticism among Catholic colleges and universities.[24] Ellis attributed the primary cause of the intellectual shortcomings of American Catholics to "an over eagerness in Catholic circles for apologetics rather than pure scholarship."[25] However, he also cites the effects of the anti-Catholicism of the majority of the population, the poverty and illiteracy of the Catholic immigrants, general American anti-intellectualism and the correlative general American suspicion of its academicians, the absence of an intellectual tradition among American Catholics, and the lack of serious reading habits as contributing causes of the lack of Catholic contributions to the intellectual life. He cites, for example, the invention of the term "egg head" to designate professors engaged in public affairs.[26] He quotes John Ireland, Archbishop of St. Paul, Minnesota, who five years after the Third Plenary Council of Baltimore made a plea for Catholic leadership in intellectual circles:

> This is an intellectual age. It worships intellect. It tries all things by the touchstone of intellect … The Church herself will be judged by the standard of intellect. Catholics must excel in religious knowledge … They must be in the foreground of intellectual movements of all kinds. The age will not take kindly to religious knowledge separated from secular knowledge.[27]

24. John Tracy Ellis, "American Catholics and the Intellectual Life," *Thought* (Autumn 1955): 351–88.

25. Ibid., 355.

26. Ibid., 357.

27. Ibid., 359, citing John Ireland, *The Church and Modern Society* (St. Paul, 1905), I:92.

Ellis concludes his essay laying the primary blame for the inadequacy of Catholic scholarship on Catholics themselves, on their "frequently self-imposed ghetto mentality which prevents them from mingling as they should with their non-Catholic colleagues," on their lack of industry and hard work, and on their failure to measure up to the tradition of Catholic learning to which they are heirs.[28]

Two years later, Gustave Weigel, SJ, outlined the continuous efforts of Christian philosophers to reconcile faith and reason in the Catholic intellectual tradition from Origen through Aquinas in a lecture to the Catholic Commission on Intellectual and Cultural Affairs.[29] Like Ellis,[30] Weigel attributed the deplorable failure of Catholic scholars to distinguish themselves in American university circles in 1957 to the "apologetic" approach to knowledge wherein every new scientific or literary discovery had to be reconciled with an already defined "truth."

Under the auspices of the North American region of the International Federation of Catholic Universities, a group of Catholic educators issued the Land O'Lakes Statement on July 23, 1967, which articulated the relationship of the modern American Catholic university to the Church and to American intellectual life.[31] It identified the Catholic university as a community "in which Catholicism is perceptibly present and effectively operative." It affirmed theology as a legitimate intellectual discipline and identified its primary task to:

> Engage directly in exploring the depths of Christian tradition and the total religious heritage of the world, in order to come to the best possible intellectual understanding of religion and revelation, of man in all his varied relationships to God. Particularly important today is the theological exploration of all human relations and the elaboration of a Christian anthropology. Furthermore, theological investigation today must serve the ecumenical goals of collaboration and unity.

28. Ellis, "American Catholics and the Intellectual Life," 386.

29. Gustave Weigel, SJ, "American Catholic Intellectualism—A Theologian's Reflections," *Review of Politics* 19, no. 3 (July 1957): 275–307.

30. Ellis, "American Catholics and the Intellectual Life," 355.

31. "The Land O'Lakes Statement," Office of University Mission and Ministry, Boston College, accessed February 25, 2015, http://www.bc.edu/content/dam/files/offices/mission/pdf1/cu8.pdf.

The statement called for dialogue within the university so that theology would confront all the rest of modern culture and all areas of intellectual study. It affirmed the autonomy of all the recognized university areas of study and disavowed any theological or philosophical imperialism at the same time that it pointed to the philosophical and theological dimension of most intellectual subjects.

Almost fifty years later, while Catholic universities have improved their stature in the academic community, most still struggle to achieve the integration of faith and knowledge envisioned by the document. The theological disciplines themselves—not to mention the various secular disciplines—have become increasingly specialized with a consequent fragmentation of knowledge. This has been accompanied by a commodification and a commercialization of knowledge in the wider university. Students increasingly choose majors for their earning power. Evaluations on ratemyprofessors.com include whether a student must read anything to pass a course. Evening television commercials advertise intensified business degrees that can be earned in a couple of years by attending class one evening a week. The hoped-for dialogue wherein theology engages all areas of intellectual study simply has not occurred to the extent either anticipated or desired. In recognition of this intellectual fragmentation, one hears increasing calls for interdisciplinarity on college campuses today. The problem is not just with theology or with faith encountering secularity, but with all knowledge being increasingly specialized and increasingly fragmented.

In the spirit of the dialogic approach to revelation and its response in faith of *Dei Verbum*, the unity of faith and reason in a Catholic university should promote dialogue between theology and the secular disciplines. In addition to creating campus structures and conversations that foster engagement across differences rather than perpetuating academic silos, however, Catholics need a contemporary intellectual framework to account for the different kinds of knowledge represented by theology and science, or theology and art, or theology and history. The category of sacrament offers such a framework, as seen in the work of George O'Brien and Michael Himes.

George Dennis O'Brien in his 2002 book *The Idea of a Catholic University* examines the models of the Church developed by Avery Dulles to determine which might offer the best vehicle for explaining the relationship between the academy and the Church. The juridical model, which establishes truth on the basis of authority, represents a methodology unacceptable to the academic freedom granted to disciplinary competence. O'Brien rejects the mystical model as evaporating visible definition and legal restrictions and therefore as not helpful in adjudicating issues surrounding the academy and the Church. O'Brien observes that although there may be anonymous Christians, there cannot be an "anonymous Catholic university" even if "some universities are pretty anonymous about their Catholicity."[32] For O'Brien, the heraldic/prophetic model and the servant model, both of which he considers more characteristic of Protestant institutions, are liable to secularism. He finds the heraldic model more appropriate to the pulpit than the professor's podium while—rightly or wrongly—he suspects the servant model as slipping into nineteenth-century Protestant liberalism, although I strongly suspect liberation theology would give this a different interpretation.

O'Brien opts for the sacramental model and extends this into a kind of knowing proper to faith within a Catholic university. He argues for the differences in the kinds of knowing among the various disciplines within a university, and identifies faith's way of knowing as sacramental such that "Catholic university = sacrament + science." According to this view, a Catholic university is "a conjunction of the sacramental and the scientific."[33] Sacramental knowledge is iconic as a way of seeing into the really real through participatory knowledge. Science or any other secular discipline provides the material "stuff," the visible reality, which functions as the icon of the really real. This "stuff" is not itself the ultimate object of knowing, but the portal, as it were, into ultimate meaning.[34]

Francis C. Wade, SJ, former professor of philosophy at Marquette University, although he does not explicitly use the category of "sacrament," points to the character of this ultimate meaning as mystery when he says that a role of the Catholic university is to be an advocate of mystery and to keep mystery alive in the world of intellect in the sense

32. George Dennis O'Brien, *The Idea of a Catholic University* (Chicago: University of Chicago Press, 2002), 154.

33. Ibid., 175.

34. This is not exactly as he explains it, but rather my interpretation of the relationships he seems to be presenting. I may be extrapolating from his thought a bit.

that things have "further and deeper meaning" and "inexhaustible possibilities for more human knowledge."[35] Ultimately, this mystery is a participation in the mystery of God, who as infinite is an inexhaustible object of knowledge. Wade says that the theological way to state this relationship is "to say that a Christian should find God in all things."[36]

Michael Himes develops the importance of the principle of sacramentality in Catholic intellectual life, stating that education is training in sacramental beholding so that "anything that awakens, enlivens, and expands the imagination, opens the vision, and enriches the sensitivity of any human being is a religious act."[37] He observes that a Catholic university "is not a place where we allow people to study mathematics or history or literature so that we can get them to sit through a religious course."[38] Any field of study is religious because it is revelatory of grace. Education in this context is a pedagogy of sacramental beholding.[39]

Yet I would argue that a sacrament is only revelatory for those of faith. Someone must point out what is to be seen. This is the role of the educator. The epiphanies encountered in the poetry of Gerard Manley Hopkins, in the film *Babette's Feast*, or in Dante's *Divine Comedy* (all examples cited by Himes) are only epiphanies if they are witnessed. That is what a faith tradition—and ultimately a Catholic university—does. It witnesses. As the writer of the first letter of John declares, "We declare to you what was from the beginning, what we have heard, what we have seen with our eyes, what we have looked at and touched with our hands, concerning the word of life—this life was revealed, and we have seen it and testify to it" (1 Jn 1:1–2).

Witnessing is not indoctrination. Witnessing does not violate academic freedom. Witnessing is telling what you see. Witnessing is a function of passing on a tradition, which is what universities do, wheth-

35. Francis C. Wade, SJ, *The Catholic University and the Faith: The Aquinas Lecture, 1978* (Milwaukee: Marquette University Press, 1978), 4, 7, 39.

36. Ibid., 8.

37. Michael J. Himes, "'Finding God in All Things': A Sacramental Worldview and Its Effects," in *As Leaven in the World: Catholic Perspectives on Faith, Vocation, and the Intellectual Life*, ed. Thomas M. Landy (New York: Sheed and Ward, 2001), 100. Himes says he could have developed the same conclusion by starting from a consideration of the Incarnation.

38. Ibid., 102.

39. Ibid., 100.

er they are religious or secular. They are the custodians of history and tradition as well as the sentinels who watch and comment on current affairs and the scouts who search out new paths in scientific discoveries. Witnessing respects a sacramental way of knowing because it incorporates a visible or audible sign that signifies and points to ultimate meaning and God's gracious presence among God's people. Witnessing is a public institutional function of Catholic universities, and not just the personal activities of individuals within them.

Practical Considerations

As we have learned from that great educator, Thomas Aquinas, that "which is received is received according to the mode of the receiver."[40] According to this maxim, the Catholic university is essential for the Church to know its membership and how to communicate to it as well as to nonmembers. The Church must know the world deeply in order to evangelize the world. The Church teaches, but first it must learn, and then it must integrate its faith and human knowledge. *Gaudium et Spes*,[41] the Pastoral Constitution on the Church in the Modern World, is a good example of the integration of theological reflection and topics touching on social and political life. The opening lines of *Gaudium et Spes* begin by identifying the concerns of the Church with those of the world, proclaiming, "The joys and hopes and sorrows and anxieties of people today, especially of those who are poor and afflicted, are also the joys and hopes, sorrows and anxieties of the disciples of Christ, and there is nothing truly human which does not also affect them" (*GS* 1). The document skillfully integrates Christology, anthropology, and eschatology with its treatment of concrete issues in the temporal order, such as marriage and the family, the proper development of culture,

40. Thomas Aquinas, *Quidquid recipitur ad modum recipientis recipitur.* Cf. *Summa Theologiae* (*ST*) Ia, q. 75, a. 5; a. 3, q. 5. In *ST* Ia, q. 12, a. 4, a more specific application of this principle is proposed according to which "a thing known exists in a knower according to the mode of a knower." "Cogitum … est in cognoscente secundum modum cognoscentis." For further references, see *ST* Ia, q. 14, a. 1, ad 3; q. 16, a. 1; q. 19, a. 6, ad 2; *Summa contra Gentiles* 2, 79, 7; *De Veritate*, q. 2, a. 3.

41. Vatican II, pastoral constitution *Gaudium et Spes*, December 7, 1965: *AAS* 58 (1966): 1025–115.

socioeconomic life, life in the political community, and the promotion of peace and encouragement of the community of nations. Each of the four chapters in Part I of *Gaudium et Spes* culminates in a reference to the return of the Lord and the kingdom to come.[42] Part II, which treats specific questions of the temporal order, follows directly from Part I insofar as temporal problems can only be addressed adequately in the light of human destiny. The text thus avoids an extrincisim wherein the world is autonomous and dealt with apart from its supernatural destiny. Similarly, the supernatural vocation of human beings is lived out amid temporal realities.

Integration of Catholicism and the academy will not happen within Catholic universities unless there are structures and activities to promote this integration. Although a critical number of intellectually committed Catholic scholars are necessary in a Catholic institution, because Catholicity is borne by people not buildings, that alone does not make the institution Catholic. Most often, Catholic faculty members are trained in secular disciplines in secular universities, and their training does not include formation regarding how to integrate their discipline and their faith. Conversely, many of those who are not Catholic are deeply committed to the mission and identity of Catholic universities. Even for Catholics, the role of faith in a university cannot be simply relegated to the private life of a faculty member any more than it should be delegated to the theology department or to campus ministry. Faith must be part of the public communal discourse of the academic community. This integration needs to be the topic of faculty development programs and seminars, symposia, and speakers. Michael Lacy has suggested that "some kind of institute for advanced study to be devoted to the needs of Catholic scholars in all of the humanities and social sciences" is a better approach than marginally improving a great, comprehensive university.[43] Whatever the solution, structures for sustained dialogue are needed so that attention to Catholic identity is not intermittent and ad hoc.

If Catholic universities are only concerned about their Catholic

42. Henri de Lubac, *Athéisme et le sens de l'homme*, vol. 4, Œuvres *complètes* (Paris: Cerf, 2006), 472.

43. Cited by David J. O'Brien in "Conversations on Jesuit (and Catholic?) Higher Education," in *A Jesuit Education Reader*, ed. George W. Traus, SJ (Chicago: Loyola Press, 2008), 226.

identity, however, that may signal only self-maintenance. The university needs to be actively engaged with Catholicism, and Catholicism, through the mediation of the university, with contemporary culture.[44] If the university is to be the place where the Church does its thinking, returning to the concerns of Gustave Weigel and John Tracy Ellis articulated in the 1950s, universities must cultivate a Catholic intellectual life. This will be more than apologetics, the defense of the faith, but will make clear the positive contribution of faith and the Church to human flourishing. Conversely, faith will be enriched by culture, which provides the context in which faith is planted, the historical time and place in which it bears witness to the sacramental dimension of all of creation. This integration is a gift that the church bears to all those who attend or work at a Catholic university, whatever their religious commitment.

44. *EcE*, 7.

[6]

How the New Evangelization Fits with Catholic Higher Education

Scott W. Hahn

> *Universities are outstanding environments for articulating and developing this evangelizing commitment in an interdisciplinary and integrated way. Catholic schools, which always strive to join their work of education with the explicit proclamation of the Gospel, are a most valuable resource for the evangelization of culture.*
>
> Pope Francis, *Evangelii gaudium*, 134

The call of the last several decades for a new evangelization finds a particularly natural setting for dialogue within the Catholic university. Evangelization—sharing the Gospel message with all people—is the Church's mission and should be a part of everything she does, including the education of young people. The nature of higher education provides a unique opportunity to integrate faith and reason, to see the

The author thanks Alicia Boyle for her assistance on this essay and graduate research assistants Alex Parra and Laura Gallant for their helpful input in preparing the original lecture.

Epigraph. Pope Francis, apostolic exhortation *Evangelii gaudium* 134, November 24, 2013: *Acta Apostolicae Sedis* 105 (2013): 1019-137, http://w2.vatican.va/content/francesco/en/apost_exhortations/documents/papa-francesco_esortazione-ap_20131124_evangelii-gaudium.html.

witness of an authentic Catholic life lived out by the faculty and staff, to engage in conversations and friendships that inspire ongoing conversion, and to participate in the evangelization of culture. These are not easy assignments. But a proper conception of both the new evangelization and Catholic institutions for higher learning demonstrates that the new evangelization can and should be an integral activity of a Catholic university.

Many in the academy and elsewhere assert that an institution for higher learning, even a Catholic one, is not a proper location for evangelization. After all, a Catholic university is neither a parish nor an evangelistic association. A university exists for the purpose of higher education. It is supposed to be academically rigorous, forming the intellect more than the will or the emotions. It is a community of students and teachers in diverse academic disciplines coming together to grow intellectually.

A Catholic school can certainly require students to learn about the Catholic faith, but it would be a violation of freedom of conscience to require belief or conversion as part of an education.[1] Most avow that the learning at a university ought to be concentrated in a classroom, not gleaned from the pulpit or a Bible study. As such, it would seem like the new evangelization does not logically fit into the mission and purpose of an institution of Catholic higher learning.

I propose that the reason so many do not see the new evangelization as a responsibility of the Catholic university can be traced to an inadequate understanding of what the new evangelization means. Evangelization is not the same as proselytization. Proper evangelization should deliver the Gospel message in a way that is respectful of other cultures and religious traditions.[2] There are many possible methods for evangelization, but all these methods lead to the center of the Gospel, which is Christ. Once we grasp the inner logic of the new evangelization and see how expansive it is, and how boldly the Church proclaims this mission in response to the great challenges we face, once we reconsider what is meant by new evangelization, we will be able to see that there is no

1. Glenn B. Siniscalchi, "No Excuses: Catholic Schools Must Evangelize," *Crisis Magazine*, March 12, 2015, http://www.crisismagazine.com/2015/evangelization-catholic-schools.

2. Ibid.

more fitting place for the new evangelization than at a Catholic institution of higher learning.

Overview of the New Evangelization

To build a proper understanding of the new evangelization, it may be helpful to trace the history of the term. The word *evangelium* ("gospel") was not prominent in magisterial or conciliar writings before the Second Vatican Council. For instance, documents of Vatican I mention "gospel" one time, and evangelization not at all. The documents of Vatican II refer to it 157 times. "Evangelization" is used 31 times, and "evangelize" is used 18 times. This increased use in the sixteen documents of the council reflects an evangelistic emphasis, which many highlight as a central theme of the council.[3]

Pope Paul VI taught extensively on the topic of evangelization during his papacy. He changed the name of the Congregation for the Propagation of the Faith to the Congregation for the Evangelization of Peoples, and he made many apostolic journeys throughout Europe as well as to Africa, the Americas, Asia, and Australia, taking the message of the Gospel to the world. His 1975 apostolic exhortation *Evangelii nuntiandi* declared that evangelization is the deepest identity of the Church; her purpose is to share the Good News of the Paschal Mystery with the world.[4]

A focus on evangelization has thus been a prominent part of the Church's dialogue in the decades following Vatican II. Pope John Paul II intensified the Church's discussion, calling for the 1990s to be an extended advent season for the new evangelization.[5] In 1990, on the twenty-fifth anniversary of *Ad gentes* (Vatican II's Decree on the Missionary Activity of the Church), he promulgated *Redemptoris missio* (viewed by many as the Magna Carta of the new evangelization), in which he says, "the mo-

3. Avery Cardinal Dulles, *Church and Society: The Laurence J. McGinley Lectures, 1988–2007* (New York: Fordham University Press, 2008), 88.

4. Paul VI, apostolic exhortation *Evangelii nuntiandi* (*EN*) 14, December 8, 1975: *AAS* 67 (1976): 5–76. English translation in *Origins* 5, no. 29 (January 8, 1976): 459–68.

5. John Paul II, encyclical *Redemptoris missio* 86, December 7, 1990: *Acta Apostolicae Sedis* (*AAS*) 83 (1991): 249–340, http://w2.vatican.va/content/john-paul-ii/en/encyclicals/documents/hf_jp-ii_enc_07121990_redemptoris-missio.html.

ment has come to commit all of the Church's energies to the new evangelization.... No believer in Christ, no institution of the Church, can avoid this supreme duty: to proclaim Christ to all peoples."[6]

What Is Meant by "New Evangelization"?

Talking about a new evangelization implies that there is an old evangelization. It is in fact ancient—the proclamation of the Good News to those who have never heard about Jesus has been the Church's mission from the beginning. This "old evangelization" is still crucially important and should not be forgotten.

The new evangelization is a reevangelization of the dechristianized.[7] The Church is not only seeking to baptize those who have been newly evangelized, which she has been doing for two thousand years, but she is also evangelizing those who have been baptized but have been progressively dechristianized by a secular culture. The culture of death, the new atheism, the dictatorship of relativism—these societal trends affect even Catholics.

As John Paul said, evangelization is not just for the clergy or for missionaries. Evangelization needs to be directed toward cultures that have become increasingly secularized. As such, evangelization is for every Christian.[8] In numerous countries where the Catholic faithful had been flourishing, the indifference to religion has grown under the influence of secularism and atheism.[9] In these places, reevangelization is necessary to "remake the Christian fabric" so the faith can grow again where it is facing serious opposition.[10] With missionary zeal, the Church must continue to preach the Gospel to those who have never encountered Jesus, but she must also reevangelize "entire portions of populations."[11]

This is not just John Paul's message. It was reinforced repeatedly by

6. Ibid., 3.

7. Ibid., 33.

8. Ibid., 71. John Paul II, apostolic exhortation *Christifideles laici* 33, December 30, 1988: *AAS* 81 (1989): 393–521, http://w2.vatican.va/content/john-paul-ii/en/apost_exhortations/documents/hf_jp-ii_exh_30121988_christifideles-laici.html.

9. *Christifideles laici*, 34.

10. Ibid.

11. Ibid.

Pope Benedict, who in *Verbum Domini* says, "Many of our brothers and sisters are 'baptized, but insufficiently evangelized' … nations once rich in faith … are losing their identity under the influence of a secularized culture. The need for a new evangelization, so deeply felt by my venerable Predecessor, must be valiantly reaffirmed, in the certainty that God's word is effective."[12]

Pope Benedict XVI established the Pontifical Council for Promoting the New Evangelization in the Roman Curia because he believed "the mission of evangelization … is necessary for the Church: it cannot be overlooked; it is an expression of her very nature."[13] Many in the world have abandoned the faith; Benedict understands the need for a new evangelization, a "constant interior renewal" of the Church.[14] The new evangelization cannot be limited to a single method; rather, "careful discernment" should be exercised to determine the best method in any situation.[15]

In 2012, Benedict called a Synod of Bishops on the New Evangelization for the Transmission of the Christian Faith. The synod identified the need for a new evangelization of those who have grown distant from the Church, that through it the Church would be a witness to God in the secularized world.[16] It reiterated that although initial evangelization and the new evangelization remain mutually supportive ideas, they should not be confused; they each remain distinct and vitally important to the Church's overall mission.[17] With his encyclical *Evangelii gaudium*, Pope Francis shows he is following his predecessors in a continuing focus on the new evangelization.

But evangelization cannot focus solely on the initial conversion of

12. Benedict XVI, apostolic exhortation *Verbum Domini* 96, September 30, 2010: *AAS* 102 (2010): 681–787, http://w2.vatican.va/content/benedict-xvi/en/apost_exhortations/documents/hf_ben-xvi_exh_20100930_verbum-domini.htmlpar.

13. Benedict XVI, apostolic letter *Ubicumque et semper*, Introduction, September 21, 2010: *AAS* 102 (2010): 788–92, http://w2.vatican.va/content/benedict-xvi/en/apost_letters/documents/hf_ben-xvi_apl_20100921_ubicumque-et-semper.html.

14. Ibid.

15. Ibid.

16. Thirteenth Ordinary General Assembly of the Synod of Bishops, "The New Evangelization and the Transmission of the Christian Faith: Final List of Propositions," 7, 8 (October 27, 2012), http://www.vatican.va/news_services/press/sinodo/documents/bollettino_25_xiii-ordinaria-2012/02_inglese/b33_02.html.

17. Ibid., 9.

individuals. Evangelization must also include ongoing personal conversion and a broader evangelization of culture. The new evangelization is a comprehensive program to reach those who have lost their faith and adopted secular worldviews. What I propose, and what John Paul regularly repeated, is that our understanding of evangelization embrace a deeper understanding of what conversion entails. This understanding of the new evangelization as conversion demands a reconsideration of what Christian formation requires. This formation is certainly an important part of the mission of the Catholic university.

Theology of Conversion

At its heart, evangelization is not just a personal relationship with Jesus, accepting him as Savior and Lord; evangelization calls for something much longer and much deeper. A distinction must be drawn between evangelization in the Catholic tradition and evangelization as practiced by many non-Catholic Protestants and fundamentalists. As beautiful and important as a personal relationship with Jesus is, this personal relationship is just the beginning of the Catholic understanding of evangelization.

Notably, the earliest accounts of the ancient Church show us how initial evangelization led to initial conversion, and the grace of this conversion made one a "convert." Following this conversion, which was the development of a personal relationship with Jesus, a convert enrolled in the catechumenate to learn the four spiritual laws and the *kerygma*, the Creed and the petitions of the Our Father, how to pray and how to fast. Catechumens underwent scrutiny and many months of catechesis, all in preparation for something even greater: entering God's covenant family through baptism, confirmation, and the reception of Holy Communion. Thus, in the ancient process of conversion, a person was evangelized, then catechized, and finally sacramentalized. This three-stage process begins with a personal relationship but culminates with a covenantal relationship.

Evangelization is like falling in love with someone, followed by engagement, when one realizes the future spouse's family will be one's own, and discovers all the commitments that marriage entails. Finally, the relationship culminates in the covenant bond of marriage. In this model, evangelization moves into catechesis, the next level, but the proclamation of the Good News does not cease. Similarly, when catechesis moves into sacramentalization, evangelization continues; it is as though the Gospel is shared and understood even more deeply. Throughout the levels of evangelization, the Good News never ceases to be internalized. Even after baptism, confirmation, and the reception of Holy Communion, there is an ongoing process of conversion. In the Catholic understanding of evangelization, conversion is a lifelong journey.

Here, the Catholic tradition offers one of the most distinctive, and largely overlooked, contributions to the theological discussion. The idea that the theology of conversion must match the depth of the theology of evangelization is deeply Catholic. The *Catechism of the Catholic Church* describes how, from the time of the early Church, the initiation of a Christian involves a journey through several stages in which "certain essential elements will always have to be present: proclamation of the Word, acceptance of the Gospel entailing conversion, profession of faith, Baptism itself, the outpouring of the Holy Spirit, and admission to Eucharistic communion."[18] The initial conversion of accepting the Gospel is only the first step, to be followed by catechesis, with conversion reaching a pinnacle in the sacramental stage. But the *Catechism* also recognizes that, with the prominence of infant baptism, a "post-baptismal catechumenate" is required because infants do not experience initial evangelization or initial conversion before their baptism.[19] The great need for the new evangelization is a call for this post-baptismal catechumenate, especially in the face of the many forms of radical secularization—the new *deevangelization*—which has been taking place for decades.

The *Catechism* is also clear that even following baptism one struggles to overcome the weakness of human nature; the struggle of the Christian life is the struggle of conversion.[20] The *Catechism* echoes the great and deep tradition that the second conversion is an uninterrupted, lifelong task for the whole Church and for each individual Christian.[21] Conversion is not a singular and static past event. Conversion is

18. *Catechism of the Catholic Church* (*CCC*), §1229.

19. *CCC*, §1231.

20. *CCC*, §1426.

21. *CCC*, §1427–28.

an ongoing and ever-deepening process, one that never becomes easy. In the Gospel of Luke, Jesus said, "If any man would come after me, let him deny himself and take up his cross daily and follow me."[22] The way of the cross always requires a grace of ongoing, ever-deepening, and lifelong conversion.

This taps into the tradition of the three stages of the spiritual life: the purgative stage, the illuminative stage, and the unitive stage. These stages have been part of the formation of religious communities for centuries. Vatican II, however, clearly affirmed the universal call to holiness—that holiness is not just for clergy and religious but for all baptized Christians—so this journey of ongoing conversion is also something for the daily life of the laity. The call to holiness and the call to conversion is the call to struggle together as a community of believers, and this is a struggle that rightly penetrates every aspect of our lives. Conversion must be both interior and exterior, private and public, spiritual and social. The university is positioned at a crucial point in this dynamic process. Therefore conversion should be found in all the departments and disciplines of a truly Catholic university.

When the *Catechism of the Catholic Church* was promulgated in 1992, the program of the new evangelization was still developing. The treatment of the new evangelization in the 2005 *Compendium of the Social Doctrine of the Church* is much more extensive. By that time, the need for ongoing conversion had become far more apparent than it had been in 1992. Another closely related feature in the *Compendium* is its emphasis on the new evangelization as integral to human society and interpersonal relations. In other words, the *Compendium*'s concept of evangelization goes beyond initial conversion, and beyond post-baptismal catechesis, to show that the Gospel should have a significant impact on every area of human life and culture.

To bridge the growing gap between the Gospel and culture, the Church must enter a new phase in which she views social doctrine as an "instrument of evangelization," emphasizing human dignity in an effort to share the Good News with others.[23] While historically an emphasis on social doctrine has focused on those who are materially poor,

22. Lk 9:23.

23. *Compendium of the Social Doctrine of the Church* (Washington, DC: United States Conference of Catholic Bishops, 2005), 523.

the growing need for reevangelization demonstrates that, in parts of the West, those who have material comfort are spiritually in need.

A mature understanding of the Church's social doctrine should be grounded in the overarching vision of human dignity and should concentrate on the Church's mission of evangelization.[24] The "witness of a Christian life … the life of holiness" proclaims social doctrine in a positive light.[25] In this way, the Church, in the lives of her members, is showcasing the beauty of the truth she advocates. The work of the Church is a perpetual effort of formation, such that Christians feel empowered to embody their faith in all aspects of their lives.[26] Therefore "Catholic educational institutions can and indeed *must* carry out a precious formative service, dedicating themselves in a particular way to the inculturation of the Christian message … the productive encounter between the Gospel and the various branches of knowledge."[27] This expresses the Church's firm belief that Catholic educational institutions provide a unique and fitting environment to advance the Church's mission of evangelization through their witness of an integrated life. At a Catholic university, students can truly experience what it means to live in the culture while not being of the culture.

Evangelization of Culture

Another aspect of evangelization growing in emphasis during the last several decades is the dialogue of the Gospel message with the culture, often referred to as the evangelization of culture. Particularly for John Paul, the evangelization of culture is essential for the success of the new evangelization. The *National Directory for Catechesis* indicates that "the dynamism inherent in the new evangelization demands both the inculturation of the Gospel and the transformation of the culture by the Gospel."[28] "Only from within and through culture does the

24. Ibid., 530.

25. Ibid.

26. Ibid., 531.

27. Ibid., 532, emphasis added

28. United States Conference of Catholic Bishops (USCCB), *National Directory for Catechesis*, 1st ed. (Washington, DC: USCCB, 2005), 47.

Christian faith become a part of history and the creator of history."[29] The inculturation of the Gospel is not meant to degrade the Good News to a simplistic or secular level simply to persuade more people to listen to the message; instead, the principle of inculturation identifies and uses the elements of culture that help people to better hear and assent to the Gospel. Inculturation involves several key levels on which a person may interact with the Gospel in order to choose to live in union with God: personally, culturally, economically, and politically.[30] We can easily see how a university is an ideal setting for precisely this type of inculturation because all aspects of the human experience come together in the little society that is a college campus.

"Education is a constitutive dimension of evangelization," and so Catholic institutions have a responsibility to participate in evangelization.[31] Catholic schools not only provide excellent academic programs but also are "effective vehicle[s] of total Christian formation."[32] All students are entitled to an education and to evangelization; as such, Catholic institutions should seek to ensure the preservation of their Catholic identity and should encourage teachers to witness to Christ through their teaching.[33] As part of this witness, Catholic universities are especially privileged places for the lay faithful to both purify and elevate the culture by boldly proclaiming the Gospel.[34]

Witness in the Catholic University

The promulgation of *Redemptoris missio* in 1990 coincided with the promulgation earlier that same year of *Ex corde Ecclesiae*. It is significant (and not coincidental) that both evangelization and higher education were on the mind of John Paul II. That year marked the twenty-fifth anniversary of the close of the Second Vatican Council, which was an

29. *Christifideles laici*, 44.

30. USCCB, *National Directory for Catechesis*, 64–65.

31. Thirteenth Ordinary General Assembly of the Synod of Bishops, "New Evangelization and the Transmission of the Christian Faith," 27.

32. USCCB, *National Directory for Catechesis*, 230.

33. Thirteenth Ordinary General Assembly of the Synod of Bishops, "New Evangelization and the Transmission of the Christian Faith," 27.

34. *Christifideles laici*, 44.

appropriate moment to reflect on the urgent need for a continuing renewal of the Church's evangelization efforts. In *Ex corde Ecclesiae*, John Paul outlined four essential marks that every Catholic university should strive to establish in order to be faithful to its Catholic identity: a Christian inspiration as a university community; an ongoing dedication to the Catholic faith in all it does, including research; a commitment to the Church's Christian message; and a disposition of service to all in the human family.[35]

In *Ex corde Ecclesiae*, John Paul does not call for Catholic universities to shy away from the traditional responsibilities of a university—study and research—rather, he calls the Catholic university to pursue all its endeavors in the light of the Catholic faith, to integrate faith and reason. In his mind, faith and reason are not competing paths to truth but two sides of a single discussion, each providing a deeper understanding of the other. An educator himself, John Paul viewed the Catholic university as a "living *institutional* witness to Christ and his message," a particularly fitting place for the advancement of the new evangelization.[36] The Church's mission is to preach the Gospel so that for individuals and their sociocultural context there is an obvious relationship between faith and life.[37] The Catholic university is to participate in the life of the local Church and enable the Church to engage in dialogue "with people of every culture."[38] A Catholic university is uniquely equipped to help its students to live integrated lives, so that what they learn in the classroom and what they experience in the world are informed and mutually deepened by the Catholic faith with which the university imbues all its activities.

In his 1821 University Sermon Number Five, *Personal Influence: The Means of Propagating the Truth*, John Henry Newman reflects on the fact that throughout the centuries the Church has confronted so many opponents, so many obstacles, and yet, faithful to its own principles, the Church has grown and prospered, often in spite of the weaknesses of her members.[39] He says this miraculous growth can be attributed

35. *EcE*, 13.

36. *EcE*, 49.

37. *EcE*, 48.

38. *EcE*, 6, 27.

39. John Henry Newman, *Sermons Preached before the University of Oxford* (Westminster, MD: Christian Classics, 1966), v. 4.

to "the influence of truth in the world at large which [arises] from the personal ... influence of those who are commissioned to teach it."[40] He concludes by saying that the truth "has been upheld in the world not as a system, not by books, not by argument, nor by temporal power, but by the personal influence of men ... who are at once the teachers and the patterns of [the truth]" they teach.[41] These teachers are not simply sharing abstract truth; they are teaching through their own personal development and imparting to their students the illumination this truth has brought them. For their part, the professors are affected by conversations with students who continually challenge them to remember that an intellectual life should not stagnate. Like conversion, the pursuit of knowledge is a lifelong journey. As Newman believed, the university is not only a place of study, but also a place where one cultivates an interior life, where students and teachers together grow in knowledge and virtue.

This same insight is evident in what Paul VI, the herald of the new evangelization, expresses in *Evangelii nuntiandi* when he writes, "Modern man listens more willingly to witnesses than to teachers, and if he does listen to teachers, it is because they are witnesses."[42] Although it is certain that students are influenced by what they are taught in the classroom, they are perhaps more affected by those who teach them. A teacher who teaches a subject with the conviction of having lived out the principles he teaches carries powerful weight in a student's consideration of the topic. Thus one sees the importance of a Catholic university's Catholic identity, wherein professors in every discipline can demonstrate their own integration of faith and reason, both in their scholarship and in daily life. At such a university, the faith is not separated from reason, is not relegated to theology class, is not the sole responsibility of the campus minister; rather, the faith is present in biology, psychology, literature, and even business and mathematics courses.[43] Catholic universities that clearly understand this responsibility

40. Ibid., v. 8.

41. Ibid., v. 26.

42. *EN*, 41.

43. Monsignor Stuart Swetland, "Catholic Colleges Are Essential Agents of Evangelization," *National Catholic Register*, September 7, 2013, http://www.ncregister.com/site/article/catholic-colleges-are-essential-agents-of-evangelization.

show the evangelistic possibilities that exist in the classroom. The exclusive goal of discussions in these academic settings may not be evangelistic, but a Catholic university should not shy away from seeking every opportunity to open a student's eyes to the beauty of the Gospel message, demonstrating that an integrated and holistic education involves the whole person—spirit and body, intellect and will. Therefore it is crucial to understand how the new evangelization is reinforced by a Catholic university aware of its true Catholic identity.

Reception of the New Evangelization among Catholic Academics

In certain quarters of Catholic academia, the call for the new evangelization was met with silence or ambivalence. Others gave it serious consideration, both in general and to its place in Catholic higher education in particular.[44] Avery Cardinal Dulles, SJ, the most influential Catholic theologian in America at the time, to the surprise of many of his colleagues, devoted considerable attention in the last fifteen years of his life to the call for a new evangelization. Dulles recognizes (not uncritically) its importance to the mission of the Church and the university and writes extensively about its application to the American situation. I am able to touch on only a few of his points in this small essay.

According to Dulles, many Catholics in the United States are hesitant to embrace evangelization, in part owing to distaste for the aggressiveness they encounter in evangelical Protestants, in part with a post–Vatican II wariness of triumphalism.[45] American Catholics "often fail to proclaim their faith with confidence," acceding to the national tradition of religion as something practiced privately.[46] As Dulles asserts, however, the new evangelization is the overriding vision in which to interpret the documents of Vatican II, and it is "the most effective remedy for the church's present ills" because it calls the faithful to share the faith and discover the beauty that comes from seeing the fruit of

44. For more on this, see my "Mass Evangelization," *America*, April 22, 2013, http://americamagazine.org/issue/mass-evangelization.

45. Dulles, *Church and Society*, 98.

46. Ibid.

conversion in the lives of others.[47] This echoes John Paul II's position that the "faith is strengthened when it is given to others."[48] "Evangelization, by concentrating on the basic Christian message, helps us to see what is supremely worthwhile about our religion."[49]

Drawing extensively from the writings of Pope John Paul II, Dulles points out that conversion builds on evangelization through catechesis and religious education at all levels. One cannot pass on to others what one does not first possess; thus catechesis is vital to helping the faithful understand the beliefs they profess. But in order to truly share the Gospel, it must permeate one's whole life through ongoing interior change and conversion.[50] Evangelization draws people into an ecumenical and interreligious dialogue and is ordered to social and cultural transformation, or what John Paul frequently refers to as the evangelization of culture.[51] All of life is deliberately included under this umbrella of the new evangelization, Dulles states, because all of life is under the Lordship of Jesus Christ.[52]

This idea that Christ is the means to draw all people together recaptures the Christocentric vision of a Gospel for all nations prominent in the writings of Vatican II, and resonates with the work of John Paul in the 1990s.[53] The new evangelization is not a passing moment. It is a long-term strategy for the revitalization of the Church.

Dulles acknowledges several general impediments for theologians to consider when adopting the new evangelization, including religious pragmatism, cultural relativism, and a false concept of freedom.[54] In

47. Ibid.

48. *Redemptoris missio*, 2.

49. Dulles, *Church and Society*, 98.

50. Ibid., 93.

51. Ibid., 95.

52. Patrick Carey, *Avery Cardinal Dulles, S.J.: A Model Theologian, 1918–2008* (New York: Paulist Press, 2010), 447.

53. Parenthetically, many thought that the 1990s was the decade of the new evangelization, and John Paul II used the term well over a hundred times throughout that decade, but in the next five years, from 2000 to 2005, he frequently spoke of the new evangelization. John Paul never referred to the 1990s as the decade of the new evangelization; instead, he referred to it as the "advent season" of the new evangelization. Just as advent is a preparatory season for ordinary time, so too when the decade was over, the new evangelization was not done; truly, it had barely begun.

54. Carey, *Avery Cardinal Dulles*, 449.

speaking to bishops of the United States, Dulles highlights within American culture four key obstacles to the Church's program of the new evangelization: American receptivity to "vague transcendence without content," the lack of appeal of many evangelical preachers, a strict understanding of the "separation of church and state, and internal Catholic divisions."[55] Demonstrating his dedication to the cause of the new evangelization, however, Dulles also believes that, though real, these impediments should not be exploited as a means to avoid the "inclusive concept" of evangelization in America.[56] Cardinal Dulles calls educators to allow Catholic theology to be renewed in the spirit of evangelization. Dulles describes the new evangelization as the realization of the *aggiornamento*, which was a key and oft-used term at the time of the Second Vatican Council, representing a renewal and updating, an opening of the Church to the world. This opening was not sought to allow the floods of secularization to come into the Church, but so that the "living water" of the Gospel might go out and bring grace to all people. In this way also, the Catholic university is a fitting place for the evangelization of culture to take place.

American Catholic Universities and the New Evangelization

Several years ago, Pope Benedict XVI came to America and addressed Catholic educators at the Catholic University of America. He stated that "education is integral to the mission of the Church to proclaim the Good News."[57] That is why Catholic colleges and universities are a prime place for the new evangelization. Only in embracing the Gospel message with conviction will Catholic universities train truly Christian leaders for all the spheres of human activity, not just for theology and philosophy, but also for politics, economics, science, art, journalism, and mass media.[58] At a vibrant Catholic university that

55. Ibid.

56. Ibid.

57. Benedict XVI, "Address to Educators," *Origins* 37, no. 46 (May 1, 2008): 742. Also available in Committee on Catholic Education, USCCB, *Catholic Mission and Culture in Colleges and Universities: Defining Documents* (Washington, DC: USCCB, 2014), 90–94.

58. Benedict XVI, "Address to Educators."

embodies Christ and his teaching, where every aspect of the community "reverberates within the ecclesial life of faith," students are drawn by the power of the Gospel and inspired to live a life of Christian witness.[59] Although there is a tendency to divide truth and faith, Benedict declares that truth is more than knowledge: "knowing the truth leads us to discover the good."[60] Thus a university striving to impart the truth to students is leading them to a deeper faith and conversion.

During his time with American Catholic educators, Benedict challenged them to make their universities about more than just the transmittal of knowledge in a classroom, and to focus on the integration of faith and reason, committing the intellect, will, mind, and heart to God.[61] Benedict, himself a former university professor, shared that, in a spirit of "intellectual charity," an educator's leading of students to the truth is a profound act of love.[62] He called all educators to be witnesses to Christ, to account for their hope and joy, to live integrated lives of prayer and study, demonstrating that it is possible to have harmony between faith, life, and culture.[63] Benedict wanted universities to be tangible expressions of the beauty of Catholicism liturgically, sacramentally, and academically.[64]

Pope Benedict identified that the current time is marked by a deep hunger, which many do not realize is a desire for God. There are many who seek to live an authentic life but need direction in order to turn to God as the fulfillment of the true desire of their hearts.[65] St. Augustine understood this desire centuries ago when he wrote "our hearts are restless until they find rest in You," but for a growing number of people, turning to God is often their last attempt to fill the void they feel

59. Ibid.

60. Ibid.

61. Timothy T. O'Donnell, "Catholic Higher Education: Heart of the Church's Evangelization," *National Catholic Register*, April 25, 2010, http://www.ncregister.com/daily-news/catholic_higher_education_heart_of_the_churchs_evangelization.

62. Ibid.

63. Ibid.

64. Ibid.

65. Benedict XVI, "Homily at the Papal Mass on the Solemnity of the Holy Apostles Peter and Paul (28 June 2010), at The Basilica of St. Paul Outside the Walls," accessed February 9, 2016, http://w2.vatican.va/content/benedict-xvi/en/homilies/2010/documents/hf_ben-xvi_hom_20100628_vespri-pietro-paolo.html.

inside.[66] This continues to highlight the role of the Catholic university as a prime place for the new evangelization. At a university, this feeling of void is often filled with superficial solutions, but when the Gospel is shared with joy, many students will find rest in the Lord rather than in the empty cures suggested by the culture.

In his *ad limina* visit with United States bishops in Rome in 2012, Benedict called Catholic schools "an essential resource for the new evangelization."[67] It is vital, he says, for American colleges and universities to "reaffirm their distinctive identity in fidelity to ... the Church's mission in service of the Gospel."[68] Benedict reinforces this by saying, "it is no exaggeration to say that providing young people with a sound education in the faith represents the most urgent internal challenge facing the Catholic community" in the United States.[69] As such, it is incumbent upon Catholic institutions of higher education in America to valiantly embrace their participation in the Church's mission of evangelization, "to challenge students to reappropriate their faith as part of ... exciting intellectual discoveries," and to afford them networks of support in a time when broken families and communities dominate the current milieu.[70]

Vision of the Catholic University as Locus for Evangelization

The basic starting point for institutions of higher learning in the Catholic Church, to fulfill the new evangelization, is to embrace their own distinctive calling; to abide in what Vatican II has imparted; to follow what John Paul, Benedict, and now Francis have recommended; and to be Christocentric, where Christ is the center of student life, of faculty life, and of the whole community of learning. In this way, they can inte-

66. Augustine, *Confessions*, 1.1.1.

67. Benedict XVI, "Address of His Holiness Pope Benedict XVI to the Bishops of the United States of America (Regions X–XIII) on their '*Ad Limina*' Visit (5 May 2012) at the Holy See," accessed February 9, 2016, https://w2.vatican.va/content/benedict-xvi/en/speeches/2012/may/documents/hf_ben-xvi_spe_20120505_us-bishops.html.

68. Ibid.

69. Ibid.

70. Ibid.

grate faith and reason in all areas of research, of study, and of teaching.

Some might object, saying evangelization is pastoral work, the responsibility of missionaries, not faculty members.[71] This is a false dichotomy for a variety of reasons. First of all, most American Catholic colleges and universities are residential, which necessarily involves a living faith community that requires vibrant pastoral ministry.[72] Second, the nature of research, study, and teaching, so essential to the university, arises from a shared hunger for the truth, and it must accord with what is true.[73] Third, every university recognizes its responsibility to form leaders who are going to go out and transform the culture.[74] But this commitment to others, this commitment to the culture, requires more than instruction, and it requires more than a diploma. It ultimately makes sense only if people understand the meaning and purpose of life under the truth of God, grasping that they must live out their own vocation in a community.

Finally, the university is the ideal place for forming not just students and scholars, but also disciples. For *mathētēs*, the Greek term for a disciple, literally bespeaks a disciplined learner who has discovered the need for disciplined study balanced with disciplined prayer and a social concord with others who are following the truth and discovering the light of the world. What else can take the place of faith in the application of reason? Where can research and intellectual growth coincide with the spiritual and moral values that make us whole, if not at a Catholic university? For this reason, not only does the new evangelization fit into Catholic higher education, but also it fits best in a Catholic university where students will discover that they are not just called to good grades but to the greatness of holiness, as well as to ministry, sharing the Good News with others.[75] The university provides instruction to help students form a Catholic worldview. This Catholic worldview is both built in the classroom and solidified through involvement with the local community, mission opportunities, and musical collaborations. Opportunities for spiritual growth abound outside the classroom through the

71. Swetland, "Catholic Colleges."
72. Ibid.
73. Ibid.
74. Ibid.
75. Ibid.

arts, campus ministry, mass, and confession. The many extracurricular activities that make up the spiritual life of a Catholic university campus show that academics are only one (albeit large) facet of the university experience. A Catholic university, with a clear Catholic identity and purpose, ought to be the setting for a student's grace-filled and holistic conversion, a conversion that will continue after they leave campus and throughout their lives.

Mentorship in a University

The new evangelization is about reevangelizing the dechristianized, which leads to a richer understanding of conversion as a process that is ongoing, ever deepening, lifelong, and holistic, for both individuals and institutions. Such a holistic view thus leads me to propose: *there may be no institution within the Church better suited to more effectively advance the new evangelization than faithful Catholic universities.* A Catholic university is much more than its classrooms. Of course, at a Catholic university professors lecture and give tests and grade papers, but they also develop mentoring relationships with the students whom they encounter on campus, at mass, and within the larger community. Speaking personally, I look back on my studies as an undergraduate and as a graduate student and realize that certain professors exercised significant formative influences on my life's direction and my outlook on the world, even more than my own parents and pastors. In mentoring relationships, these influential professors extended my own experience of conversion beyond repentance and faith to a true and lasting *metanoia*, a complete and total change of mind. At a university, mentoring and formation lead to transformation. This is exactly what the new evangelization calls for and why it fits so well in a Catholic university. It is difficult to identify a better-suited institution to accomplish the life-changing long-term goals of the new evangelization than a Catholic university.

Recent anecdotal evidence indicates that a Catholic university can have this kind of lasting impact on its students. *Our Sunday Visitor Newsweekly* reports how a legion of students who attended Franciscan University of Steubenville in the 1990s went on to work in—or found—a multitude of prominent Catholic apostolates. Those students describe their experience at Franciscan and how the faith was not merely a topic for rigorous study and classroom discussion, but something lived and shared by professors and students alike.[76] Within a community of faith, they discovered a "fertile environment for spiritual growth, study and Christian friendship," which inspired them to find ways to evangelize the culture and minister with the mind of the Church.[77] Additional examples from other Catholic colleges and universities could be cited, but this may suffice to show the effect that a Catholic university can have not only on its students, but also on the entire Church and the broader culture. Through the various ministries these students touch, the new evangelization is happening boldly throughout the Catholic Church in the United States.

All the Church's institutions are called to participate in the mission of evangelization. But the reach of a parish or retreat center is often limited to the lives of its parishioners and retreatants because many come to these places to be individually nourished but may not feel particularly called to participate in the evangelization of others. Yet, at a vibrant Catholic university, students see the powerful integration of faith and life, and often feel drawn to share their experience of the Gospel. As the *Our Sunday Visitor Newsweekly* article shows, when the Catholic university embodies the new evangelization, seeking to preach the Gospel to all, the university's participation in the Church's mission can bear unending fruit as its alumni hunger to transform those around them.

76. Susan Klemond, "Apostolate of Friendship," *Our Sunday Visitor Newsweekly*, September 16, 2015, at:https://www.osv.com/OSVNewsweekly/Article/TabId/535/ArtMID/13567/ArticleID/18221/%E2%80%98Apostolate-of-friendship%E2%80%99.aspx.

77. Ibid. Klemond observes how students "who attended Franciscan University of Steubenville in the 1990s have gone on to become some of the Church's leading evangelizers ... Called by the Holy Spirit to immerse themselves in the Catholic Faith, a diverse group arrived at Franciscan University of Steubenville in the 1990s and soon forged an 'apostolate of friendship' as they studied the Faith together and prepared for God's next big assignments. The small campus set in the hills of northeastern Ohio served as the launching pad for these friends to start national and international ministries. Two decades later, they continue to help each other promote the Faith to millions. The roughly two dozen ministry leaders—including Jeff Cavins, Patrick Coffin, Tim Gray, Marcus Grodi, Sister John Dominic, Curtis Martin, Curtis Mitch, Tom Nash, Leon Suprenant and Edward Sri, among others—were drawn to Franciscan by the university's intellectual fervor, by the teachings of Pope St. John Paul II and [professors] who shared with them [a] deep understanding and zeal for ... the Faith."

When a university is passionately Catholic in a true and honest way, it requires both academic excellence and rigorous scholarship because to study properly enhances prayer, but to pray properly is not an exemption from hard study. In fact, proper prayer should motivate us to go back and study harder and learn truth more deeply and then share it more generously, allowing the virtue and the holiness of God's spirit to grow in our lives and to reach others as well. After reflecting on all these reasons, it should be clear that the new evangelization has no more appropriate place to flourish than in a vibrant institution of Catholic higher education committed to the Church's mission.

The Catholic University and the Church's Mission

For the Church's mission to evangelize all people to truly succeed, Catholic institutions of higher learning must understand and embrace their role in sharing the Good News with the world. The time has come for all professors, administrators, and trustees of Catholic universities to seek a Christocentric vision for their institutions; to integrate faith and reason; to see that a student's experience in the classroom, the chapel, and the dormitory should be an ongoing assimilation; and to desire to send forth disciples who will transform the world and the culture. If Catholic universities embrace John Paul's vision in *Ex corde Ecclesiae*—seeking to be all that "they are called to be," seeking to embody a vibrant Catholic identity, seeking to mentor students in an authentic Christian life—then these universities will answer the Church's urgent call to evangelize the culture.[78] This task cannot be overlooked; the need to reevangelize the dechristianized grows daily. Catholic institutions of higher learning are uniquely poised to provide the means to live out the call for the new evangelization. Through a deeper understanding of the ongoing conversion that empowers evangelization, and a deeper understanding of the Catholic university's opportunity and responsibility to be an instrument for this conversion, one can clearly see that the success of the new evangelization necessitates the participation of the Catholic university in this preeminent mission of the Church.

78. Swetland, "Catholic Colleges."

[7]

In Service

Shaping the Culture, Serving the Church

Anne Hendershott

More than fifty years ago, a then-obscure Catholic college professor published an essay in a long forgotten journal accusing faculty on Catholic campuses of "perpetuating mediocrity" by giving too great a priority to the moral development of students instead of scholarship and intellectual excellence.[1] Within six months, as historian Philip Gleason points out in his book *Catholic Modernity*, more than 3,500 reprints had been distributed, and it had been commented on in the Catholic press, noted by *Newsweek*, read aloud in the refectories of many religious communities, and discussed at meetings of Catholic educators, including two sessions at the National Catholic Educational Association's 1956 convention.[2] The author, Monsignor John Tracy Ellis, became a Catholic celebrity—and Catholic higher education has yet to recover.

Looking back today as we celebrate the twenty-fifth anniversary of the release of the apostolic constitution *Ex corde Ecclesiae*, it is difficult to understand how this essay could have generated such emotional debate among faculty and administrators on Catholic campuses in 1956. With further reflection, however, we can begin to see that Ellis's analy-

1. John Tracy Ellis, "American Catholics and the Intellectual Life," *Thought* 30 (Autumn 1955): 351–88.

2. Philip Gleason, *Contending with Modernity: Catholic Higher Education in the Twentieth Century* (New York: Oxford University Press, 1995), 290.

sis may have, as Gleason suggests, "popped the cork on long-suppressed discontents."[3] At the time, Ellis noted the absence of Catholic scholars from the national dictionaries of science and letters and decried the dearth of scholarship on Catholic campuses. He accused Catholic faculty members of "living within a ghetto mentality" that prevented them from "mingling as they should with their non-Catholic colleagues" and lamented the undue emphasis placed upon the virtue of humility for Catholic faculty without compensating warnings against the "evils of intellectual sloth." Ellis concluded that Catholic academics would never achieve parity with their counterparts on secular campuses unless they overcame their sense of inferiority and began to act like scholars.[4]

Catholic leaders joined Ellis, including Rev. John J. Cavanaugh, former president of Notre Dame, whose own essay asked, "Where Are the Catholic Salks, Oppenheimers, and Einsteins?" Cavanaugh, like Ellis, suggested that Catholic faculty do not have a sense of dedication to an intellectual apostolate. Both concluded that "cultural and attitudinal factors were the most important causes of Catholic intellectual backwardness."[5] The fulfillment of Ellis's goal for Catholic higher education was realized in 1967, when Catholic college and university officials gathered at Notre Dame's retreat center in Land O'Lakes, Wisconsin, and decided that the Catholic identity of their schools was a liability in achieving upward mobility in an increasingly secular age. The opening paragraph of the 1,500-word statement began: "To perform its teaching and research function effectively the Catholic university must have a true autonomy and academic freedom in the face of authority of whatever kind, lay or clerical, external to the academic community itself."[6]

The Land O'Lakes statement ushered in a new era for Catholic higher education as most Catholic colleges moved to laicize their boards of trustees. Some colleges went even further. Manhattanville College of the Sacred Heart and Webster College publicly and officially declared themselves "no longer Catholic." Manhattanville promptly dropped part of their name, deleting the now too Catholic-sounding "College of the Sacred Heart." Webster, under the direction of the Sisters of Loretto,

3. Ibid., 290.

4. Ellis, "American Catholics and the Intellectual Life."

5. Gleason, *Contending with Modernity*, 290.

6. Ibid., 317.

was not the earliest Catholic college to announce that it was choosing to relinquish its Catholic identity; its president, Sister Jacqueline Grennan, SL, renounced her religious vows and withdrew from her own religious order to become a lay leader so that she too could function as president of the now secular institution "without the embarrassment of being subject to religious obedience."[7] Indeed, obedience to the authority of the Church became an embarrassment for many Catholic colleges and universities. While Catholic colleges had been accused of "mediocrity and moralism" in the 1950s, faithful Catholics shifted their attention in the '60s, '70s, and '80s to concerns about the loss of the Catholic identity on these same campuses.

The release of *Ex corde Ecclesiae*, the papal document identifying the centrality of Catholic higher education, changed the conversation—and forced us all to pay attention to what was happening on these campuses. Literally translated as "from the heart of the Church," Pope John Paul II's *Ex corde Ecclesiae* called on Catholic colleges to revitalize what the Holy Father viewed as the "authentically Catholic character" of the Church's colleges and universities. And although *Ex corde Ecclesiae* acknowledges that the Catholic university, as a university, possesses the institutional autonomy necessary to perform its functions effectively and guarantees its members academic freedom, the document reminds those working on Catholic campuses that this freedom must be always be viewed "within the confines of the truth and the common good,"[8] and that there must be "fidelity" to the Christian message as it comes to us through the Church.

Toward that goal, *Ex corde Ecclesiae* states that the "honor and responsibility of a Catholic University is to consecrate itself without reserve to the cause of truth."[9] Faculty and administrators at Catholic colleges and universities are held responsible for pursuing and proclaiming that truth. For Pope John Paul, the pursuit of truth is the university's way of serving both the dignity of man and the good of the Church, maintaining that it is in the context of the "impartial search for truth that the relationship between faith and reason is brought to light and meaning."[10]

7. Ibid.
8. *EcE*, 12.
9. *EcE*, 4.
10. *EcE*, 5.

Faithful Catholics found *Ex corde Ecclesiae* an affirming joyful document that celebrates the importance of Catholic higher education, yet many Catholic college faculty and administrators have spent much of the past twenty-five years protesting—or ignoring—*Ex corde Ecclesiae*, refusing to comply with its requirements. In fact, so alarmed with the initial release of what they perceived as the demands of the document were Boston College's then president, Donald Monan, and Edward Malloy, then president of Notre Dame, that they published an article warning that the papal document would threaten the status of their institutions: "The universities' acceptance of the obligations spelled out here would mean the sacrifice of many of those prerogatives that make Catholic universities and their professional staffs the respected and influential members of the higher education community that they are."[11] Concerned about the same loss of status and academic inferiority that Ellis identified in 1955, the presidents of Notre Dame and Boston College wrote that they desired a document for Catholic colleges and universities that "by reason of its literary style, as well as its content, they would be proud to display to sister institutions of higher education."

Describing the decree as "unworkable and dangerous," the editors of *America* warned that the impact of the norms of *Ex corde Ecclesiae* would be "disastrous" for Catholic colleges and universities. In an especially hyperbolic article, Loyola University of Chicago theology professor Jon Nilson likened the approval of *Ex corde Ecclesiae* to the "doomsday clock" for Catholic higher education. With the metaphor of the doomsday clock, a vestige of the Cold War, the Bulletin of Atomic Scientists showed how close the world was to the midnight of mass nuclear annihilation. Nilson warned of a similar annihilation for Catholic colleges:

> If there were a doomsday clock for Catholic higher education in the United States, its hands moved closer to midnight in November, 1999, when the bishops approved *Ex corde Ecclesiae*. The hands moved still closer this past November when the bishops accepted draft procedures for implementing the Applications requirement of a mandatum for theologians. The hands are still moving, counting down to the moment when the American experience of

11. J. Donald Monan and Edward A. Malloy, "*Ex corde Ecclesiae* Creates an Impasse," *America* 180, no. 3 (January 30, 1999): 6–12, http://209.35.85.31/articles/excordeecclesiae monan-malloy/cfm.

independent but church related colleges and universities as envisioned and enacted by Theodore Hesburgh, Timothy Healy, Joseph O'Hare, Raymond Baumhart, J. Donald Monan, Raymond Fitz, Alice Gallin, Paul Reinert and so many others, will be terminated.[12]

Nilson was joined by other theologians who were critical of what they viewed as the "Vatican's inability to appreciate a system of Catholic higher education independent of the Church's juridical control," seeing the document as an attempt by Rome to "put theologians on a short leash" in the application of the requirement of a *mandatum* for theologians.[13] These theologians were concerned about the requirement that all theologians receive a *mandatum*—an acknowledgment by the bishop that the Catholic professor of a theological discipline is a teacher within the full communion of the Catholic Church. The mandate also recognizes the professor's commitment and responsibility to teach authentic Catholic doctrine—requiring that the professor refrain from putting forth as Catholic teaching anything contrary to the Church's Magisterium.[14]

In the early years after the release of the document, angry Catholic theologians began a series of counter-initiatives. Theresa Moser, then the president of the College Theology Society and an assistant dean at the University of San Francisco, dismissed the document as "going against our tradition in the University."[15] Terrence Tilley, chairman of University of Dayton's religious studies department, wrote that the norms of the document "sent the wrong message" and suggested that "Implementing *Ex corde Ecclesiae* will discourage the most able Catholic students of theology and religious studies from studying at Roman Catholic institutions."[16] Some theologians openly defied the document.

12. Jon Nilson, "The Impending Death of Catholic Higher Education," *America* 184, no. 18 (May 28, 2001): http://americamagazine.org/content/article.cfm?article_id=927.

13. Ibid.

14. National Conference of Catholic Bishops Ad Hoc Committee on the *Mandatum*, "Guidelines Concerning the Academic *Mandatum* in Catholic Universities (Canon 812)," Article 1, a–b, in Committee on Catholic Education, United States Conference of Catholic Bishops (USCCB), *Catholic Mission and Culture in Colleges and Universities: Defining Documents: 1965–2014* (Washington, DC: USCCB, 2014), 234–49.

15. Beth McMurtrie, "Catholic Bishops Offer Revised Guidelines for Carrying Out Papal Statement," *Chronicle of Higher Education* 46 (October 1, 1999): A18.

16. Ibid.

Claiming that *Ex corde Ecclesiae* did not apply to them, the faculty senate at Notre Dame voted unanimously for the guidelines to be ignored.[17]

Other dissenters from the document have chosen a more creative approach. Rather than public dissent, Rev. Raymond Collins, then dean of the religious studies department at the Catholic University of America, advised faculty members to "selectively dissent" from *Ex corde Ecclesiae* by refusing to implement the parts they disagreed with. In an attempt to avoid outright confrontation with Church authorities, Collins advised that theologians should "set aside Church teachings that they found wanting, but without fuss, thus implementing the *Ex corde* guidelines selectively—being faithful in their fashion."[18]

This appears to be the route taken today by many faculty and administrators on Catholic campuses as they choose Catholic teachings they find acceptable, including most teachings on economic justice, and the preferential option for the poor, and rejecting others, especially those focusing on the role of women in the Church, reproductive rights, homosexuality, same-sex marriage, and, increasingly, transgender rights and assisted suicide. Some theologians publicly proclaim that they—not the pope or the bishops—are the true authority, or the "alternative Magisterium" on what the Church teaches.[19]

On many of these same campuses, the academic deans provide "Catholic" cover for them. Mark Roche, then dean of Notre Dame's College of Arts and Sciences, is one example of an academic dean who has led by example in openly defying authoritative teachings on abortion in his 2004 op-ed piece in the *New York Times* titled "Voting Our Conscience Not Our Religion."[20] Likewise, Nicholas M. Healy, formerly the Dean of the College of Arts and Sciences at the University of San

17. Ralph McInerny, "Picking and Choosing Church Doctrines," *Beliefnet*, accessed September 8, 2017, http://www.beliefnet.com/Faiths/Christianity/2000/04/Picking-And-Choosing-Church-Doctrines.aspx.

18. Ibid.

19. Nicholas M. Healy, "'By the Working of the Holy Spirit': The Crisis of Authority in the Christian Churches," *Anglican Theological Review* 88, no. 1 (Winter 2006): 5–24, http://www.anglicantheologicalreview.org/read/article/506/.

20. Mark W. Roche, "Voting Our Conscience, Not Our Religion," *New York Times*, October 11, 2004, http://www.nytimes.com/2004/10/11/opinion/voting-our-conscience-not-our-religion.html.

Diego, has suggested that a "profound change" in Catholic leadership is needed to address what he sees as the "crisis in authority." "The crisis of authority in the Roman Catholic Church," he writes, "cannot be resolved by demanding blind obedience to judgments the rationales of which seem lacking in cogency, and by stifling constructively critical theological inquiry."[21]

Clearly, rather than being "in service" to the Church, many Catholic colleges and universities have decided to conform to the greater culture on issues like reproductive rights and same-sex marriage. The Cardinal Newman Society recently released a major study on the ties between abortion provider Planned Parenthood and Catholic colleges. It seems that sixty-three Catholic colleges have ties to Planned Parenthood. Boston College, DePaul, Mount St. Mary's, Seattle University, Stonehill College, the University of Dayton, and the University of San Diego all offer internships—and career opportunities—for undergraduate students. For example, the University of San Diego's website recommends potential careers at Planned Parenthood for students who have majored in women's studies.[22]

Worse, there are faculty members of many Catholic colleges who have also worked at Planned Parenthood, or who are concurrently working at Planned Parenthood. Fairfield University's Michael Pagano, an assistant professor of communication, worked as a physician's assistant at Planned Parenthood. A nursing professor at University of San Diego proudly posts on her vita that she received a certificate in OB-GYN through a joint program at the University of California, San Francisco, and Planned Parenthood. Georgetown University has two faculty members in their nursing program who worked as certified midwives at Planned Parenthood. Georgetown Law School has two faculty members who worked as general counsel at Planned Parenthood. When Loyola Marymount University held a search for a new dean in arts and sciences, the two finalists had both worked for Planned Parenthood. One was a former dean at Fairfield University and had served on the board of Planned Parenthood throughout her years in Connecticut.

21. Healy, "'By the Working of the Holy Spirit.'"

22. Cardinal Newman Society, "A More Scandalous Relationship: Catholic Colleges and Planned Parenthood," August 18, 2015, https://cardinalnewmansociety.org/scandalous-relationship-catholic-colleges-planned-parenthood/.

As revelations emerged on Planned Parenthood's role in the selling of fetal organs and body parts, one might have expected Catholic colleges to distance themselves from the now stigmatized organization. Rather, a new generation of pro-choice lawyers trained at some of the nation's premier Catholic universities has stepped up to defend the barbaric practice. Law Students for Reproductive Justice (LSRJ), a student law school organization on several Catholic campuses, has been helping Catholic law schools "train and mobilize law students and new lawyers across the country to foster legal expertise and support for the realization of reproductive justice."[23] Collaborating with Catholics for Choice, LSRJ aims to produce a new generation of abortion advocates to help convince Catholics and others that "reproductive justice"[24] means access to full reproductive rights—including the right to an abortion. Catholics for Choice is an important partner for LSRJ, and for the Catholic university law schools that host LSRJ. In fact, the national LSRJ was so grateful to Catholics for Choice that they recently (2014) awarded the Allied Organization Award to Catholics for Choice for its help in creating the LSRJ initiative "Keeping Faith in the Conversation" event tool kit. The tool kit aids in creating a panel for an on-campus event sponsored by LSRJ chapters, especially those on Catholic campuses. This tool kit allows chapters to bring speakers to campus who can help them share information on "the intersection of faith and abortion rights."

With chapters at DePaul University College of Law; Fordham Law; Georgetown University Law; Loyola Law School, Los Angeles; Loyola University Chicago School of Law; Santa Clara University Law School; Seattle University School of Law; St. Louis University School of Law; University of Detroit Mercy School of Law; University of San Diego School of Law; University of San Francisco School of Law; and Villanova University School of Law,[25] LSRJ has made real progress in helping to create a new generation of Catholic law school graduates who are ready, willing, and able to defend organizations like Planned Parenthood.

Far from challenging the mainstream culture, the reality is that too many Catholic colleges and universities have contributed to the culture

23. Available at website for Law Students for Reproductive Justice, http://lsrj.org/motivation/.

24. Ibid.

25. See the website for Law Students for Reproductive Justice, http://lsrj.org/chapters/.

of death. This is counter to the important mandate Pope John Paul II gave to Catholic colleges in *Ex corde Ecclesiae* when he asked Catholic colleges to make scholars available to "speak uncomfortable truths which do not always please public opinion, but which are necessary to safeguard the authentic good of society."[26] Far from making scholars available to speak the "uncomfortable truths" about the unborn child, or end-of-life care, or the sanctity of marriage, it seems to faithful Catholics that many scholars on Catholic campuses have sided with the opposition—against the Church—on all of these issues. This has been the real tragedy of the twenty-five years following the release of *Ex corde Ecclesiae*. Rather than being in service to the Church, many scholars are in service to their disciplines—creating their academic disciplines as "little deities" that proclaim the truth as they see it—a multiplicity of truths, as George Dennis O'Brien, a former college president, described it in his book.

Rather than using their research and writing to help in the search for truth as revealed to us by God through the Church, or to help influence public opinion in order to shape the culture, scholars on many Catholic colleges have been conscripted to fight for the other side. *Beyond the Abortion Wars*,[27] by Fordham philosophy professor Charles Camosy, promises that "the argument put forth in this book is consistent with defined Catholic doctrine," but then Camosy goes on to try and convince us that Catholic doctrine allows for early term abortion. In fact, Camosy suggests that the use of RU 486 is not a direct abortion; rather, it is a form of "indirect abortion":

> The drugs present in RU 486 do not by their very nature appear to attack the fetus. Instead, the drug cuts off the pregnancy hormone and the fetus is detached from the woman's body . . . Some abortions are indirect and better understood as refusals to aid.[28]

26. *EcE*, 32.

27. Charles C. Camosy, *Beyond the Abortion Wars: A New Way Forward for a New Generation* (New York: Eerdmans, 2015).

28. Ibid., 82–83.

Shaping the Culture Surrounding the Marriage Wars

Beyond the abortion wars, we now are faced with the war surrounding marriage. But rather than defending marriage as a union of one man and one woman, many philosophy, theology, and social science professors on Catholic campuses have been lobbying against the Church's teachings on marriage. In fact, there are scholars at Georgetown, Notre Dame, Manhattan College, Boston College, Seattle University, and other Catholic campuses like the University of San Francisco who have actually lobbied to "end" marriage—or to "move beyond" marriage. And these Catholic college faculty have received funding to mount those attacks on their own Church. As a result, some of the most brutal attacks on Magisterial teachings on marriage are funded through Catholic colleges and universities. Sometimes these Catholic colleges are paid to make these attacks. Gay billionaires John Stryker and Tim Gill are doing everything they can to use Catholic colleges and universities to discredit Church teachings on sexual morality by directly attacking the Magisterium. Both Stryker's Arcus Foundation and the Gill Foundation have made their aims explicit in their grant-making materials and on their IRS 990 reporting forms. In their 2012 filing (available at Guidestar.org) to the Internal Revenue Service, the Arcus Foundation described itself as a private grant-making foundation that supports nonprofit organizations around the world working in two areas: lesbian, gay, bisexual, transgender, and queer (LGBTQ) human rights and conservation of the world's great apes.

In the LGBTQ area, Arcus provides money to those organizations—including, most notably, Catholic colleges as well as progressive faith-based organizations—who are working toward "full inclusion" of gays and lesbians, including access to same-sex marriage. For example, hundreds of thousands of dollars have been awarded to the Women's Alliance for Theology Ethics for seeking to achieve social justice through the Arcus LGBT Rights Program. The goal of the $70,000 grant to Women's Alliance for Theology, Ethics, and Ritual (WATER) in 2010 was identified by Arcus as intending to "create a cadre of Catholic, lesbian, bisexual and transgender women and their allies that would assume a leadership role within the Catholic community."[29] Escalating their attack in 2011,

29. Forms 990 Filing 2011, Arcus Foundation EIN#383332791, Attachment D, p. 9,

in their IRS 990 form, filed on December 31, 2012, Arcus disclosed that the $180,000 awarded to WATER that year was to be used to "Identify, network, train and amplify the voices of lesbian feminist Catholics,"[30] many of them teaching on Catholic campuses, and in so doing, creating a counter-voice to the Catholic hierarchy that "respects, values and affirms people of all sexual orientations and gender identities."[31]

The Arcus strategy is to help progressive Catholic organizations—including Catholic colleges and universities—convince Catholics of the goodness and morality of gay and lesbian behavior by providing large sums of money to them. For example, Fairfield University was a perfect choice for funding from Arcus because it houses theology professors like Paul Lakeland, an embittered ex-priest and current head of Fairfield's Catholic Studies Department. Lakeland, whose books *Liberation of the Laity* and *Catholicism at the Crossroads* demand dramatic changes in the Church—including the abolition of the College of Cardinals as well as changes in Church governance and teachings on reproductive rights, women's ordination, and the inclusion of gay and married priests—received a $100,000 grant from the Arcus Foundation in 2010 "to hold four forums at four Catholic colleges and disseminate information from these forums in order to expand the current discussion on homosexuality within Roman Catholicism to include the diverse opinions of progressive Catholic thought leaders and theologians."[32]

In 2011, Arcus provided $37,938 to the National Gay and Lesbian Task Force Foundation for a project called "Roman Catholic Thought Leaders Convening." The goal of the project was "to strengthen and expand a network of pro-LGBT Catholic thought leaders working to promote the moral and civil equality of LGBT people."[33] While Jon

---

Guidestar.org, accessed March 10, 2016, http://www.guidestar.org/FinDocuments//2011/383/332/2011-383332791-08b29556-F.pdf.

30. Forms 990 Filing 2012, Arcus Foundation EIN#38332791, Attachment C, p. 15, Guidestar.org, accessed March 10, 2016, http://www.guidestar.org/FinDocuments//2012/383/332/2012-383332791-09b48e8c-F.pdf.

31. Ibid.

32. Arcus Foundation, *2011 Annual Report*, accessed September 8, 2017, http://beta.arcusfoundation.org.s3.amazonaws.com/wp-content/uploads/2011/01/Arcus-Foundation-Annual-Report-2011.pdf.

33. Non-profit Profile, Forms 990 for Arcus Foundation, Guidestar.org, accessed December 13, 2015, http://www.guidestar.org/organizations/38-3332791/arcus-foundation.aspx.

Stryker's Arcus Foundation uses a subtle strategy of attacking Church teachings through persuasion and conversations on campuses like Fairfield University, Tim Gill's foundation directly attacks the Magisterium with systematic assaults on individual bishops through organizations like Faith in Public Life and its subsidiary, Faithful America. Last year's media attack on, and petition against, San Francisco Archbishop Salvatore Cordileone was funded in large part through Gill's Movement Advancement Program, which is described in Gill's IRS filings as helping to "speed equality for lesbian, gay, bisexual and transgender people. MAP's work helps educate and persuade public audiences (such as policymakers, allied organized funders, media and the American public) and helps to support LGBT movement audiences." Toward the goal of educating the American public on the goodness of homosexual acts and same sex marriage, the Gill Foundation provides hundreds of thousands of dollars to organizations like the Center for American Progress and Media Matters.

Gill knows that the biggest stumbling block to "speeding equality" for the LGBT community is the Catholic Church. To neutralize the teachings of the Church on sexual morality, he employs organizations like Catholics United and Faithful America, both organizations with close ties to scholars on Catholic campuses throughout the country. Board members for Catholics in Alliance for the Common Good have included Catholic college faculty: Lisa Sowle Cahill of Boston College, Stephen Schneck of Catholic University, and others. The success of this movement is clear in San Francisco, where Archbishop Cordileone has been under attack, sometimes from faculty at the Catholic colleges and universities in his own diocese. During the spring of 2015, as the archbishop was attempting to ensure that San Francisco's Catholic high schools remain faithful to the Church and that teachers there teach the truth, some on the faculty and staff at the University of San Francisco (USF) took sides against his commitment to defending marriage as a union between one man and one woman. In fact, USF hosted some of the most brutal attacks on Archbishop Cordileone's attempt to ensure that San Francisco's Catholic high schools remain Catholic.

On March 17, 2015, the University of San Francisco hosted a forum that was described in *National Catholic Reporter* as an opportunity to "galvanize opposition to Archbishop Salvatore Cordileone's changes to a handbook for teachers at four high schools."[34] Leading the charge against the archbishop was Brian Cahill, retired executive director of Catholic Charities/Catholic Youth Organization in the Archdiocese of San Francisco. Angry about Catholic teachings on homosexuality, Cahill has been protesting these teachings for more than a decade, long before Archbishop Cordileone ever arrived in San Francisco. A longtime advocate of same-sex "marriage" and adoption of children by gay parents—even during the time he headed San Francisco's Catholic Charities—Cahill publicly denounced Catholic teachings on homosexuality. On March 13, 2011, Cahill published an op-ed in the in the *San Francisco Chronicle* titled "My Gay Son: The Face of Church's Lack of Respect," which began: "I am a Catholic who voted against Proposition 8 in 2008 and contributed $1,000 to the No on 8 Campaign."[35] Archbishop Cordileone was a leader of the Proposition 8 campaign, which sought to ensure that marriage remain a union between a man and a woman.

Joining Cahill at the University of San Francisco forum was Jim McGarry and his wife, Kathy Curran, both of whom appear to have made a commitment to changing Catholic teachings on marriage and homosexuality. And, like Cahill, Curran and McGarry made that commitment more than a decade ago, long before Archbishop Cordileone arrived in the Bay Area. In December 2008, the couple coordinated a demonstration along with Dignity USA, New Ways Ministry, and Call to Action in a candlelight vigil to protest Vatican opposition to a United Nations resolution on homosexuality. In his opening speech at the event at the University of San Francisco on March 17, Cahill helped set the tone for the evening when he charged that "Cordileone, who with his imported crew of orthodox, smugly ideological and intentionally provocative zealots, is trying to shove his sex-obsessed version of Catholic identity down the throats of Catholic high school students and teachers."[36]

34. Mandy Erickson, "Hundreds Attend Forum Opposed to San Francisco Handbook Changes," *National Catholic Reporter*, May 11, 201, https://www.ncronline.org/news/parish/hundreds-attend-forum-opposed-san-francisco-handbook-changes.

35. Brian Cahill, "My Gay Son: The Face of Church's Lack of Respect," *SFGate*, March 13, 2011, http://www.sfgate.com/opinion/article/My-gay-son-the-face-of-church-s-lack-of-respect-2389568.php.

36. Erickson, "Hundreds Attend Forum."

Following the US Supreme Court's 5–4 ruling in *Obergefell v. Hodges*, regarding same-sex marriage, USF sent out a message celebrating the decision to allow same-sex couples access to marriage.[37] According to the Cardinal Newman Society, "The tweet, which was originally distributed by the University's Leo T. McCarthy Center for Public Service and the Common Good, was then retweeted on the official USF Twitter account."[38] The Cardinal Newman Society captured the tweet—even though it was later removed by USF president—after pressure from many Catholics.[39] A post from the university's official Facebook account read, "Proudly part of the city that defines the word pride." The post also featured the university's official logo. "Love Wins" read the Twitter post. The official USF mascot attended the pride parade wearing a sticker that stated, "proudly part of the city that defines pride." Several employees and students of USF wore T-shirts that read, "Pride 2015 University of San Francisco." Andrea Wise, co-chair of the USF LGBT Caucus for Faculty and Staff, boasted that she has helped grow the USF involvement in the San Francisco Pride parade from seventy-five people in 2013 to two hundred this year. She also added that USF is committed to the Jesuit calling of respecting the dignity of every person—and that the Supreme Court ruling was something to celebrate at USF.

For our purposes in relation to *Ex corde Ecclesiae*, the most disconcerting part of the USF Facebook postings were the ones that stated that USF is "proudly part of the City that defines gay pride." Counter to the intention of *Ex corde*, USF has allowed the culture of the city of San Francisco to begin to shape the university itself, rather than helping to shape the culture of the city. No longer "in service" to the city, USF is now part of that city's culture. While the Holy Father stated in *Ex corde* that Catholic universities are essential to the growth of the Church and

37. Justin Petrisek, "University of San Francisco Celebrates SCOTUS Marriage Ruling Despite Catholic Mission," *Cardinal Newman Society*, July 2, 2015, http://www.cardinalnewmansociety.org/CatholicEducationDaily/DetailsPage/tabid/102/ArticleID/4273/Univ-of-San-Francisco-Celebrates-SCOTUS-Marriage-Ruling-Despite-Catholic-Mission.aspx.

38. Ibid.

39. Justin Petrisek, "University of San Francisco President Deletes Tweet Celebrating Same-Sex Marriage," *Cardinal Newman Society*, July 16, 2015, http://www.cardinalnewmansociety.org/CatholicEducationDaily/DetailsPage/tabid/102/ArticleID/4290/Univ-of-San-Francisco-President-Deletes-Tweet-Celebrating-Same-Sex-Marriage.aspx.

to the development of Christian culture and human progress, I do not think he ever could have anticipated what has happened at USF. Rather than an institutional commitment to the service of the people of God and of the human family, USF is now in service to San Francisco and its ideals, attitudes, and principles. This is not to suggest that those at USF see themselves as defying the Church—they don't reject the Church. But they have redefined the Church's commitment to social justice in order to accommodate those of same-sex orientation, to make sure they do not feel left out or unloved. This is a form of sentimentality.

Sentimentality on Catholic College Campuses

His Eminence Raymond Leo Cardinal Burke talked about the danger of sentimentality when he visited the Franciscan University of Steubenville campus during the fall semester of 2015.[40] He was speaking of those who want to change the unchangeable teachings of the Church on marriage and said that many of them seem to be motivated by a misguided sense of sentimentality, a kind of tenderness that seems compassionate and kind and tells people what they want to hear. Cardinal Burke reminded those gathered that such misguided sentimentality has cut itself off from the person of Christ and his teachings. In some ways, Cardinal Burke was echoing Catholic writers Walker Percy and Flannery O'Connor, who have both reminded readers that "tenderness can lead to the gas chamber."[41]

To truly be "in service" to the Church, we must continue to be inspired by the light of the Christian message—being both a community of scholars representing various branches of human knowledge, and a place where Catholicism is vitally present and operative. We need to be a "living union" of individuals dedicated to the search for truth—a truth that continues to be "profoundly inscribed on the heart of the human person." That search for the truth—a truth that has already been

40. Raymond Leo Burke, "The Synod on the Family: Addressing the *Instrumentum Laboris*," Henkels Lecture at Franciscan University of Steubenville, Ohio, September 8, 2015, http://www.franciscan.edu/Henkels-Lecture/Burke/.

41. Walker Percy, *The Thanatos Syndrome: A Novel* (New York: Picador, 1999).

inscribed on our hearts—is the only way we can truly devote ourselves to the service of the Church and to each other. The late sociologist Philip Rieff once wrote that the central purpose of culture is to regulate the relationship between the "no" imposing voice of commandment and the "yes" seeking desires of the individual.[42] He was not a strongly religious man, but he still believed that religion stamps our inner lives with creeds that deliver us from slavery to instinct. In fact, he believed that these creedal truths are what keep us from becoming barbarians. As a society, we have always believed that religion played an important role in our socialization. Sociologists have always taught that religion was one of the major socializing agents, but the newest editions of introductory-level sociology textbooks have deleted religion as a "socializing force." Rather, the media is viewed as a primary agent, rivaling the socializing influence of the institutions of the family and the Church.

Pope John Paul II knew the importance of culture. In some important ways, it seems that concern about culture was a motivating force in much of the wording in *Ex corde*. The Holy Father knew that any living culture—including the culture of the Catholic Church—is constantly under attack by those who want to change it. Cultural work, then, is the matter and manner of disarming competing cultures both inside and outside the Church. Sociologists have always known that no institution, especially one like the Catholic Church, exists without conflict over contested cultural issues like the ones we are talking about here. If we truly believe that what the Church teaches is true, then these culture wars will continue—and faithful Catholics who accept the truth of these teachings must be willing to engage in that fight.

The truth is that we can never really get beyond the culture wars. Rieff's books remind us that where there is culture there is struggle. For Rieff, culture is war by other normative means.[43] By its very nature, the work of culture is the matter and manner of disarming competing culture—something that always threatens sacred order. This does not mean that the Church is resistant to all change. The Catholic Church, like all institutions, is constantly being re-created in certain ways. Some

42. Philip Rieff, *Charisma: The Gift of Grace and How It Has Been Taken Away from Us* (New York: Pantheon, 2007).

43. Philip Rieff, *Fellow Teachers* (New York: Dell, 1972).

change is inevitable—it is inherent to culture as it emerges through conflict. But this re-creation cannot be guided by the changing values of a secular culture. And the Church cannot change her infallible teachings, including those concerning the dignity of the human person, the sacredness of the family. These nonnegotiable teachings are the definitive teachings of the Church and will never change. As such, the Catholic culture wars will never end. And they should not end because there will always be those on Catholic campuses—and beyond—who want to change these teachings. *Ex corde Ecclesiae* simply calls on us to defend them, and we should be grateful to the Catholic colleges and universities still willing to do just that.

[8]

Canonical Issues and US Catholic Universities

Twenty-Five Years since *Ex corde Ecclesiae*

James J. Conn, SJ

What a delight it was to be at Franciscan University for the Fidelity and Freedom Symposia! I am especially grateful to Father Sean Sheridan for arranging the invitation. He and I first met some years ago while he was working on his doctoral dissertation in canon law at the Catholic University of America and I was visiting a Jesuit classmate who had been Fr. Sheridan's liturgy professor at the Washington Theological Union. Father Sean and I share an interest in canonical questions relating to Catholic universities, and I have followed his scholarly and academic journey with enthusiastic interest. My more immediate connection with Steubenville can be found in two recently ordained Jesuit priests whom I taught at our School of Theology and Ministry at Boston College. They both were undergraduates here and speak in glowing terms of their college experience. They are both among the finest students I have known in my forty-four years of teaching. They were eminently well prepared for their seminary-level studies; they think clearly, write and speak eloquently, and argue persuasively. Of greater importance still, I hasten to say, is their lively Catholic faith and zeal for souls. If they are typical of Steubenville graduates, I will never stop singing its praises and recommending it to young people and their families who are seeking the best in Catholic higher education.

Canonical Issues and US Catholic Universities

My role in the Fidelity and Freedom Series is to reflect on some of the canonical dimensions of St. John Paul II's landmark apostolic constitution *Ex corde Ecclesiae*, whose twenty-fifth anniversary we observed in 2015.[1] Not altogether coincidental is this same year's fiftieth anniversary of the Second Vatican Council's declaration *Gravissimum educationis* on Catholic education. Thinking about the intersection of church and school has in one way or another occupied most of my life. In the 1950s, because of a visual disability that I have always had, I was what the good Sisters in Philadelphia used to call a "public school boy." In those days I was, and hope I still am, as you in Steubenville proudly proclaim, passionately Catholic. I was a faithful participant in twice weekly catechism classes and learned their lessons well. Our mostly Protestant public school teachers were not sympathetic to the faith and not too subtly let those of us in the Catholic minority know it. Ecumenism had not yet taken root in the City of Brotherly Love. I finally made it to Catholic school at 7th grade and spent my adolescent years—which were coterminous with Vatican II—under the influence of the Jesuits at St. Joseph's Preparatory School in my hometown. That experience changed my life; I would not exchange that peerless education with any other.

Wanting to be like my Jesuit teachers when I grew up, I entered the order at age eighteen, and even as a novice heard the first reflections of some of my elders about how the "spirit of the Council" would affect what we then still called "our universities." I confess that in my youthful enthusiasm I was seduced by visions of "entering the mainstream" of American higher education and "loosing the shackles" of ecclesiastical control. At that time, the leaders of Catholic higher education were meeting at Land O'Lakes, Wisconsin, to assert the "true autonomy and academic freedom in the face of authority of whatever kind, lay or clerical, external to the academic community itself."[2] One of the early effects of "the spirit of the Council" on religious formation was the move away

1. The English texts of most official Church documents mentioned in this essay can be found in Committee on Catholic Education and United States Conference of Catholic Bishops (USCCB), *Catholic Mission and Culture in Colleges and Universities: Defining Documents: 1965–2014* (Washington, DC: USCCB, 2014).

2. "Land O'Lakes Statement: The Nature of the Contemporary Catholic University (1967)," in *American Catholic Higher Education, Essential Documents, 1967–1990*, ed. Alice Gallin (Notre Dame, IN: University of Notre Dame Press, 1992), 7–12.

from isolated rural seminaries to university campuses so that we young religious could study with our lay classmates, in my case at Fordham University in New York City. In the late 1960s, many of us protested and rebelled with those same classmates. I did only a little of that, preferring instead to make friends with Jesuit administrators and offer to assist them in their more bureaucratic tasks. At a tender age, I conceived an ambition to follow in their distinguished footsteps. I was treated nicely by these elder brothers of mine and enjoyed life in their academic and social fast lane.

By the mid-1970s, when I was ordained to the priesthood, the transformation of much of Catholic higher education had already taken place. Needless to say, my own experience was, for the most part, limited to the twenty-eight Jesuit colleges and universities, especially those in the Northeast. The most significant juridical change they had undergone was a separation of the institutions from the religious order that founded and until then governed and directed them. The universities had long since obtained civil charters and corporate bylaws, but the religious superior of the local religious house had always been the president of the college, and his religious council constituted the board of trustees of the institution. Around the time of that Land O'Lakes meeting, the two entities gradually began to move away from each other, making it official in the eyes of the civil law by effecting a separate incorporation of the religious community and its assets. Lay trustees, often in large numbers, were added to the boards in such a way that in short order the religious did not occupy enough seats even to prevent action taken by a supermajority. The offices of superior and president were occupied by two different members of the community, and the lines of authority between them and their subordinates quickly blurred. Other changes—far more significant from the point of view of Catholic identity—included extending faculty appointments to non-Catholics, some of whom, along with some of their Catholic colleagues, were less than passionate about the institutions' Catholic identity. Such indifference and even antipathy were reflected in curriculum and a host of factors involving student life and activity.

Little of this should be news to most readers of this volume. But I rehearse it as some background to my own more immediate formation as a scholar and would-be leader in Catholic higher education. I listened to some naysayers at the time who questioned whether the institutional leaders had gone too far and may even have violated, unwittingly perhaps, the law of the Church in fashioning their institutions' new structures. I had considered the leaders' motivation to be basically good: to make Catholic universities as outstanding as they could be and competitive with highly rated secular institutions in our country. But perhaps I, along with some of my confreres, had failed to consider how the values of secular higher education were in some respects inconsistent with the Catholic aspirations that we took for granted.

My 1980 assignment to pursue doctoral studies in canon law in Rome would show me the way, I naively thought, to balance the complementary values of institutional autonomy and Catholic identity. *Sapientia christiana*, the apostolic constitution governing ecclesiastical universities and faculties, had just been promulgated, and the leaders of Catholic universities in the United States were assured that its detailed provisions did not pertain to their institutions. But John Paul II promised a companion document addressing his concern for the many higher-level institutions that are not exclusively dedicated to the sacred sciences. At the same time, the Church was in the last stages of drafting a new *Code of Canon Law*, and the US university presidents were among the most active and vocal lobbyists against any prescriptive norms in that code that would limit their institutions' autonomy. How foolish I was to think that I could help them to fulfill their hope and more foolish still to imagine that their hope was in the Church's best interests.

As a teacher of canon law, I try to bear three objectives in mind. The first is to help my students to know as accurately as possible what a norm of law requires, allows, or prohibits—and to distinguish those prescriptive norms of law that do such things from those that are either descriptive or precative. The second objective is to assist the students in discovering the *ratio legis*, that is, the reason for the law and the reason (or reasonableness) of the law—the theological or ecclesiological value that the law is meant to safeguard or promote. The third objective goes beyond the immediate parameters of the norm itself when I suggest practical means of applying the norm in concrete settings.

In the rather protracted preparation of my doctoral thesis, I quickly learned that the few canons of the 1983 Code of Canon Law that treat Catholic universities have a clear rationale and that the provisions of those canons safeguard important principles. My acceptance of this truth helped me to finish my thesis. The first principle, notwithstanding the contrary objections of the university leadership, was that a Catholic university is a participant in the life of the Church and that therefore the Church and its pastors have a role in university life and are not external to it. The lobbying of the leadership, based on the Land O'Lakes rhetoric, would gladly have seen no reference to Catholic universities in the 1983 code and no apostolic constitution on Catholic universities.

But a closer look at these documents reveals what is not simply the result of pressure from the leadership. Rather, the Church's understanding of the nature of a Catholic university is the rationale for its minimal provisions for the direct involvement of ecclesiastical authority in institutional governance. University autonomy has deep roots in Western culture, even if it was otherwise implied in the 1917 code, where all Catholic educational institutions were treated under a single heading. The 1983 code, like the Council, treated universities separately from schools, assigning schools, Catholic universities, and ecclesiastical universities individual chapters in the code. While the 1917 code, treating all educational institutions univocally, attributed to bishops the right to appoint and remove university-level teachers (can. 1381 §3), the current code, in order to acknowledge and promote the value of autonomy, recognized that function as belonging to the authority determined in the university's statutes. Canon 810 §1 nonetheless declared the criteria for appointment and removal: first, the scientific and pedagogical qualifications that are to be expected of university-level teachers as well as a further requirement proper to a Catholic institution, namely, integrity of doctrine and probity of life. Because nothing further is specified about these qualities, it can be concluded that the institutional statutes could determine their meaning and procedure of application more specifically. In any case, the substantive *ratio legis* on this matter is perfectly clear. An institutional commitment to participate in the Church's teaching mission through instruction, research, and service simply requires a critical mass of persons who are so committed. This does not necessarily exclude non-Catholics, as *Ex corde Ecclesiae* specifically recognizes (art. 4, §§3–4) when it distinguishes Catholic teachers who are to be faithful to Catholic doctrine in their teaching and research on the one hand, from all others who are obliged to respect it. What does *Ex corde*

Ecclesiae say of the critical mass? It asserts in article 4, §4: "In order not to endanger the Catholic identity of the University ... the number of non-Catholic teachers should not be allowed to constitute a majority within the Institution, which is and must remain Catholic." I have elsewhere conducted a careful examination of the texts of *Ex corde Ecclesiae* and its national application or *Ordinationes* produced by the United States Conference of Catholic Bishops (USCCB), along with their various journeys toward promulgation.[3] There is no time and little value to repeating much of that here, but for the purposes of this reflection, I point out a major problem that I have encountered in my study of what I call the US Particular Norms (PN). Both the apostolic constitution and the *Ordinationes* are divided into two parts: the first is an introduction seeking to describe what a Catholic university is. The second is a normative section that has the binding force of ecclesiastical law whether universal or particular. It might be safely said that the introductory part can be something of a *ratio legis* for the normative part. The national *Ordinationes* were prepared by the USCCB over a stormy ten-year period of consultation between bishops and several Catholic university presidents chosen by their peers. To make a long story short, the presidents were fairly united, with a central desire to have a document that was minimally prescriptive. The bishops were divided, but a good number of them were disposed to honor the position of the university leadership. Various drafts appeared. The earlier ones were brief, aspirational, and quite general. The Holy See would not confirm the conference's proposed document until it produced norms of a more juridical nature. A special subcommittee of bishops who were also canonists was appointed to draft a further document that satisfied the required supermajority of the conference, though not the university leadership. Though this document eventually received the required *recognitio* of the Holy See, it was, as a legal document, significantly flawed. My reference above to the critical mass and the Catholic-majority provision in *Ex corde Ecclesiae* is a case in point. The purpose of the national norms was to apply to the concrete political, social, and academic situation of var-

3. See "The Mandate of can. 812 Revisited," in *Iustitia in Caritate*, ed. James J. Conn and Luigi Sabbarese (Rome: Urbaniana University Press, 2005), 227–48, and "National Norms for Catholic Universities Twenty Years since *Ex corde Ecclesiae*," *Seminarium* 50 (2010): 733–64.

ious nations throughout the world the General Norms of the pontifical document. But the objectivity of the General Norms was not to be lost, only made more specific. To ensure this, the Congregation for Catholic Education (the Vatican department in charge of Catholic education at every level) had issued several directives calling for concrete procedures ensuring that the General Norms would be properly applied on the national scenes. The USCCB's PN provided, for the most part, no concrete means or procedures for achieving such objectives as recruiting professors committed to Catholic identity; orienting new faculty members to the Catholic mission of the institution; ensuring statutory provisions for mission-based hiring and firing; and the granting, withholding, or removal of the *mandatum* for teachers of theological disciplines. Instead, the language of the pontifical document was softened by adding "to the extent possible" to such expectations that the majority of the board and faculty members be Catholic. And although these board members were to be "Catholics committed to the Church," no such further specification was made for faculty members, nor was the case of lapsed, indifferent, or hostile Catholics addressed, as may have been usefully done in the context of the United States.

In article 4, §1, *Ex corde Ecclesiae* addresses the "quality of teachers" and in a footnote repeats the text of Canon 810 §1 and its reference to integrity of "doctrine and probity of life." This is translated in the PN where they say at article 4, §4b: "All professors are expected to exhibit not only academic competence and good character but also respect for Catholic doctrine." Any further detail is left to the statutes, including possible distinctions to be made in this matter between Catholics and non-Catholics, as well as just what is meant by good character. Finally, on the matter of academic freedom, I note that the General Norms of *Ex corde Ecclesiae* article 2, §5 makes the following affirmation: "Freedom in research and teaching is recognized and respected according to the principles and methods of each individual discipline, so long as the rights of the individual and of the community are preserved within the confines of the truth and the common good." The US Particular Norms address academic freedom in article 2, §3, suggesting that concern for the common good is what should characterize the bishop's "duty to recognize and promote the rightful academic freedom of professors in Catholic universities in their search for truth." The PN further condition the promotion of Catholic identity and fostering of Catholic teaching and discipline by respect for the religious liberty of individuals. It would have been more helpful had the notions of truth and the common good as conditions to academic freedom been further explored and applied to the national scene by the PN.

Canon 810 §1 imposes an obligation, at least implicitly, that Catholic university statutes guarantee Catholic identity through the doctrinal and moral commitment of university personnel. By contrast, Canon 810 §2 sets forth a right and duty of the hierarchy, specifically the conferences of bishops and diocesan bishops, "of being watchful so that the principles of Catholic doctrine are observed faithfully in these same universities." Here, too, the *ratio legis* seems clear. As the pastors and teachers of the Church, bishops are bound to exercise vigilance, lest the integrity of faith and morals be threatened by any forces that oppose that teaching either directly or indirectly. Such negative influences may come from a wide variety of sources outside the Church: agents of government and politics, the broader academic world, and the news and entertainment media are but a few examples. Bishops are obliged to recognize such dangers and speak out clearly in their preaching and writing to urge the faithful to be discerning about the influences that these sources have on their moral choices and attitudes, on the lives of their families, on the education of their children, and on the conduct of their professional, social, and political lives. More particularly, this duty of vigilance extends to Catholic institutions, including those dedicated to healthcare, charity, social service, and education. Institutions that depend directly on the bishops' authority are certainly the objects of their vigilance, but so are those institutions that are related to the Church in one manner or other, even though they retain a high degree of autonomy, as is the case with most Catholic universities. Vigilance can be said to be an episcopal art. It includes a high level of familiarity with its object, good sources of information, personal presence both formal and informal, praise, encouragement, admonition when needed, and at times judicious public comment. The scope of vigilance regarding Catholic universities is broad. As *Ex corde Ecclesiae*, article 2, §2 affirms, "A Catholic University as Catholic, informs and carries out its research, teaching, and all other activities with Catholic ideals, principles and attitudes." We have only to think of articles in the press, on Catholic blogs, and in statements of those organizations that have made themselves the watchdogs of Catholic higher education to recognize some of the neuralgic issues: honorary degree recipients, speakers invited to campus, plays produced there, and various issues dealt with by student affairs and health services personnel. In some of these areas, we have seen public disputes between bishops and Catholic universities, sometimes to the embarrassment of one or both parties. For this reason, it is regrettable that the USCCB failed to heed adequately the admonition of *Ex corde Ecclesiae* that the episcopal conferences adopt procedures for resolving disputes "concerning ... Catholic character," which the bishops have the right and duty to preserve and strengthen. The US bishops seemed to presume that such disputes would arise more readily between theologians and the Church's Magisterium, but experience has taught us that problems tend to arise more frequently in the other areas mentioned above. At many institutions, there are good lines of communication open between bishops and university presidents. But these may not be enough. Closer cooperation between lower-level university and diocesan officials may effectively prevent potential fires. And when the fire spreads in such a way that even the bishop and president cannot extinguish it, various formal means of dispute resolution, such as those suggested in Canons 1733*ff.*, should be employed so that the objectives of both parties are considered and, if possible, met in some mutually acceptable way.

It is, in my opinion, further regrettable that the list of eight "essential elements of Catholic identity," including a "Commitment to create a campus culture and environment that is expressive and supportive of a Catholic way of life," was transferred from the normative section of the USCCB document, as in a prior draft, to its introductory, nonjuridical section. Reference is made to those commitments in PN article 2, §5, which adds that the university's commitments are not limited to these. Courageously and honestly confronting vexing issues in advance could preclude any regrettable last-straw action, such as that provided for by John Paul II in his encyclical *Veritatis Splendor* 116, where he wrote:

> A particular responsibility is incumbent upon Bishops with regard to Catholic institutions ... Bishops can canonically erect and recognize these structures and delegate certain responsibilities to them. Nevertheless, Bishops are never relieved of their own personal obligations. It falls to them, in commu-

nion with the Holy See, both to grant the title "Catholic" to Church-related schools, universities, health-care facilities and counselling services, and, in cases of a serious failure to live up to that title, to take it away.

It seems that the pope is not using a simplistic nominalist interpretation of the "title Catholic" of Canon 808. He means institutions that hold themselves out as Catholic. In my opinion, the universities' honest, good-faith attempt to observe the Church's modest norms designed to preserve that Catholic identity can go far to safeguard them from such radical action on the part of ecclesiastical authority.

It is difficult to say how successful this provision about episcopal vigilance over universities has been. The university presidents seem untroubled by it because it does not even suggest control. And they are likely to have been pleased by the lengthy discussion in the introductory section of the US document about mutual trust between university and Church authorities, close and consistent cooperation between them, and continuing dialogue between university representatives and the hierarchy. There have been, however, ample complaints from some quarters about how Catholic universities are neglecting their Catholic identity or acting in ways contrary to it. These same complainants are critical of what they see as the bishops' failure to exercise adequate vigilance or oversight. Nor has the Holy See seen fit to intervene, except perhaps to turn to the universities' sponsoring religious institutes and their superiors to assist in safeguarding Catholic identity. St. John Paul II makes reference to this source of support in number 25 of the introductory section of *Ex corde Ecclesiae*, where he says: "Many Catholic Universities were founded by Religious Congregations, and continue to depend on their support; those Religious Congregations dedicated to the apostolate of higher education are urged to assist these Institutions in the renewal of their commitment, and to continue to prepare religious men and women who can positively contribute to the mission of a Catholic University."

My own public and published sympathy with the role of the bishops in Catholic higher education moved the center of my apostolic efforts away from Catholic university administration and toward the unexpected work of priestly formation, until recently with diocesan seminarians in Baltimore and in Rome and with graduate students in canon law in Washington and in Rome. In more recent years, however, it has been my privilege to teach and assist in the religious formation of my own younger Jesuit confreres. I have been greatly pleased that most of these young religious are blessed with a healthy ecclesial mindedness. Those destined for work in higher education—and many of them are dedicated to the sacred sciences—are not inclined to fight the battles of former generations and seem intent on centering their work in higher education, present and future, at the heart of the Church. Similarly, the emerging leaders of Catholic universities are laypeople who seem less shy about asserting their institutions' Catholic identity than were clerics of former years, who were concerned instead with emphasizing the commonality of their institutions with those led by their secular peers.

Having considered Canon 810 and the complementary roles of institutional and ecclesiastical authorities, I would like to turn now to what for two decades was the single most controversial issue concerning Catholic higher education, first in the revision of the code in the 1980s and then in the preparation of *Ex corde Ecclesiae* and the USCCB companion document: Canon 812 on the *mandatum*. In case some readers have not committed it to memory, it reads as follows: "Those who teach theological disciplines in any institutes of higher studies whatsoever must have a mandate from the competent ecclesiastical authority." During the drafting period, the most vexing question was, quite simply, what is a mandate? From a canonical point of view, the word is a strange one, since elsewhere in the code it means something different from what has now been accepted to be its special meaning in this context. Elsewhere it means the conferral by an authority of some element of his otherwise exclusive authority on someone else, who would ordinarily not have that authority. Few in the Catholic world would say that theologians, even the most orthodox and faithful of them, are, as it were, substituting for the bishops when they teach. The bishops, of course, are teachers, but in a quite different way. Well over thirty years ago, my fellow student of canon law, Robert Deeley, now Bishop of Portland, Maine, drew in his doctoral research an important conclusion that this academic mandate, with its source in the conciliar decree on the laity, is to be understood as the means by which a bishop recognizes the ecclesial activity of another precisely for what it is in itself. The mandate is a recognition and declaration that a theologian is working in communion with the Church and its teaching authority and is not offering as Catholic teaching anything that is not Catholic teaching.

In *Ex corde Ecclesiae*, the mandate is mentioned only once. Article 4, §3 of the General Norms reads as follows: "In ways appropriate to the different academic disciplines, Catholic teachers are to be faithful to, and all other teachers are to respect, Catholic doctrine and morals in their research and teaching. In particular, Catholic theologians, aware that they fulfill a mandate that they receive from the Church, are to be faithful to the Magisterium of the Church as the interpreter of Sacred Scripture and Sacred Tradition." This is followed by a footnote that recites the canon in full. The words "fulfill a mandate" created some distress among university people who rejected the notion that bishops were making academic appointments, a notion that the deference to university authorities guaranteed in Canon 810 §1 contradicts. The PN at article 4, §4.e.ii has a lengthy discussion of the mandate and makes a number of negative assertions: "The *mandatum* should not be construed as an appointment, authorization, delegation or approbation of one's teaching by ecclesiastical authority." And, positively, it says at article 4, §4.e.iii: "The *mandatum* recognizes the professor's commitment to teach authentic Catholic doctrine and to refrain from putting forth as Catholic teaching anything contrary to the Church's magisterium."

The *ratio legis* for the first norm we considered today is a Catholic university's internal desire and commitment to safeguard its Catholic identity by what has come to be called "hiring for mission." There are various ways to do this, and it is fitting that the institution make the appropriate statutory provisions to regulate and evaluate faculty for their service of mission—and to determine the "remedy," as the PN put it, when faculty do not meet these standards. Otherwise, Catholic character would be likely to suffer irreparable damage. The rationale for the second norm is the unique role of the hierarchy to be vigilant for the protection of Catholic faith and morals in every quarter where Catholics live and work, and where the Church bears witness to evangelical values. Such vigilance is even more crucial in institutions related to the Church. Now we need to consider the *ratio legis* for the *mandatum*. It is focused less directly on faculty quality in general or on the wide range of faith-based issues that call for the bishop's vigilance, but on the special place of theology in the Church and the university and the relationship between bishops and theologians. More than any other right, in my opinion, what this norm protects is that of the faithful to rely on Catholic theologians to present Catholic teaching authentically.

There are many highly technical issues concerning the *mandatum* that remain of timely or at least theoretical interest to canonists but that we have no time to consider here. We should take our leave of the subject, appropriately perhaps, at a footnote 41 to the US document. Here is hidden some valuable and practical information. It affirms that Canon 812 "is grounded in the right and responsibility of bishops to safeguard the faithful teaching of Catholic doctrine to the people of God and to assure the authentic presentation of the Church's magisterium." It repeats the notion that those "with such a *mandatum* are not agents of the magisterium; they teach in their own name, not in the name of the bishop. Nonetheless, they are not separate from the Church's teaching mission. Responding to their baptismal call, their ecclesial task is to teach, write and research for the benefit of the Church and within its communion. The *mandatum* is essentially the recognition of the ecclesial relationship between the professor and the Church (see Canon 229 §3)."

Teaching "in the name of the bishop or of the Church's magisterium" is different from teaching in the name of the Church. The 1990 instruction *Donum veritatis* of the Congregation for the Doctrine of the Faith affirms that it is the Magisterium's mission "to set forth the Gospel's teaching, guard its integrity, and thereby protect the Faith of the People of God," whose right it is "to receive the message of the Church in its purity and integrity and not be disturbed by a particular dangerous opinion." This responsibility may lead the Magisterium to take serious measures, as "when it withdraws from the theologian, who departs from the doctrine of the faith, the canonical mission or the teaching mandate it had given him." Such action should not be considered a violation of justice, the instruction maintains, when it affirms that "the theologian who is not disposed to think with the Church … contradicts the commitment he freely and knowingly accepted to teach in the name of the Church" (no. 37).

In an address on "The Church and the Theologian" at the University of St. Michael's College in Toronto on April 15, 1986,[4] Cardinal Joseph

4. Joseph Ratzinger, "The Church and the Theologian," *Origins* 15 (1986): 761–70.

Ratzinger observed, "the freedom of the individual instructor is not the only good under the law nor it is the highest good to be safeguarded." He affirmed that "the Church's main job is the care of the faith of the simple." A professor's opinions, he goes on to say, "are given a weight which they could not possibly deserve on their own, precisely because he teaches on behalf of the Church. Believers have confidence in the Church's word and so naturally transfer that confidence to those who teach in her name."[5]

What, then, is the university's role? Footnote 41 of the US document tells us that seeking the *mandatum* is the professor's responsibility, not the university's. What happens if the professor teaches without the *mandatum*? Referring to Canon 810 §1, the footnote declares: "the university must determine what further action may be taken in accordance with its own mission and statutes."

Few Catholic universities have altered their governing documents to reflect the juridical norms of *Ex corde Ecclesiae* or the USCCB's Particular Norms. The institutions, for the most part, are indifferent with regard to the *mandatum* for teachers of theological disciplines, and do not make it a condition for appointment under the institutional statutes and contracts. Many bishops, including those who grant the *mandatum*, do not publish a list of those theologians who have it, nor do the universities, preferring instead to view the canonical formality as a private matter between the theologian and the bishop. As a result, the faithful are left without a convenient means of determining whether one or other theologian is teaching in communion with the Church's magisterium. Because the law of the Church safeguards this right of the faithful, it is incumbent finally upon bishops to provide the information, most suitably by issuing a list of those who have been granted the *mandatum*. Without this public character of the act, the norm of canon 812 would have no practical meaning or value. If the faithful are not given the assurance to which they have a right, they may seek recourse from the Apostolic See.[6]

As I look back on the twenty-five years since the promulgation of *Ex corde Ecclesiae*, especially through the lens of the USCCB's Particular

5. Ibid., 769.

6. Further reflections on the publicity of the *mandatum* can be found in my "Mandate of can. 812 Revisited," 247–48.

Norms, I wonder how effective these documents have been in strengthening or, in some cases, restoring the religious identity of Catholic universities. The connection between reason and law presumes a shared vision between the legislator and the persons and institutions being governed. It is, in my opinion, a grave wound to the heart of law when it is ignored by those subject to it and even by those charged with its implementation and enforcement.

I believe that higher education is not at the top of the US bishops' list of priorities. My guess is that the leadership of the mainstream of Catholic universities is too strong to oppose. Perhaps the law has succeeded in inspiring some Catholic universities to freely choose Catholic identity as a priority of priorities. Both Canon 810 §1 and the normative section of *Ex corde Ecclesiae* defer largely to institutional statutes to guarantee Catholic identity. But most Catholic universities in the United States specify in their statutes either minimally or not at all concrete and measurable means to guarantee Catholic identity. I propose that as individual institutions or associations of likeminded ones, they could embody in their statutes the self-regulation and Catholic autonomy that the law intended in the first place. So, in closing, I offer, according to the structure of *Ex corde Ecclesiae*, some model statutes for such universities, which I call for convenience CARS (Catholic affiliated, related, sponsored).

Article 1

This CARS university acknowledges that it is accountable for the faithful observance of the apostolic constitution *Ex corde Ecclesiae* and its USCCB Application. Internal and external (e.g., a special accrediting agency) mechanisms will be put in place to assure compliance.

Article 2

1. This CARS university affirms a commitment to its Catholic identity. As a Catholic university, it pledges to promote the twelve elements of Catholic identity contained in the USCCB Application, part 1, section 7.

2. It upholds the academic freedom of professors in teaching and research within, as *Ex corde Ecclesiae* affirms, the confines of the truth and the common good. The truth, with respect to Catholic doctrine, is based on the Church's ordinary and extraordinary Magisterium. The diocesan bishop will be the arbiter of the common good.

3. It safeguards its autonomy, except as limited by civil or canon law.

4. The program of studies and student activities both reflect and foster the Catholic identity of the university.

Article 3

This CARS university will identify itself from among the different types of Catholic universities listed in *EcE* Norms, Article 3.

Article 4

1. This CARS university will choose as trustees practicing Catholics and, as may seem opportune, non-Catholics who understand and formally pledge to uphold the Catholic identity of the university. Due process will see to the removal of trustees who gravely fail in this obligation.

2. The majority of faculty members are to be practicing Catholics.

3. Having used appropriate means of hiring for mission, the university will provide extensive programs in orientation of new staff in issues of identity and mission.

4. Catholic faculty members must formally pledge to be faithful to Church teaching in ways proper to their discipline.

5. Non-Catholic faculty members must formally pledge to respect Catholic teaching.

6. Catholics who teach theological disciplines are to have a mandate from competent ecclesiastical authority. Except when it is otherwise provided for by canon law, this will be the diocesan bishop of the institution's principal seat.

7. All faculty members are to exhibit probity of life by observing the university's code of personal and professional conduct.

8. Those who fail to observe points 4–7 are to be removed or suspended from office or otherwise disciplined according to the code of conduct.

9. Standards for promotion and tenure will include a faculty member's commitment and contribution to the university's identity and mission.

Article 5

1. Each year this university will prepare a written report to the local diocesan bishop and major religious superior that treats especially those issues that affect the Catholic character of the university.

2. Once each year, the bishop or his delegate and the major superior or his delegate should be invited to meet with the board of trustees on matters of mutual interest.

3. In the event of difficulties that may arise concerning the Catholic character of the university, the bishop will meet with the president, the rector of

the religious community, and the chair of the board of trustees to attempt to forestall crisis situations. If such difficulties remain unresolved, the institution and the bishop will engage in a previously agreed-upon means of dispute resolution before having recourse to higher ecclesiastical authority.

Article 6

1. The diocesan bishop will approve the appointment of any staff member who carries the title of Catholic chaplain.

2. The university's ministry staff will observe all universal and particular norms that concern catechesis, sacred space, sacramental discipline, liturgy, ministry, preaching, and ecumenism.

Article 7

1. This CARS university will make special efforts to cooperate with other Catholic institutions: other universities, secondary schools, and seminaries.

2. Cooperation with secular institutions and government programs will not compromise the university's Catholic character.

PART III

Pastoral and Practical Reflections

[9]

The Bishop and the Catholic University

Cultivating Dialogue and Cooperation

Jeffrey Monforton

Praised be Jesus Christ. I wish to thank Fr. Sean Sheridan and Franciscan University for the invitation to speak at this symposium series celebrating the twenty-fifth anniversary of the promulgation of the apostolic constitution *Ex corde Ecclesiae* (*On Catholic Universities*). How profound that the beginning text, from which the title is usually derived in a papal document, goes as such: "*Born from the Heart of the Church*, a Catholic University is located in that course of tradition which may be traced back to the very origin of the University as an institution."[1]

I am grateful for our collaboration these past three years of my episcopate both today and in the years to come. I am at your disposal as both your diocesan bishop and as your brother in Jesus Christ. As I have mentioned previously, many of my friends pursued undergraduate and graduate studies at Franciscan University and have fond memories of their time there.

The fact is I consider myself truly blessed to have Franciscan University within the boundaries of my pastoral responsibilities as a diocesan bishop. But the question remains: how do the bishop and the university continue to cultivate dialogue and consequently cooperate in an effective manner to influence a world beyond the borders of the rigors of formal academic studies and local episcopal governance? How does

1. *EcE*, 1.

this happen in a world that holds sovereignty as a virtue and casts a suspicious eye on authority in general?[2]

I begin with an excerpt from 1 Peter 5:4, which is quoted at the beginning of chapter 4 in the *Directory for the Pastoral Ministry of Bishops*: "Tend the flock of God that is your charge, not by constraint but willingly, not for shameful gain but eagerly, not as domineering over those in your charge but being examples to the flock. And when the chief Shepherd is manifested you will obtain the unfading crown of glory." This passage is a clear episcopal mandate to live by example and to seek to foster a living encounter with Jesus Christ. Coercion, complacency, and entitlement have no place in this life because, as the *Directory* emphasizes, all credit belongs to God's grace as we "come to live in Christ." To a certain extent, and in a unique manner, a Catholic university may also embrace this mandate, entrusted with teaching and forming the people of "God to live in Christ through his grace."

I address, then, our common Christian pilgrimage in this postmodern world of ours, identifying the complimentary yet distinct roles of the bishop and the Catholic university, and explore how our dialogue and cooperation may best serve the universal call to evangelize. Let us begin with my role as diocesan bishop: the chief shepherd of this local Church.

2. The sources I reference, in addition to Sacred Scripture, include *Ex corde Ecclesiae*; *Pastores gregis* : post-synodal apostolic exhortation of St. John Paul II, *On the Bishop, Servant of the Gospel of Jesus Christ for the Hope of the World*, October 16, 2003: *Acta Apostolicae Sedis* (*AAS*) 96 (2004): 825–924, http://w2.vatican.va/content/john-paul-ii/en/apost_exhortations/documents/hf_jp-ii_exh_20031016_pastores-gregis.html); "Final List of Propositions from the 13th Ordinary General Assembly of the Synod of Bishops," presented at the 13th Ordinary General Assembly of the Synod of Bishops, October 28, 2012, http://www.vatican.va/news_services/press/sinodo/documents/bollettino_25_xiii-ordinaria-2012/02_inglese/b33_02.html; and Congregation for Bishops, "Directory for the Pastoral Ministry of Bishops," March 9, 2004, http://www.vatican.va/roman_curia/congregations/cbishops/documents/rc_con_cbishops_doc_20040222_apostolorum-successores_en.html. The latter were shared with my newly ordained brother bishops and me in September 2012, when we attended the conference for newly ordained bishops. Two years ago, I gave a presentation titled "A Shepherd's Perspective on Higher Education." In preparation for this essay, I gleaned much from that talk for substance and direction.

The Bishop (The Ordinary)

As I said upon the occasion of my ordination and installation here at Franciscan University, "I am yours." This brief statement succinctly states my role in relation to my flock, for, as Our Holy Father states time and time again, the bishop is one who has the responsibility to be among his people. That is what a pastor does. Moreover, Jesus is quite direct in John's Gospel, "The Good Shepherd lays down his life for his sheep" (10:11b). This quote graced my holy card upon ordination to the priesthood in 1994, and then my episcopal ordination holy card in 2012, communicating the continuity of my service to Jesus Christ and his Church. Then, for my episcopal motto, I chose Romans 10:12: "Faith comes from hearing." In other words, I am my brother's keeper, especially when it comes to the stability of his faith, for in the 2003 post-synodal apostolic exhortation *Pastores gregis*, St. John Paul reminded the bishop of his threefold *munera* to teach, to sanctify, and to govern. These three offices are mutually inclusive, as one cannot stand without the other two, and their dutiful fulfillment is, St. Augustine of Hippo states, an office of love: *amoris officium*.[3]

The episcopal ministry is founded upon the Trinity. A testament to this foundation is seen in my bishop's chair, a symbol of paternal authority. At my episcopal ordination, I put on Jesus Christ, the Good Shepherd, to be Shepherd and Spouse. The Holy Spirit himself, at my anointing, gave me the ability to be "a living continuation of the mystery of Christ for the Church." The collegial vocation I possess is not limited to me with my brother bishops but embraces God's people. Recall the words of St. Augustine, "For you I am a Bishop, with you I am a Christian."[4]

I am grateful to refer to two bishops who provided me with the so-called pastoral template for the relationship between a diocesan bishop and the Catholic university within his own diocese. I had the privilege to serve and to collaborate with Cardinal Adam Maida and Archbishop Allen Vigneron when I was rector-president of Sacred Heart Major Seminary from 2006 to 2012. I appreciated their pastoral direction, as well as their confidence and trust in me, as I maintained the helm of a

3. Cited in John Paul II, *Pastores gregis*, 9.

4. *Pastores gregis*, 10.

seaworthy ship that negotiated the ever-growing secular-oriented society and an economy on the brink of the Great Recession. The relationship between the Archdiocese of Detroit and Sacred Heart Major Seminary was symbiotic; namely, the health of one had a direct impact on the status of the other. Although the relationship between a diocesan seminary and the diocesan bishop is not the same as an autonomous Catholic university and the Ordinary of the diocese in which the university resides, I do believe presuppositions to an effective bishop-university relationship do exist.

One virtue is obedience, which tends not to be characterized as a good word at all by many in our culture or even within our own Church—ordained, consecrated, and laypeople alike. This word, obedience, culturally charged as it is, has a principal role in the discipline of teaching. For me, I am reminded again by the apostolic exhortation that, taking on the very features of Jesus, I am to be a "model and promoter of a spirituality of communion, carefully and vigilantly working to build up the Church, so that all (I say and do) will reflect a common filial submission in Christ and in the Spirit to the loving plan of the Father. As a teacher of holiness and minister of the sanctification of (my) people, (I am) called to carry out faithfully the will of the Father. My obedience must be a lived example … of the obedience of Christ himself, who said that he came down from heaven not to do his own will, but rather the will of the One who sent him."[5]

Obedience shares an inseparable link with community. As *Pastores gregis* further instructs, the communal dimension of my office compels me "to live out my obedience by overcoming all temptations to individualism and by taking upon (myself), within the wider context of the mission of the College of Bishops, (yes, I am still in school), concern for the good of the whole Church."[6] My obedience is not insufferable, but joyful and without end.

Finally, in the same apostolic exhortation, St. John Paul touches upon the theme to teach (to evangelize!) in his third chapter. "Go into the world and preach the Gospel" (Mk 16:15) are Jesus's own words as he empowers the disciples to evangelize, to inform humanity that the *Kingdom of God is at hand.*

5. *Pastores gregis* 19; cf. Jn 6:38, 8:29; Phil 2:7–8.

6. *Pastores gregis*, 19.

As your chief shepherd, I have the distinct role to proclaim "the Gospel (which) is incumbent upon the whole Church and each of her children." By virtue of my episcopal ordination, within this apostolic succession, one of my "principal responsibilities (is) the proclamation of the Gospel: 'with the courage imparted by the Spirit, to call people to faith and strengthen them in living faith.'"[7]

For example, early in my episcopal ministry, I introduced my media ministry, *Ask the Bishop*, an e-initiative on our diocesan website that is also published monthly in the *Steubenville Register*. I did not begin *Ask the Bishop* because I needed one more thing to do. No, rather, from my time as a parish priest, both as a parochial vicar and as a pastor, I saw the need to invite questions from my younger brothers and sisters in the faith. If they ask questions about their faith, then their faith matters to them. It means the Catholic faith is on their daily "radar," along with many other thoughts and concerns. The Church is relevant for them.

Time and time again, *Ask the Bishop* has reminded me that the Holy Spirit's purpose eternally exceeds my humble intentions. Whether at the grocery store or the hardware store, adults have approached me and shared their gratitude for *Ask the Bishop*. They even have gone as far as to disagree with me (as to my intended audience), asserting that its audience is not limited to Kindergarten through 12th grade. *Ask the Bishop* has had unintended consequences: this initiative is not limited to our children but has reached out to all of God's children.

My vocation as your bishop is not limited to the human gifts Jeffrey Marc Monforton possesses. For me to exercise my "office of love," I must remain close to the source of my episcopal calling: God the Father, God the Son, and God the Holy Spirit. In my complete obedience, I am free to serve God and his people with the threefold functions I received at ordination. By centering on Jesus Christ, and not on myself, I allow the Holy Spirit to work through me as I show our brothers and sisters how to follow the will of our Heavenly Father.

7. *Pastores gregis*, 26; see Vatican II, decree *Christus Dominus*, October 28, 1965: *AAS* 58 (1966): 673–96.

The Catholic University

To begin this section on the Catholic university, I want to express my profound love and unwavering support for Franciscan University. You constantly keep the heart of the Church close and dear to you. I again quote St. John Paul, rightfully so since at the ushering in of the third millennium of Christianity he turned a page in the Universal Church's history with a call for the new evangelization. He writes: "From the beginning, this mission of evangelization has been an integral part of the Church's identity. The Apostle Paul was well aware of this when he wrote: 'If I preach the Gospel, that gives me no ground for boasting. For necessity is laid upon me. Woe to me if I do not preach the Gospel!'"[8]

We should allow the following quote to form our academic, missionary, identity:

> BORN FROM THE HEART of the Church, a Catholic University is located in that course of tradition which may be traced back to the very origin of the University as an institution. It has always been recognized as an incomparable center of creativity and dissemination of knowledge for the good of humanity. By vocation, both the universal magisterium and the scholars are dedicated to research, to teaching and to the education of students who freely associate with their teachers in a common love of knowledge. With every other University it shares that *gaudium de veritate*, so precious to Saint Augustine, which is that joy of searching for, discovering and communicating truth in every field of knowledge. A Catholic University's privileged task is "to unite existentially by intellectual effort two orders of reality that too frequently tend to be placed in opposition as though they were antithetical: the search for truth, and the certainty of already knowing the fount of truth."[9]

Yes, St. John Paul is getting much credit today for this vision, and rightfully so.

He continues by stating, "A Catholic University pursues its objectives through its formation of an authentic human community animated by the spirit of Christ.[10] The source of unity is a common dedica-

8. *Pastores gregis*, 26; 1 Cor 4:15.

9. *EcE*, 1.

10. *EcE*, 21, emphasis added.

tion to the truth, a common vision of the dignity of the human person and, ultimately, a faith in the person and message of Christ which gives the institution character."[11] St. John Paul then underscores the need for freedom, charity, and mutual respect, fellow charioteers that enable us to search for and to teach the truth. Thus the Catholic university participates in the daily life of the local Church, for the university is not an ivory tower of knowledge beckoning for one to scratch and claw in the pursuit of intellectual ascent. That gnostic approach has no room in the Catholic curriculum. No, the Catholic university freely shares the truth of Jesus Christ and in turn further fortifies the local bishop's teaching office in the pastoral setting of the community.

Dialogue and Cooperation

The *Directory for the Pastoral Ministry of Bishops* highlights the bishop's ministry in the Church. As the Ordinary, it is imperative that I be the visible principle and the foundation of the Diocese of Steubenville. Just what does that mean? It means that I am mandated—better yet, three years ago I *promised*—to "promote unity in faith, in love and in discipline, so that (all in) the diocese [are] aware (they) form a vital part of the whole people of God ... not in sterile conformity, but (encompassing) legitimate diversity."[12] This promise must be fulfilled through pastoral visits combined with timely refection and prayer in order to ascertain the general spiritual health of the diocese, of which Franciscan University is a vital member. Constant dialogue with the university is paramount, not just for the sake of my knowledge of the academic community, but for the members of the university to be confident of my shepherd's care and support.

The postmodern university landscape seems to be constantly in flux, so I am obliged to engage in constant dialogue with all the faithful here, especially in timely meetings with the president of the university. Yet you most certainly do not need a "helicopter bishop" hovering over the university each and every day!

In this area of dialogue, then, the bishop is exhorted to encourage

11. *EcE*, 21.

12. Congregation for Bishops, "Directory for the Pastoral Ministry of Bishops," 58.

the creative work of theologians and to fortify research that respects the theological method. Within the discipline of dialogue, the university seeks to more effectively communicate the meaning of Christian revelation as transmitted in Scripture, tradition, and the Church's Magisterium, essential pillars to any Catholic university's transparent Catholic identity. To that end, as the university pursues St. Anselm's definition of theology as *faith seeking understanding*, there should remain steadfast respect of the bishop's authority and Catholic doctrine. Consequently, dialogue between the Ordinary and theologians is essential, and "this is especially true today, when the results of research are so quickly and so widely communicated through the media."[13] This was stated by both St. John Paul and the Congregation for the Doctrine of the Faith some twenty-five years ago. In other words, both St. John Paul and his successor, Pope Emeritus Benedict XVI, saw this cooperation as essential.

Let us move from the theme of dialogue to that of cooperation. Catholic ecclesiology of communion teaches that all Christians should be involved in the one mission of the Church. The principle of cooperation and the principle of subsidiarity instruct that all Christians possess the right and duty to cooperate in the mission of Jesus Christ entrusted to his Church. This comes about through our own God-given vocation and the gifts we have received from the Holy Spirit. My role as bishop is to communicate to you your sense of responsibility, both as individuals and as part of a university community. Instead of creating an atmosphere of distrust and fear, I am to communicate to you my full confidence that you will accept with utmost zeal the task before you to evangelize our fellow brothers and sisters.

As outlined in the apostolic constitution *Ex corde Ecclesiae*, "each Catholic University must recognize its relationship to the local Church that is essential to its identity. As an institution of scholarship and inquiry, the university participates directly in the life of the particular Church and contributes to her life and mission."[14] Each year, when the academic school year begins, the Catholic population of the Diocese of Steubenville grows by over two thousand souls. The Franciscan University administration, faculty, staff, and students do not remove their Franciscan identity when they attend local off-campus churches. On the

13. *EcE*, 29.
14. *EcE*, 27.

contrary, they proudly, and rightfully so, wear their university identity for all to see.

Essential to the local Church is the Catholic university's *institutional* fidelity to the Church, especially in the matter of faith and morals. The annual Oath of Fidelity Mass, usually celebrated at Franciscan each August, does not simply ensure the university's identity; this particular moment is a *burning light for all to see* in the entire world of Catholic education. In our mutual cooperation, you fortify my teaching role by reaching out to a vast community that would be impossible for me to reach otherwise. Moreover, you strengthen the position of my brother bishops, especially those who may be in arduous situations with other universities whose teaching is inconsistent with their Catholic identity.

Now I am not taking the "coward's way out" when I say that much of what I just said about my role applies also to the laity. Remember, the Kerygma—the announcement of our salvation in Jesus Christ—is highly contagious. Our eyes must always be on Jesus Christ, morning, noon, and night.

St. John Paul, in his introduction, provides clear direction for the Catholic university when he states,

> It is the honor and responsibility of a Catholic University to consecrate itself without reserve to *the cause of truth* … It does this without fear but rather enthusiasm, dedicating itself to every path of knowledge, aware of being preceded by him who is "the Way, the Truth, and the Life" (Jn 14:6). We are fully aware that the Catholic University is the very stage where faith and reason dialogue. Here is where the world witnesses the harmony between faith and reason, thus pointing at the unity of all truth.[15]

It seems to me that the challenge of the Catholic university, as well as the bishop, is that we must find a way for others to understand that this dialogue is even relevant. A Catholic theology department is not limited to "preaching to the choir," but it is "teaching the choir" to go out and sing, to sing well enough to catch another's attention so that they wish to sing along. How do we go about doing it? We begin by having a personal relationship with Jesus Christ, by accepting our role as ambassadors of Jesus Christ, and being unafraid to make mistakes if it takes us to the right answer. Finally, for the Catholic university to be

15. *EcE*, 17.

truly effective in the promotion of the truth, it must enjoy the complete support of the diocesan bishop. I promise to uphold my end of the bargain. I am quite aware you are upholding yours. May we ever keep our focus on the fact that our mission of service is for the good of society in the name of Jesus Christ, our Lord and Savior.

Complementary and Collaborative Roles

The Fidelity and Freedom Symposia offer a striking reminder that our role as theologians is not to "convert the converted" but to instead formulate a protocol—a game plan, if I may—to stoke the flames of faith in whom faith is dormant. *Metanoia* is not some inconsequential Greek word of long ago. Remember, above all, our lives are living encounters with Jesus Christ. Waving the Bible or the *Catechism of the Catholic Church* at someone is not going to force them into spiritual *metanoia.* Evangelization must first begin within us. If you and I do not have a personal relationship with Jesus Christ, if we do not obey our Lord and God, unconvincing witnesses and unproductive stewards we will be. We must remain acutely aware that we are witnesses in what now is an increasingly secularized world.

I recall an interview I had with Emily Stimpson early on in my episcopate. We discussed the reality of lukewarm or even disinterested fellow Catholics. While I focused on the Catholics who were perhaps angered with the Church or too embarrassed to return, Stimpson rightfully underscored the need to reach out to our brothers and sisters who simply do not see the Church as being relevant to their lives. Although baptized and even confirmed, they have lost touch with Jesus Christ. Unfortunately, I believe this is the larger group of disengaged Catholics, those who need the *faith* that *comes from hearing.* This is no time for despair, however, for we bear witness to the Gospel message of salvation and "are called to be salt and light of the world" (Mt 5:13–16). The Kerygma is timeless. Our role is to promote our faith in the language and delivery of the third millennium.

Conclusion

The Diocesan Bishop and the Catholic university possess distinct yet complementary roles. Neither exists in a vacuum: the people of God depend on the dialogue between faith and reason for clarity. As one defending the deposit, I am obligated to assist the Catholic university, enabling it to promote the truth through critical thought and steadfast fidelity to God and his Church. The principle of subsidiarity is crucial to the local Church's ability to reach out and to teach.

Perhaps these words from C. S. Lewis best summarize the work before us as fellow laborers in the Lord's vineyard: "The task of the modern educator is not to cut down jungles, but to irrigate deserts." You and I must remember that the Lord's vineyard may not just need tending, but it may be a desert in need of growth.

In Pauline terminology, you and I are ambassadors of Jesus Christ. You and I matter in the sharing of the Good News. But we cannot embrace our roles by being stationary; we must be in motion. St. John Paul, quoting directly from Jesus, has called us: *Duc in altum!* (Lk 5:4). Yes, we must "put out into the deep" if we are to be effective. According to St. John Paul, "These words (of Jesus) ring out for us today, and they invite us to remember the past with gratitude, to live the present with enthusiasm, and to look forward to the future with confidence 'Jesus Christ is the same yesterday and today and forever' (Heb 13:8)."[16]

And so together, as we venture onward as intrepid pilgrims endeavoring to share the Good News, we prayerfully ask for the intercession of the Mother of the Church, Patroness of the Diocese of Steubenville: Immaculate Heart of Mary, pray for us. St. Francis of Assisi, pray for us. And the patron saint of universities, St. Thomas Aquinas, pray for us. God bless you all.

16. John Paul II, apostolic letter *Novo Millennio Ineunte* 1, January 6, 2001: *AAS* 93 (2001): 266–309, https://w2.vatican.va/content/john-paul-ii/en/apost_letters/2001/documents/hf_jp-ii_apl_20010106_novo-millennio-ineunte.html.

[10]

Reflections on the Dialogue between Faith and Reason and the Relationship of a Diocesan Bishop with Local Catholic Universities

Mark L. Bartchak

I appreciated the opportunity to be a part of the second symposium commemorating the twenty-fifth anniversary of the promulgation of St. John Paul II's apostolic constitution *Ex corde Ecclesiae*, with a focus on the dialogue of faith and reason. In response to my request for some directions regarding my participation, Jonathan Sanford gave the following list of some of the relevant questions that speakers would address. What is faith? What is reason? Does faith ground reason? Does reason ground faith? Can one exercise one without the other? What happens to faith when divorced from reason? What happens to reason when divorced from faith? What can we learn from the recent history of Catholic higher education and competing ways of understanding the relationship between faith and reason? What role does the apostolic constitution *Ex corde Ecclesiae* have in addressing these questions?

I thoroughly enjoyed listening to the other presenters as they brought these questions to life. Sanford asked me to focus on two questions:

1. What is my understanding or interpretation of the relationship between faith and reason according to *Ex corde Ecclesiae*?

2. How does my interpretation or understanding of the relationship between faith and reason according to *Ex corde Ecclesiae* offer guidance to me in relationship with the Catholic universities in the Diocese of Altoona-Johnstown, where I serve as bishop?

The Relationship between Faith and Reason in *Ex corde Ecclesiae*

Before I give my positive answer to the first question, I want to mention that as I prepared this essay, I encountered the commonly held view that there is no easy answer to the question of the relationship between faith and reason. In an article in the *New Catholic Encyclopedia* under the title "Faith and Reason," the authors state:

> There have been and still are many different ways in which the faith-reason relationship might be conceptualized. Yet, in spite of ecclesiastical statements of principle, there is still no generally accepted view as to the manner in which the relationship in question is best explained.[1]

This article characterized in various ways the relationship between faith and reason:

1. There is no distinction between faith and reason because faith absorbs, dominates, and eliminates the need for reason, as in fideism or traditionalism.
2. Reason can totally encompass matters of faith as in rationalism, scientism, or modernism.
3. The distinction between faith and reason is entirely due to the limitations of abstractive thinking, and such a distinction does not express the real state of affairs, as in naturalism or supernaturalism.
4. A real distinction may be asserted because faith and reason are contrary to each other as two modes of thinking that remain independent in human thought and activity.
5. Either faith or reason provides the human person with firm, adequate knowledge, while the other is only a vague approximation.

1. Edmund F. Byrne and Edward A. Maziarz, CPPS, "Faith and Reason," in *New Catholic Encyclopedia*, vol. 5 (Washington, DC: Catholic University of America Press, 1967), 807.

6. Faith and reason are distinct but interrelated in a highly complex way that each believer and each generation of believers must rethink, reclarify, and reunify in order to understand, suggesting that it's all relative.

7. Faith is an assent to truths and to what Christ said, rather than a way of life, committed to the person of Jesus Christ.

It was a surprise to find no mention amid the myriad hypotheses in that 1967 article of the teaching of the Second Vatican Council in *Gaudium et Spes.* This document explicitly addresses:

1. faith and reason as "two orders of knowledge," as expressed in the teaching of the First Vatican Council;

2. the freedom of individual persons to search for and express the truth, within the limits of doctrine, morality, and the common good;

3. the valid practice of the arts and sciences according to their own proper methods and principles;

4. the integral perfection of the human person, the good of the community, and the whole of society;

5. the advancement of each person in their knowledge of God; and

6. the need for religious practice to keep pace with scientific knowledge and ever-advancing technology.[2]

It was a disappointment to find that the authors of the 1967 article did not propose their own understanding of the relationship between faith and reason, nor did they suggest any pathways for dialogue. They simply offered what they saw as the state of the question, and it was not at all encouraging.[3]

Pope John Paul II recognized that these disparate views about the relationship between faith and reason were still operative in the final decade of the twentieth century. This is evident in the text of *Ex corde Ecclesiae* and in his encyclical letter *Fides et ratio*, to which I refer below.

2. Vatican II, pastoral constitution *Gaudium et Spes*, December 7, 1965: *Acta Apostolicae Sedis* (*AAS*) 58 (1966): 1025–115, chap. II, "The Proper Development of Culture," nn. 53–62.

3. Byrne and Maziarz, "Faith and Reason." The first sentence of the article has this disclaimer: "The complexity of the relationship between faith and reason suggests that this article present (1) a clarification of terms, (2) a historical survey of the principal positions adopted on their relationship, and (3) some critical remarks on the problem today."

This same recognition of "a crisis of truth that is the result of the exaltation of technology and science, as well as the continued impact of rationalism, materialism and unbridled instinct" continues to be acknowledged in these early years of the twenty-first century in the writings of both the pope emeritus and Pope Francis.[4]

But where others have seen only challenges, problems, and obstacles that discourage them from engaging culture in a conversation that includes both faith and reason, Pope John Paul II saw privileged, joyful, and life-giving opportunities for dialogue about the things that are most important. In the opening paragraph of the apostolic constitution *Ex corde Ecclesiae*, he stated that the privileged task of a Catholic university is "to unite existentially by intellectual effort two orders of reality that too frequently tend to be placed in opposition as though they were antithetical: the search for truth, and the certainty of already knowing the fount of truth."[5] John Paul II reminded us that this task is constitutive of the mission of a Catholic university. It is a vocation that comes from the heart of the Church. This is the first principle of the approach he set forth, saying, "It is the honor and responsibility of a Catholic university to consecrate itself without reserve to the cause of the truth."[6] This cause, he said, serves the dignity of the human person, and it also serves the Church. Pope John Paul II described this search for truth as a disinterested service, one that does not disregard useful or practical knowledge but engages in a free and impartial search for the whole truth about nature and the human person, and ultimately seeks the wisdom that comes from God who is the source and end of all truth.[7]

4. See Benedict XVI, Discourse to the University of Regensburg, "Faith, Reason and the University: Memories and Reflections," September 12, 2006, http://w2.vatican.va/content/benedict-xvi/en/speeches/2006/september/documents/hf_ben-xvi_spe_20060912_university-regensburg.html; Benedict XVI, "Address to Educators," *Origins* 37, no. 46 (May 1, 2008): 742. Also available in Committee on Catholic Education, United States Conference of Catholic Bishops, *Catholic Mission and Culture in Colleges and Universities* (Washington, DC: United States Conference of Catholic Bishops, 2014), 90–94; Francis, encyclical *Lumen Fidei*, June 29, 2013: *AAS* 105 (2013): 555–96, esp. nn. 2, 24–25, and 32–34, which addresses "The dialogue of faith and reason"; and Francis, apostolic exhortation *Evangelii gaudium*, November 24, 2013: *AAS* 105 (2013): 1019–137, nn. 132–34.

5. *EcE*, 1.

6. *EcE*, 4.

7. *EcE*, 4.

I find it important that Pope John Paul II underscored what is at risk if this disinterested service is lacking. He mentioned especially the potential loss of the fundamental values of freedom, justice, and human dignity. These are the issues that I often hear about when I interact with the universities in my diocese, a topic I touch upon below in addressing the second question. Having described the role that Catholic teaching has in providing "a kind of universal humanism," Pope John Paul II proposes how the relationship between faith and reason is able to be known and its proper meaning expressed through this impartial search for truth. He recalls the words of St. Augustine (as well as St. Anselm): "think so as to believe; believe so as to understand" (*Intellege ut credas; crede ut intellegas*). The exhortation applies especially to Catholic universities because they are called to explore courageously the riches of revelation and of nature. Pope John Paul II also addressed the many Catholic scholars engaged in teaching and research in non-Catholic universities. Their task as academics and scientists should be lived out in the light of the Christian faith, and even their presence should be a "stimulus to the selfless search for truth and for the wisdom that comes from above."[8] Through a united endeavor of intelligence and faith, people will be able to come to the full measure of their humanity. And that full measure refers to their creation in the image and likeness of God, their renewal or redemption in Christ after sin, and their shining forth in the light of the Holy Spirit.[9]

In furthering my understanding of the dialogue between faith and reason according to Pope St. John Paul II, I have come to appreciate even more his encyclical letter *Fides et ratio*,[10] promulgated eight years after *Ex corde Ecclesiae*. According to protocol, as an encyclical, *Fides et ratio* is addressed to bishops, but because the dialogue of faith and reason is also a dialogue with culture, his real audience are university professors, scholars, and researchers of all disciplines.

Cardinal Avery Dulles, SJ, observed in a commentary on *Fides et ratio* that Pope John Paul II has softened the dualism of reason and faith that was present in earlier Church teaching, including Vatican I. Dulles also noted that John Paul II does not reject the distinctions between

8. *EcE*, 2.

9. *EcE*, 5.

10. John Paul II, *Fides et ratio*.

reason and faith or philosophy and theology. For Pope John Paul II, there is no competition between faith and reason; instead, he sees a relationship between them such that neither is isolated from the other.[11]

He thus offers two images of the dialogue between faith and reason. The most important image illustrates the relationship between theology and philosophy:

> The relationship between theology and philosophy is best construed as a circle. Theology's source and starting-point must always be the word of God revealed in history, while its final goal will be an understanding of that word which increases with each passing generation. Yet, since God's word is Truth (cf. Jn 17:17), the human search for truth—philosophy, pursued in keeping with its own rules—can only help to understand God's word better. It is not just a question of theological discourse using this or that concept or element of a philosophical construct; what matters most is that the believer's reason use its powers of reflection in the search for truth which moves from the word of God towards a better understanding of it. It is as if, moving between the twin poles of God's word and a better understanding of it, reason is offered guidance and is warned against paths which would lead it to stray from revealed Truth and to stray in the end from the truth pure and simple. Instead, reason is stirred to explore paths which of itself it would not even have suspected it could take. This circular relationship with the word of God leaves philosophy enriched, because reason discovers new and unsuspected horizons.[12]

Pope St. John Paul II uses another image for the complementary relationship between faith and reason in the preamble to *Fides et ratio*.

> Faith and reason are like two wings on which the human spirit rises to the contemplation of truth; and God has placed in the human heart a desire to know the truth—in a word, to know himself—so that, by knowing and loving God, men and women may also come to the fullness of truth about themselves (cf. Ex 33:18; Ps 27:8–9; 63:2–3; Jn 14:8; 1 Jn 3:2).

As Dulles observes about these images, "The implication would seem to be that truth is unattainable without both (faith and reason) together."[13] I would say that Pope John Paul II does more than imply

11. Avery Cardinal Dulles, SJ, "Faith and Reason: From Vatican I to John Paul II," in *The Two Wings of Catholic Thought: Essays on Fides et Ratio*, ed. David Ruel Foster and Joseph W. Koterski (Washington, DC: Catholic University of America Press, 2003), 201.

12. John Paul II, *Fides et ratio*, 73.

13. Dulles, "Faith and Reason," 201.

the necessity of the dialogue of faith and reason in the search for truth.

In *Ex corde Ecclesiae*, Pope John Paul II explains that integration of knowledge is a necessary process, one that will always remain incomplete, especially where there is a rigid compartmentalization of knowledge within individual academic disciplines. He writes,

> University scholars, aided by the specific contributions of philosophy and theology must engage in a constant effort to determine the relative place and meaning of each of the various disciplines within the context of a vision of the human person and the world that is enlightened by the Gospel, and therefore by a faith in Christ, the Logos, as the center of creation and of human history.[14]

For Pope John Paul II, promoting this integration of knowledge is "a specific part of a Catholic university's task of promoting dialogue between faith and reason, so it can be seen more profoundly how faith and reason bear harmonious witness to the unity of all truth."[15]

What a rich, complimentary, and integral view that St. John Paul II has in mind when he speaks of the relationship between faith and reason. Unlike the dreadful exposition of that relationship as presented in the encyclopedia article in 1967, Pope John Paul II offers an invitation to engage in the dialogue and, if we pay attention to his teaching in both *Ex corde Ecclesiae* and *Fides et ratio*, it provides us with the principles that will make the dialogue meaningful.

Implementing *Ex corde Ecclesiae*'s Principles in Relation to the Universities in My Diocese

The application of *Ex corde Ecclesiae* to Catholic universities in the United States went into effect in 2001, with a decision that a review of the application would be made after ten years. Beginning in January 2011, then, bishops were to conduct conversations with the presidents of Catholic universities in their dioceses as part of the review.

I was appointed Bishop of Altoona-Johnstown on January 14, 2011, but was not ordained and installed until April 19, 2011. So I missed the

14. *EcE*, 16.
15. *EcE*, 17.

opportunity to be part of the *Ex corde Ecclesiae* review that was directed by the United States Conference of Catholic Bishops.

I should explain that there are two Catholic universities in the Diocese of Altoona-Johnstown. St. Francis University in Loretto, Pennsylvania, was founded in 1847 and continues to be sponsored by the Franciscan Friars of the Third Order Regular, Province of the Most Sacred Heart of Jesus. The President of St. Francis University is Malachi Van Tassell, TOR. The governance of the university is the responsibility of a board of trustees that is composed of some Franciscan Friars of the Third Order Regular, Province of the Most Sacred Heart of Jesus, with laypeople comprising most of the board membership. The chairman of the board is the Minister Provincial of the Franciscan Friars.

Mount Aloysius College in Cresson, Pennsylvania, was founded in 1853 by the Religious Sisters of Mercy. It is one of eighteen Mercy-sponsored colleges and universities in the United States and is a member of the Conference for Mercy Higher Education. The president of Mount Aloysius College is Thomas Foley, JD, a Catholic layperson. The governance of the college is the responsibility of a board of trustees that is composed of some Religious Sisters of Mercy, with laypeople comprising most of the board membership. The chairman of the board is elected and is currently a non-Catholic layman.

Even though I did not participate in the 2011 *Ex corde Ecclesiae* review process, I have had frequent contact with the presidents of both Catholic universities in the diocese and have made frequent visits to both places for liturgical celebrations and other activities. I have experienced a rapport with the presidents of both universities that is on par with the "positive and engaged" relationships that most bishops in the United States reported in the 2011 review of the application of *Ex corde Ecclesiae*. In fact, over time, I have begun to experience more substantive dialogue, as has been the experience of bishops with university presidents in a number of dioceses.[16] I was invited to Mount Aloysius College to give a lecture to faculty, students, and guests on some aspects of *Ex corde Ecclesiae* as part of a symposium on hospitality. And I was invited to be the first to speak at the inauguration of the current pres-

16. "Bishops, Colleges Find Good Collaboration in *Ex corde* Review," *Catholic News Service*, January 11, 2013, http://ncronline.org/news/theology/bishops-colleges-find-good-collaboration-ex-corde-review.

ident of St. Francis University, which afforded me the opportunity to offer a few ideas taken from *Ex corde Ecclesiae*.

Obviously, much more can and should be done. The question is where to begin. Both Catholic universities under my care offer undergraduate and graduate degrees in the arts and sciences, and each is proud of the success of its students within its respective academic programs. For the undergraduates, it is their readiness for further study at the graduate level, and for the graduate students it is their readiness for employment in fields that expect that level of study. St. Francis University offers undergraduate degrees in philosophy and religious studies, while Mount Aloysius Colleges does not offer undergraduate degrees in those disciplines but has a core requirement of six credits in philosophy/religious studies. Neither has a school, department, or chair of theology.

Because the relationship between faith and reason is about a dialogue, I am intrigued with the idea of a dialogue that is suggested by Joseph A. Appleyard, SJ, professor emeritus at Boston College. It comes from his idea of a "framework for thinking strategically about formation of students." Appleyard suggests that part of the framework of student formation should be "an idea of the university that genuinely values empirical disciplines and professional models of training and the knowledge they produce, but intentionally places these into conversation with religious accounts of human existence."[17]

As I mentioned, the Catholic universities located in the Diocese of Altoona-Johnstown take pride in the results of the empirical disciplines and professional models of training and the knowledge they impart to their students within their programs of study. In *Ex corde Ecclesiae*, Pope John Paul II affirms the value of empirical disciplines and professional models of training and the knowledge they produce. But he cautions that this is insufficient. The search for the truth should also be conducted through a dialogue between faith and reason. The Catholic intellectual tradition has no difficulty with science, when science limits its conclusions to what can be known through an empirical exploration of nature.[18]

17. Joseph A. Appleyard, SJ, "Student Formation in Catholic Colleges and Universities," in *American Catholic Higher Education in the 21st Century: Critical Challenges*, ed. Robert R. Newton (Chestnut Hill, MA: Linden Lane Press at Boston College, 2015), 46–47.

18. James L. Heft, SM, "Leadership in Catholic Higher Education," in *American Catholic Higher Education in the 21st Century*, 94.

I agree with Appleyard, who argues, "The mission of the Catholic university is to create conditions in which Christians, non-Christians, and post-Christians can engage in conversation about a shared, lasting human good and how to bring it about." He explains that this shared, lasting human good has to do with the instinct for human progress, that life matters, and the efforts of life are not lost in time or in death. He says that the instinct to articulate and achieve such a shared, lasting human good is found in the Christian faith experience, and it is expressed in numerous cultures and is accessible to everyone independent of their beliefs.[19]

I have no doubt that the extent of the belief systems of many of the students in the Catholic universities in the Diocese of Altoona-Johnstown may be characterized as Christian, non-Christian, or post-Christian. All the more reason why these Catholic universities must effectively fulfill the mission of creating conditions in which students benefit from the dialogue between faith and reason. Appleyard believes that this is first and foremost a matter of formation of the students. But the challenge extends to other key segments of the university community, especially to the board of trustees responsible for governance, and to the professors responsible for teaching. The board of trustees is a key entity at any university, with its responsibility for the financial well-being of the institution and the decisions that must be made regarding buildings, programs, equipment, and so on.

It is no longer realistic to expect that the board members individually or collectively can rely on a sense of the charism, spirit, or tradition of the religious congregation that founded the university. There are Religious Sisters of Mercy on the Board of Trustees at Mount Aloysius College, but that is the extent of their contact with the college. Not unlike other Catholic universities founded or sponsored by a religious order, the number of Sisters of Mercy at Mount Aloysius continues to diminish, and there is little prospect of other Sisters taking their place. Without a living presence of the Sisters of Mercy on the college campus, there is a danger that the "Mercy" charism will be reduced to a concept.

Returning to Appleyard's suggestion of a "framework for thinking strategically about formation of students," I see two other groups that

19. Appelyard, "Student Formation in Catholic Colleges and Universities," 48–49.

could benefit from the kind of formation he envisions: the president and those in administrative offices, and especially the professors, who are in the classroom.[20] I think the "idea of the university that genuinely values empirical disciplines and professional models of training and the knowledge they produce" would be a great starting point to engage the confidence of professors who may be suspicious that this formation would focus on the teachings of the Church.

On a small scale, I have seen this kind of formation take place with college students when the conversation turns to sharing accounts of human existence, particularly where it is endangered by any number of ideologies, programs, technologies, or structures that lack a reference to the truth about the human person as found in our Catholic tradition. In *Ex corde Ecclesiae*, Pope John Paul II reminds us that when the empirical disciplines are applied without reference to what is transcendent, their limits and deficiencies expose the thirst for truth, which is inscribed in the heart of the human person. He says that's where "a University, and especially a Catholic University, has to be a 'living union' of individual organisms dedicated to the search for truth." That is where the contributions of philosophy and theology aid in providing a synthesis of knowledge that makes up for the shortcomings of compartmentalized knowledge within individual academic disciplines. Limited and fragmented views of the human person can be replaced with a vision of the human person and the world that is enlightened by the Gospel, and therefore by a faith in Christ, the *Logos*, as the center of creation and of human history.[21]

I also want to mention my renewed appreciation for the service that a Catholic university should provide to the Church and the community. It is stated explicitly that "through teaching and research, a Catholic University offers an indispensable contribution to the Church. In fact, it prepares men and women who, inspired by Christian principles and helped to live their Christian vocation in a mature and responsible manner, will be able to assume positions of responsibility in the Church."[22] One area of service that involves positions of responsibility in

20. This view of the necessity and not just the importance of formation for university trustees, presidents, administrators, and professors and the pitfalls of not providing such formation is highlighted by Heft, "Leadership in Catholic Higher Education," 109–14.

21. *EcE*, 16.

22. *EcE*, 31.

the Diocese of Altoona-Johnstown is that of Catholic school teacher and administrator. Many elementary and secondary teachers and principals in Catholic schools within the diocese have received their undergraduate and graduate studies at St. Francis University or Mount Aloysius College.

Those programs of study lead to academic degrees and to professional certification according to standards established by the state. More important is that these one-time students are now responsible for handing down the Catholic faith to the next generation, and the effectiveness of their Catholic teaching is dependent upon the dialogue of faith and reason that they encountered while at university.

Before concluding, I offer some observations about just two of the General Norms that are found in Part II of *Ex corde Ecclesiae*—it's the canon lawyer part of me finally coming through! Under Article 2, "The Nature of a Catholic University," §5 states:

> A Catholic University possesses the autonomy necessary to develop its distinctive identity and pursue its proper mission. Freedom in research and teaching is recognized and respected according to the principles and methods of each individual discipline, so long as the rights of the individual and of the community are preserved within the confines of the truth and the common good.

In his article on "Leadership in Catholic Higher Education," James L. Heft, SM, briefly touches on the issue of academic freedom under the heading "The Challenge of Relating to the Hierarchy." Like many authors, he underscored the anger, anxiety, and consternation that the *mandatum* aroused in many theologians at Catholic universities. Heft states, "Although *Ex corde Ecclesiae* supports academic freedom 'properly' understood, precisely what that proper understanding is remains a matter of debate among both theologians and bishops." Then, without explanation, he adds, "If the local bishop often assumes an adversarial position, the recruitment of faculty becomes more difficult."[23]

Without intending to sound adversarial, I think that in fairness it should be said that Catholic universities will have less difficulty in the recruitment of faculty provided that all interested parties understand that the job description calls for applicants who wish to exercise their

23. Heft, "Leadership in Catholic Higher Education," 99–100.

role as researcher, scholar, and teacher in a manner consistent with the principles set forth by Pope John Paul II in *Ex corde Ecclesiae*. The most important principle in that regard is that academic freedom properly understood is situated within the relationship between faith and reason, a relationship that is expressly considered a dialogue of such nature that there will be lively reflection and discussion on the meaning of things in light of the truth that is revealed by God.

As a closing comment on the topic of academic freedom, Heft poses an important question: "How should (university) presidents protect the necessary academic freedom of theologians while at the same time maintaining a cordial relationship with the local bishop?"[24] It is an important question, but it could be better worded. This is how I would pose it: "How should (university) presidents and bishops protect the necessary academic freedom of theologians while at the same time maintaining a cordial relationship?" I think this formula works better because it captures the reciprocity of the relationship between a bishop and a university, as it is an episcopal duty to safeguard and promote the good of Catholic universities, including those who establish them, direct them, teach in them, and learn in them.[25] As a result of my study and reflection in the context of this symposium, I have a more positive view about the opportunities to provide for academic freedom so that all who teach and learn in a Catholic university will benefit from the highest level of scholarship in the Catholic intellectual tradition, whether it is in the field of philosophy, theology, arts, or sciences.

Finally, Article 5, "The Catholic University within the Church," §3 states:

> Periodically, each Catholic university, to which Article 3, §1 and §2 refers, is to communicate relevant information about the University and its activities to the competent ecclesiastical authority.

24. Ibid., 100.

25. Congregation for Bishops, *Directory for the Pastoral Ministry of Bishops Apostolorum successores* (Vatican City: Libreria Editrice Vaticana, 2004), n. 135. Additionally, this is supported in the directory by certain "General Principles for the Pastoral Governance of the Bishop," esp. n. 57, "The Principle of Truth"; n. 58, "The Principle of Communion"; n. 59, "The Principle of Cooperation"; n. 60, "The Principle of Respecting the Competence of Others"; n. 61, "The Principle of the Right Person for the Right Job"; and n. 62, "The Principle of Justice and Legality."

According to this norm and to the norm of Canon 810 §2, and as Bishop of Altoona-Johnstown, I am the competent authority for St. Francis University and Mount Aloysius College. That authority regarding this norm in *Ex corde Ecclesiae* should not lead to potential adversarial relationships, as suggested previously regarding academic freedom. What is significant about this norm is that it highlights the importance and even necessity of communication between the Catholic university and the diocesan bishop. In many instances, problems that arise can be exacerbated through neglect, albeit unintentionally.

The value underlying this norm, then, is to facilitate proactive communication between the Catholic university and the diocesan bishop. I have no need or desire to know everything that goes on in the two Catholic universities within my diocese. But sometimes there is a major initiative, an important address, a distinguished guest, a commemoration of an anniversary, or an award to a student or faculty member that is worth bringing to the attention of the bishop. Sometimes also there are problems, which can and should be resolved under the jurisdiction of those responsible for the governance of the university (i.e., president and/or board of trustees) within their respective competence. In the end, this norm is about communication and sharing of information, with the possibility that the substance of the information may require some action or response.

Communication, sharing of information, and especially posing questions are all essential to dialogue. This symposium has been about the dialogue between faith and reason, which is a most important dialogue for a Catholic university. Dialogue makes for good relations and partnerships. Among the highlights of my study and reflection on the questions posed to me in view of the apostolic constitution *Ex corde Ecclesiae* is the realization of the importance of the relationship between faith and reason, a relationship that should always be directed toward the truth and guided by the truth. So, I conclude with an observation made by Pope Benedict XVI in 2007 at the Angelus on the feast of the preeminent theologian and doctor of the Church, St. Thomas Aquinas:

> When Christian faith is authentic, it does not diminish freedom and human reason; so, why should faith and reason fear one another if the best way for them to express themselves is by meeting and entering into dialogue? Faith presupposes reason and perfects it, and reason, enlightened by faith, finds

the strength to rise to knowledge of God and spiritual realities. Human reason loses nothing by opening itself to the content of faith, which, indeed, requires its free and conscious adherence.[26]

I didn't realize it at the time, but I began to learn that truth when I was only seven years old. My teacher asked, "Who made me?" And we responded, "God made me." And my teacher asked, "Why did God make me?" And we responded, "God made me to know him, to love him, and to serve him in this world, and to be happy with him in the next." I lost nothing when my mind was opened to that truth enlightened by faith. What I did not know then but I gradually learned from further dialogue is this: God knows me (and you); God loves me (and you); and God humbled himself to serve me (and you) in this world, especially by the passion and death of his Son Jesus Christ, so that I can be truly happy in the next.

It makes all the difference for these truths to remain at the center of such an amazing dialogue. Thank you.

26. Benedict XVI, Angelus Message, January 28, 2007, http://w2.vatican.va/content/benedict-xvi/en/angelus/2007/documents/hf_ben-xvi_ang_20070128.html.

[11]

The Heart of the Matter

Richard Jusseaume

The twenty-fifth anniversary of *Ex corde Ecclesiae* is a wonderful opportunity to reflect on its influence and its role in the development of a small Catholic university in the Midwest. I was grateful for the invitation to be part of the Faith and Freedom symposium for three reasons:

1. It caused me to reminisce, reflect, and reenergize my familiarity with the document and its impact on Walsh University.
2. It led me to refocus on that history and refresh my own passion for what it has meant to Walsh.
3. It allowed me to share a story, a theory, and a model that might be of assistance to other Catholic organizations.

As I work my way through the seventeenth year of my presidency, I appreciate the call to share because it reminds me that Catholic identity is not something to be given only token attention.

About Walsh University

Walsh University was founded by the Brothers of Christian Instruction in 1958. Its predecessor, LaMennais College in Alfred, Maine, was a tiny institution that prepared young men to be teachers and to staff the Brothers' schools from New England to Detroit, Michigan. Opening day for Walsh was November 17, 1960, and sixty-seven young men began classes at this commuter college for men only. The founding religious order had no plan, no land, no money, no buildings, and no employees. What they did have was unbounded faith. As they looked across the alfalfa field that was the McDowell Farm, one of them said, "I can see *un petit collége*." Over the first forty years, the sleepy little college grew, added ten or so buildings, became coeducational, and enrollment reached about 1,400. Financially, there were some modestly successful years, and some crisis years during which only borrowing from the congregation kept the doors open.

Today, there are three thousand students, twenty-six buildings, and five external campuses (three in Ohio, one in Rome, Italy, and one in Uganda). There are nearly eighty majors, eight master's programs, and two doctoral programs. We have over eight hundred full- and part-time employees, and we are proud to be members of the Cardinal Newman Society, along with Franciscan University.

In 1990, when Pope John Paul II issued *Ex corde Ecclesiae* defining his vision of Catholic higher education, Walsh University was thirty years old, enjoying modest success, and wondering how it would transition to its first non–Brothers of Christian Instruction president. In the previous ten years, five Nobel Peace Prize winners (including Blessed Mother Theresa) visited Walsh. The goals were to establish financial stability, and to do so in a faith-based environment wherein service to others was paramount.

Acceptance and Adoption of *Ex corde Ecclesiae*

Things moved along at a moderate rate. It took a while for university personnel to get familiar with the document. During the mid-1990s, a simple strategy was implemented. Copies of the document were made available on campus, and many discussion groups were organized. Faculty members gathered in several events to discuss the key elements of the document. Members of the board of directors discussed the document among themselves, and with faculty and professional staff. Students engaged mostly in classroom discussions. By 2001, three former presidents had read and analyzed the document, shared thoughts with faculty, and sought to define the apostolic constitution in terms of a landmark pronouncement that potentially affected Walsh.

The plan introduced by Vatican officials called for the president and a majority of faculty members and directors to be Catholic. It also asked that theologians who teach Catholic doctrine seek approval from their bishops. Of course, each institution could author its strategy for its own campus.

When I arrived on the scene as president in 2001, I came to the subject of *Ex corde Ecclesiae* with the perspective of a board member rather than a college administrator or cleric. I confess the topic had not made my top-ten list of things that needed to be done. But as I sought to devise a plan to stabilize finances, grow enrollment, develop campus facilities, and strengthen the brand and marketing image of Walsh University, I found myself reminiscing about those foundational years of the institution. I had arrived on campus in 1963 as a student from Massachusetts. I knew the founding administration and the early faculty. I also knew that I came to Walsh because it was Catholic, safe, and a continuation of twelve years of Catholic education. Students were required to take eighteen credits of theology and philosophy. Crosses, crucifixes, statues, and a variety of Catholic art were on display; every class, event, and meal began with a prayer, and teaching Brothers and Scholastics roamed the campus in black cassocks. And, of course, several Catholic nuns taught education classes.

But now it was thirty-five years later. No nuns—no cassocks—no prayer before classes—fewer required theology classes—no dedicated chapel—no vocations—and no branding tied to Catholic origins. In my first few weeks in office, I met with several senior administrators who politely warned me that it would be a serious mistake and an obstacle to enrollment growth to emphasize our Catholic identity and traditions. "Young people who have been in Catholic education for twelve years mostly do not want to continue in a Catholic institution" (though they admitted that might not be a problem for the University of Notre Dame or Georgetown University). I thought about that for a while and reviewed my thirty-seven-year history with Walsh and why I was willing to work here again after seventeen years in the corporate world. A few days later, I called them back and announced that I had decided the only way to build Walsh was to return to our founding mission, emphasize our Catholic identity, and proclaim that we were a "beacon of Catholic higher education in northeast Ohio." As they listened in silent frustration, I spoke of special scholarships for graduates of Catholic high schools, tuition discounts of 60 percent for diocesan employees, free use of our facilities for any Catholic groups, crucifixes in every room on campus, pilgrimages to Catholic shrines, a freestanding chapel, and more. I also knew that only one of six vice presidents was Catholic, but decided that could wait until I could see how they supported this plan and how effective they were in their positions.

In the midst of all this, I met with the new Bishop of Youngstown who was, *ex officio*, a voting member of the Walsh board. Bishop Thomas Tobin's role was simple because Walsh was not a diocesan college. His direct question to me was, "What about the *mandatum*?" This is when my rudimentary knowledge of *Ex corde Ecclesiae* paid off. At my inaugural mass, I had taken a public oath of fidelity. I had taken that oath because I believed in it, and I was aware that Pope John Paul II's constitution spoke to what I believed and to what I thought Walsh needed to be.

In part, I promised: "I shall always maintain personal communion with the Catholic Church in the words I speak and in the way I act. I also promise to preserve the deposit of faith as expressed in the Creed, hand it on faithfully, and help make it shine in the faith-based community at Walsh. And, I promise to carry out the responsibilities by which I am bound with great care and fidelity, and to exercise my service within the requirements of the Catholic Church."[1]

Effectively, I had fulfilled my *mandatum*. A few weeks later, I hosted a luncheon with Bishop Tobin and the faculty of theology. He had been on the commission that authored the document, and he explained the basis for the *mandatum* and how the bishops had arrived at a final draft. He welcomed questions and comments, and invited them to contact him if they had issues. He encouraged them to sign the *mandatum* and send it to him if they agreed with the terms. No pressure—no threats—no timelines. Within ten days, he had received a signed document from each.

The process had worked: a year of study and discussion; board adoption; a president who had taken his own oath; a bishop who led a conversation and encouraged dialogue; a group of Catholic theologians

1. Cf. Congregation for the Doctrine of the Faith, "Profession of Faith and Oath of Fidelity," June 29, 1998: *Acta Apostolicae Sedis* 90 (1998): 542–51, http://www.vatican.va/roman_curia/congregations/cfaith/documents/rc_con_cfaith_doc_1998_professio-fidei_en.html.

who respected the process, felt valued by the bishop, and knew that the presidential vision was an authentic Catholic university faithful to the Magisterium of the Church.

A few months later, I issued a statement that made the signing of the *mandatum* a condition of employment in the Theology Department. I wish I could regale you with stories of the epic battles over the coexistence of faith and reason and academic freedom and fidelity to the Church. Alas, there were none.

The question of academic freedom among faculty is always a topic of discussion on campus. Faculty are comfortable expressing views that oppose Catholic teaching. They bring non-Catholic exegetes on campus to speak and discuss. The Catholic-Jewish Studies Institute welcomes thousands of lifelong learners to explore all sorts of issues in a multicultural context. We ask only one thing: somewhere in the conversation, we must identify and define the Catholic position on the ongoing discussion.

Why would it be academic freedom to hire professors to teach beliefs that contradict our very identity as Catholic? Because I interview every prospective faculty member, I have the opportunity to explain who we are and what we stand for. I ask them to consider whether they would be comfortable in this environment, and I encourage them to look elsewhere if they could not be. While most of our professors are Catholic, many are not. They understand our position and are free to accept it or not. They are not "free" to launch a campaign or expostulate on what they think is wrong with Catholic Church teaching—unless they first respect, present, and identify the Catholic position on the topic.

Personally, I believe that our "fidelity" to the Catholic Church teaching "frees" us to act, using that teaching as a benchmark, so to speak, to begin the discussion:

- Should we have a Students-for-Life Club on campus? Absolutely.
- Can students display crosses in the quadrangle to remind us of the tragedy of aborted babies? Of course.
- Should we honor (or even invite) a speaker who militates against Catholic teaching? Why would we?
- Will there be masses celebrated daily, adoration daily, rosary events, daily reconciliation, Bible study groups, Divine Mercy celebrations, retreats, pilgrimages, and more? Most certainly.

And what about service and the development of leaders in service to others? What is the theological and philosophical basis of engaging in this work? At Walsh, it is Catholic social teaching inspired by the Gospels themselves.

Fidelity to our faith does not limit our freedom. In fact, it frees us to wander through the somewhat indefinable beliefs and practices of centuries of human thought and action while providing an anchor—a measuring stick if you were—that enables us to evaluate against an inspired standard that unites us, directs us, protects us, and frees us. No subject need be off limits; no opinions need be silenced. But, ultimately, amid conflicting thoughts, Catholic teaching—the core of our identity as a Catholic university—restores stability, brings comfort, and helps us to navigate the troubled waters of our culture.

Where Are We Now?

Pope John Paul II wrote the following:

> It is the honor and responsibility of a Catholic University to consecrate itself without reserve to the cause of truth. This is its way of serving at one and the same time both the dignity of man and the good of the Church, which has an intimate conviction that truth is (its) real ally . . . and that knowledge and reason are sure ministers to faith. Without in any way neglecting the acquisition of useful knowledge, a Catholic University is distinguished by its free search for the whole truth about nature, man and God. The present age is in urgent need of this kind of disinterested service, namely of proclaiming the meaning of truth, that fundamental value without which freedom, justice and human dignity are extinguished. By means of a kind of universal humanism a Catholic University is completely dedicated to the research of all aspects of truth in their essential connection with the supreme Truth, who is God.[2]

It seems to me that for someone to present the Catholic Church's teachings on a variety of core issues, one would have to read the New Testament, the identified Church teaching as presented in various documents, and most importantly live a life that embodies those teachings. Anything less admits of disbelief and confuses the listener. Can one

2. *EcE*, 4.

speak about how it feels to be a father while not being one? Can one speak of love while not loving?

A few months ago, I was at a meeting of Catholic university presidents. The question of gay and lesbian rights was a discussion topic. I asked what they would do if a male residence director announced in August that he had married Harry—his soul mate. The president of a large Catholic university suggested I was raising an issue that was settled several years ago, and that the battle I proposed was lost years ago. A New York Catholic college president agreed the battle was lost, and our efforts had to go to matters other than Catholic teaching on this matter. It was clear that at most Catholic colleges and universities, few wanted to take a stand against those opposing the Catholic teachings on marriage, contraception, gay issues, and more.

Some weeks later, I was aware that the president of a large, state-funded university told the humanities and history faculty that they would be asked to participate in the recruiting of prospective students, perhaps even off campus. One professor argued that the university did not have the authority to tell faculty what to do in such matters. The new president, recently recruited from the West Coast and a veteran of faculty legal battles and claims, looked him in the eye and said, "You're fired!"

The Catholic priest president was not willing to defend Church teaching. Yet the public institution's president would not back down to his uncooperative critic. What an object lesson illustrating strength of leadership. I found when I made signing the *mandatum* a condition of employment that it ceased to be a discussion topic. When students petitioned for permission to start a lesbian, gay, bisexual, and transgender (LGBT) club, I told them that I needed to pray first. A week later, I spoke of my oath of fidelity, of the Church teaching on homosexuality, and on remedies. I told them we would continue to meet on the subject but that it was nonnegotiable. There would be no approved club because promoting the homosexual agenda would be a contradiction of Catholic teaching. The students hardly blinked, said they expected "no," and were pleased to hear that I was giving them a permanent seat on our Diversity Council.

When all is said and done (usually a lot more is said than done), we need to live our faith, proclaim it everywhere, and not wait until the moment of decision has passed.

I was present at Catholic University in Washington, DC, on April

17, 2008, when Pope Benedict XVI spoke to presidents of Catholic colleges and universities. After "reaffirming the great value of academic freedom," he also noted that any appeals to academic freedom "to justify positions that contradict the faith and teaching of the Church would obstruct or even betray the university's identity and mission."[3]

He said this in an address in which the press had predicted he would deliver a stern message to the leaders of Catholic colleges. *The Washington Post* said the Pope's message would be a rebuke. Instead, Benedict spoke of the extraordinary importance of Catholic education at every level. His teaching was thoughtful, respectful, challenging, and invitational. Yet his position was clear: a Catholic university must articulate Catholic teaching and must not use the university as a means of opposing Catholic thought.

In many venues, the declaration by Pope John Paul II, and the subsequent *mandatum*, were received with an attitude of challenge, opposition, contradiction, change, and denigration. It became a rallying point for those who questioned papal authority, for those who wanted to be liberated from Catholic control, and for those whose battle cry was "academic freedom."

The truth was that, after the declaration's threatening (or at least controversial) prepublication publicity, many institutions settled into a ritual of distribution, discussion, tactical disagreement, and even some denial. Others engaged in the discussions, determined the document and its accompanying *mandatum* were not threatening, used it to strengthen their identity as Catholic institutions, and moved on to live their mission.

For me, the real threats come from a culture and a government that disavow the essence of a Catholic university. We are forced to comply with laws that restrict religious freedom and individual conscience.

When Catholic presidents share with me conclusions such as:

1. The gay and lesbian agendas (including same-sex marriage) are here to stay, so accept them.

2. In New York State, there is nothing we can say or do that will not bring punishment or recriminations.

3. Benedict XVI, "Address to Educators," *Origins* 37, no. 46 (May 1, 2008): 742. Also available in Committee on Catholic Education, United States Conference of Catholic Bishops, *Catholic Mission and Culture in Colleges and Universities* (Washington, DC: United States Conference of Catholic Bishops, 2014), 90–94.

3. Don't worry about Health and Human Services mandates. It is a lost battle.

4. Focus on academics. Jobs are far more important to students and parents than religious issues.

5. The Church must change, because right now it cannot lead.

And these are Catholic presidents at Catholic universities!

The situation is disconcerting at best. Yet for those of us who welcomed *Ex corde Ecclesiae* as a blessing rather than a threat, the outcomes have been generative. It helped Walsh to move to acceptance by the Newman Society. It helped Walsh to define itself. It helped Walsh establish standards of acceptance. It was and is not a threat. Rather, it engendered a healthy conversation that continues.

If, under the banner of academic freedom, we choose to oppose Catholic teaching, then certainly the constitution is a threat. But if the *modus operandi* is a survey of dissenting opinions, combined with the articulation of the Catholic teaching and a defense of its parameters, then the word "threat" becomes inappropriate. Honest discussion is possible within the context and environment of a Catholic university. Diversity of opinion is not anathema; overt and/or subversive attacks on Catholic doctrine are.

Walsh University has flourished over the past decade. Our motto, *Sed Deus dat incrementum*, reminds us that "God gives the increase." In our case, the issue has been one of integrity.

- If I violate my oath of fidelity, I lack integrity.
- If faculty compromise the *mandatum*, they lack integrity.
- If Walsh University markets itself as a deliberately "Catholic university of distinction" but opposes Catholic doctrine, it lacks integrity.

For Walsh University, *Ex corde Ecclesiae* has never been a moment in time. It has been an inspiration to grow, develop, and fulfill our mission. The document speaks of the "heart" of the Church—not the mind of the Church. As we look back over the twenty-five years of this constitution, we at Walsh University reflect on a seminal document that has challenged us to be better and has committed us to be who we say we are—a Catholic university of distinction. Indeed, God has granted the increase.

Thank you.

[12]

Ex corde Ecclesiae at the University of Mary

James P. Shea

> *The courage to engage the whole breadth of reason, and not the denial of its grandeur—this is the program with which a theology grounded in Biblical faith enters into the debates of our time. To rediscover it constantly is the great task of the university.*
>
> Pope Benedict XVI, *Regensburg Address*

How good it was to celebrate the silver jubilee of the promulgation by St. John Paul II of the apostolic constitution *Ex corde Ecclesiae.* For many reasons, I was honored by the invitation to participate. Not least among these reasons is that Franciscan University has been so notable in our country for the study and implementation of *Ex corde.*

Three of my younger brothers are alumni of Franciscan University; one of them is now also a priest. Their lives have been much enriched by the education and formation they received here. I remember being here for commencement as a new priest and teacher, and experiencing the profound joy of the baccalaureate mass, gazing out over so many well-formed and well-educated students. And in the culmination of their studies together, I saw that they were singing with one accord the praises of God. This made a lasting impression on me as a vision of education in faith and reason, the important topic we have taken up in our present symposium.

It has been twenty-five years since *Ex corde Ecclesiae* was signed into

Church law and presented by Pope John Paul II to the Church's academic community. In looking back over the response to this important document and assessing its impact on Catholic colleges and universities in the United States, one has the sense that *Ex corde* has been received in some quarters as a document that may no doubt provide a number of interesting insights but that, if applied consistently, would get in the way of serious intellectual work. Or perhaps it has been admired as the work of a pope who was also a saint and is therefore seen as providing a formula for fostering a vibrant devotional life among the university community amid the more serious work of the academy that is outside the document's proper purview. But I am not satisfied with that kind of response. When I look around at certain encouraging developments in the Catholic world, when I consider the education my brothers received here, when I call to mind my own undergraduate years at the Catholic University of America, and especially when I think of what I witness in our students at the University of Mary, I am moved by what I take to be evidence of an awakening that is not simply spiritual but rather involves genuine *intellectual* discovery. In the light of that experience, I argue that *Ex corde* lays down a blueprint for a good university, whether that university be Catholic or not. It provides us with a compelling and coherent vision ordered to intellectual excellence.

The Place of Faith in the University Project

Every university, every educational endeavor that goes beyond a specific and limited purpose, is animated by a set of principles concerning God, the human person, and the natural world. To insist on this is not to say that educational projects *should* be so animated; it is to claim that they always *are*, whether their practitioners recognize the fact or not. These foundational principles are not themselves mainly matters arrived at by university studies; they are the starting point and the basis upon which all study and teaching goes forward. Such first principles can be studied, refined, and articulated, but they are the intellectual foundation stones, the bases of thought that an educational project needs to assume and accept if it is to begin at all. In this sense, one could say that they are taken on faith: not that they are blindly embraced, but that they are understood either as self-evident or as revealed; not as provable *by* study, but as the necessary condition *for* study. It is a good Aristotelian maxim: if nothing is assumed as true at the beginning, no line of thought can proceed.

The modern secular university, by necessity, is based on its own set of "faith" commitments, its own assumed propositions and attitudes. In this sense, the secular university is not a faithless place or even a faith-neutral place. The dogmas it operates by are largely those of modern materialist naturalism, principles that the university community cannot prove but rather assumes as true. Granted, this secular academic faith is not robust; it does not have the resources to address the deepest questions of life: the immortal nature of man, the being of God and the invisible world, and the fundamental meaning of life. When it comes to such important questions—Why am I here? Whom am I supposed to love, and how? What is the point of my life? What is right and wrong? Why should I get up this morning and fight life's battle?—our secular universities increasingly do not have the interest or wherewithal to offer meaningful answers. Our culture instead turns elsewhere: to daytime television, talk radio, or the latest self-help bestseller.

Universities were not always so hapless in addressing life's most important questions. The university arose as an institutional form in the twelfth century as an outgrowth of a society that was hungry for greater knowledge about these questions, and was eager for the greater systematization of that knowledge. The early university was reared upon a set of assumptions that had provided the groundwork for the civilization as a whole: the pursuit of reason inherited from the Greeks, given clarity and rootedness by Christianity in the revelation of the divine *Logos*, reason incarnate. Those civilizational principles were enfleshed in the Catholic faith, which was the soil, intellectual as well as spiritual, in which the universities took root. This assumption of first principles by the nascent universities for the pursuit and clarification of knowledge and wisdom was an entirely natural, even a necessary, process. Without some such assumed philosophical basis, universities would never have arisen at all.

From their beginnings, universities, founded upon a Christian view of reality, understood themselves as places of dialogue between faith and reason, a dialogue that allowed the truest understanding of reality to emerge. The term "faith" used in this context did not refer to a subjective feeling, or a devotional state, or a privately held opinion. Faith was rather a source and a repository of genuine knowledge. Faith gave the possibility of appropriating knowledge that, while not unreasonable, was not simply accessible to reason or experimentation. Reason could only grope in the dark concerning such matters as the inner nature of God, the purpose of God in creating the world, the mystery of evil, or the general movement of history and therefore the meaning and proper interpretation of an individual life. All these questions gained clarity through faith. When the university assumed the knowledge that came from revelation, it was like having a new set of eyes that opened the mind to key aspects of reality.

The Catholic university held that the articles of the Catholic faith were true, not simply as a private subjectively held opinion, but as objective reality. They thought it true that God existed, a likely philosophical proposition, and that God was the source of goodness and truth, again a reasonable philosophical insight. They held that this God, who could be ascertained using philosophic reason, had spoken to humanity and revealed important things about himself, about the world and about the destiny of humanity. The conviction of the truth of that revelation came from numerous sources: among others, the testimony of the early disciples, the triumph of the faith in the ancient world, and the remarkable fittingness of revelation with their observation and experience of life. These revealed truths, buttressed by reason, were the basis for the medieval understanding of the cosmos, and therefore they naturally found their place in the university, an institution specially dedicated to the pursuit of knowledge.

These Catholic first principles were not unsophisticated assumptions. They had been subjected to significant scrutiny and purification over the centuries. The whole discipline of theology, so central to the life of the university from its beginnings, was developed to allow reason to act upon the data of revelation in order to determine its cogency, its proper limits, and the way its various aspects interrelated with one another and with knowledge arrived at by other means. The integrated synthesis that resulted from this long process was an impressive achievement. It is not an exaggeration to say that the Western Christian intellectual tradition has been among the deepest and most sophisticated the world has seen.

It is well known that the liberal arts tradition, the *trivium* and *quadrivium*, first articulated by the Greeks and come to mature form in Hellenistic, Greco-Roman society, was taken up by the Christians to form the structure of the Western educational ideal. What is less widely acknowledged or celebrated is that Christianity not only used that Greek discovery and benefitted from it, but also salvaged it and deepened it. Christianity provided the needed metaphysical ballast for the liberal arts tradition to maintain its vitality, without which it tended to turn in upon itself and lose its liberating clarity. The union of Christian faith and Greek *paideia*, as the Greek educational ideal was called, was the fertile ground for educational and civilizational renewal through much of the next two thousand years. That Greek-Christian tradition—first digested by the Church Fathers, then taken up by Benedictine monks, then by the mendicant orders and the universities, and then by Renaissance humanists culminating in the Jesuit *Ratio Studiorum*, and lasting in different forms even to our own day—provided the undergirding for the ideal of the civilization as a whole: it identified the kind of person the civilization understood itself to be forming. Enlightenment thinkers, critical of Christian civilization, tended to equate the "ages of faith" as the "dark" ages, holding that Christianity had corrupted and tainted the purity of the ancient educational ideal, and had maintained it almost accidentally and in diminished form. The opposite is the case: Christianity has been the means by which that ideal has been able to survive and thrive for so long.

The secular university arose in the late eighteenth and early nineteenth centuries. Its promoters, who wanted to overthrow the traditional Christian dialogue between faith and reason they had inherited, sought to radically reorient the university. They wanted to establish a different kind of academic institution, a secular one, based on a redefinition of knowledge. They equated faith with superstition and therefore considered it a kind of blindness, certainly not as a means of gaining genuine knowledge. They hoped that by purging the university of its faith, the doors would now be open to all true knowledge, and a new golden age of reason would arrive. The ironic result has been that reason itself has become reduced and fragile. It is precisely in academia, the supposed stronghold of reason, that reason has been most aggressively attacked. The deniers of faith found that they could no longer affirm rationality.

So, I return to a basic principle that I have been insisting on here, namely, that there is no such thing as a coherent university that is not founded on some kind of faith; every intellectual project is rooted in a set of first principles and understandings that are not argued *for*, but are rather argued *from*. The insistence on such principles is not a Catholic "add-on." It is an intellectual necessity. The modern secular university, by refusing to acknowledge its own assumed commitments, has not thereby avoided them. It has only rendered them confusing, incoherent, and exempt from careful consideration. In the absence of a coherent and examined guiding philosophy, at least two developments may be observed in modern universities. (1) There must be some kind of guiding philosophy, but because it is unacknowledged and therefore exempt from investigation and scrutiny, it functions badly, often coercively; this set of assumptions is what currently goes by the name of "political correctness." The real problem with this annoying and intellectually debilitating phenomenon is not that it is keeping the university from its proper stance of neutrality. No university can be neutral about first principles. The problem is rather that, because the modern university pretends to neutrality when it does not and cannot possess it, its assumed principles and their resulting moral stances are at best confused and at worst manipulative and dishonest. (2) In the absence of a coherent philosophy of God and man, with a resultant lack of intellectual and moral resources for pursuing life's most important questions, the modern university has been reduced to the pursuit of power, a pursuit that comes mainly in the form of an undue accent on technical education and growth in the applied sciences, disciplines that are increasingly unmoored from clear moral and anthropological guidelines.

From the time of the Greeks, it has been understood that intellectual and moral activity run together: the intellect and the will are integrally connected and cannot be divorced. This has always meant that to think well leads to acting rightly, and to act wrongly leads to thinking poorly. Hence for the Greeks, and later for the Christians (and Jews and Muslims), education was both an intellectual and a moral training: moral because intellectual. According to the Greek and Christian theory of the human, all intellectual formation was ultimately moral. This meant that intellectual disorders would result in moral disorders, and moral chaos would tend to produce intellectual confusion. It also meant that an intellectual community could not function without an agreed-upon moral order. The only question was: What sort of moral order would be agreed upon, and what would the intellectually grounded basis for that order be? The Catholic university has a coherent and honest answer to that question. The modern secular university does not, and as a result it struggles with intellectual coherence and moral integrity.

Both before *Ex corde* and perhaps in somewhat stronger terms since, we have faced the claim that a Catholic university is a contradiction in terms. It has been insisted that a university founded on "opinions" provided by the faith cannot, by that very fact, be a place of the honest pursuit of knowledge. Yet it would be more true to say that a *secular* university is a contradiction in terms, because without a commitment to truths of faith, to clear first principles, no serious intellectual activity can take place at all.

A consequence of the foregoing discussion is that fostering a genuinely Catholic university does not (mainly) mean having a lot of extracurricular Catholic things going on, valuable as they are. Rather, to build a Catholic university is to found the intellectual project of the university itself on a sound basis, on a coherent philosophy of God and man and nature that will allow each of the disciplines to be fruitful in the broadest sense, fruitful not just in acquiring bits of technical knowledge, but in attaining to a vision of the whole of the cosmos, and of gaining wisdom for the betterment of individual and corporate human life. All the disciplines studied at the Catholic university properly spring from an agreed-upon set of first principles, and all will, in various ways, be molded by them. In the humanities and the social and medical sciences, the applications are obvious and constant. But even in the natural sciences and mathematics, there is an understanding of the world behind their study that helps direct lines of inquiry and areas of application, and leads to an integrated and holistic vision of reality.

Developments at the University of Mary

All of this has been important for us in the ongoing development of the University of Mary as a seriously Catholic university. During the past academic year, we offered a series of four-day formation retreats on the Catholic intellectual tradition for all of our full-time faculty. The faculty of the four schools of the university—the School of Arts and Sciences, the School of Business, the School of Health Sciences, and the School of Education and Behavioral Sciences—have each had the opportunity to step in out from the wind, as it were, and to enjoy a time of examining the intellectual assumptions of their university, with great texts and with each other. Together we have read and wrestled with *Ex corde*, along with readings from Blessed John Henry Newman, Alaisdair McIntyre, James Burtchaell, Pope Benedict XVI, Pope Francis, T. S. Eliot, John Senior, Walker Percy, Don Briel, and many others. We have even watched some Sister Wendy Beckett, and have rehearsed and performed Robert Bolt's *A Man for All Seasons*! The response to this communal, intentional engagement with a coherent vision of truth and education and life has surpassed our best hopes. Catholic and non-Catholic faculty alike have experienced an encounter with a bracing intellectual vision in which they can participate both as a community of scholars and as individuals, each in his or her own way. The faculty have found that robust discussion and debate and the development of consensus around the integration of knowledge and the ultimate complementarity of faith and reason do more than simply bolster the Catholic *ethos* of the university; they strengthen the academy in its essential mission.

The School of Health Sciences at the University of Mary is our largest. Nursing is a legacy program for us, one of our original two majors when we were founded, and in September 2014 we received a $10 million gift that will allow us to offer the senior year tuition-free for nursing students. Two of our three doctoral programs are in the health sciences, with another soon to come; there are more than three hundred applicants on our waiting list each year for entrance into our physical therapy program. At our Billings campus, we recently launched the first occupational therapy program in the state of Montana. To ground and deepen all of our outreach and instruction and research in the health sciences, we are now in partnership with the National Catholic Bioethics Center in Philadelphia. We are working together to craft and deliver a master of science degree in bioethics; the ethicists at the NCBC are also assisting us with ongoing faculty development efforts and are providing case-specific consultation to our faculty. All faculty in our School of Health Sciences receive personal copies of the NCBC's publications, *Ethics & Medics* and *The National Catholic Bioethics Quarterly*. This concerted effort to ground a school of health sciences in a Catholic vision of the human person and the human person's relationship to God is not to throw in a bit of arbitrary spiritual content; it is to strengthen the intellectual project, to give it clarity, purpose, direction, and animation. At the risk of belaboring the point, if it is not a Catholic philosophy that guides the school, it will be another philosophy, probably neither better nor clearer.

The University of Mary places a strong accent on hiring for mission, a concern and priority we received from our founding Sisters and personally passed on to me by my predecessor, Sister Thomas Welder, who served the university as president for thirty-one years. When we hire for mission at the University of Mary, we do not intend a process that will yield a candidate who is incidentally both Catholic and happily possessed of the skills or expertise we seek. It is not unusual that the best candidate for mission is not even among the Catholic candidates for a given position. Rather, we look for those with the generosity of heart to move beyond their personal projects and pour themselves out for the university community and the common good, who have the capacity and willingness to grasp an integrated vision, who understand their lives and their work in the context of the search for truth, and who sense that there is a mystery that runs beneath all things. I do not mean to be vague or poetic; I mean that such capacities are necessary to do scholarly work and to participate meaningfully in our mission as a Catholic university, as well as to serve our students well in their education and formation. Praying the rosary and mixing chemicals are perfectly admirable skills, but simply knowing how to do both does not a good scholar or teacher make.

Campus Life and the Intellectual Mission

If faith and reason are intimately connected, and if the intellect and the will are inseparable in education, then in addition to a clear guiding philosophy for the intellectual project of the university, there will need to be a concern for the proper intellectual, moral, and spiritual environment to be fostered such that the formation the university provides can rightly take root in the lives of faculty and students. *Ex corde Ecclesiae* gets at this by speaking about the university as a Catholic community. A Catholic university is not just a neutral institution mainly populated by Catholics, like a Walmart that might happen, in a given town, to have a majority of Catholics as workers and shoppers. A Catholic university is an intentionally Catholic community, a moral and spiritual as well as an intellectual community. Or, to put it differently, because it is an intellectual community, it is also a moral and spiritual one. This is what gives the Catholic university so much potency for the transformation of those who enter it, and so much possibility as a source of creativity and life for the wider society.

Practically speaking, this means paying attention to things like good living arrangements, opportunities for prayer and service, an atmosphere that encourages genuine friendship, and creative ways of keeping youthful passions from burning the place down. To attend to these matters is not, in the parlance of the modern secular university, a question of maximizing health and averting risk, a matter of "wellness"; it is part of the intellectual project appropriate to the university.

To do this well requires a good deal of ingenuity. At the University of Mary, we have a thriving Catholic Studies program, envisioned not simply as yet another curricular department but as a unifying apostolic endeavor. We have discernment residence halls for men and for women, with the diocesan vocation director in residence with the men, and two Benedictine Sisters living with the women. Cardinal Timothy Dolan was on campus last year to bless our new pub, Chesterton's, which has afforded us the much-needed opportunity of engaging our students concerning questions of alcohol, virtue, and culture. Our campus in Rome is now in its fifth year of operation, and our new campus in Peru has just been launched with a small group of students this semester. In an effort to build deeper engagement between the academy and the pastoral work of campus ministry, we have hired a well-published scholar and gifted professor as our director of campus ministry; he also holds a joint appointment in the School of Arts and Sciences. Such efforts as these, along with many others, in evidence at Catholic colleges across the nation, require a particular kind of thinking to conceive and sustain.

Seeing Catholicity as a University Advantage

For the last fifty years or so, Catholic institutions of higher education have more or less followed the wider societal academic pattern, in most cases with little resistance. Catholics educators subscribed to the reduced notion of reason promoted by secular academia, tacitly accepting the view that only what can be proven rationally or demonstrated experimentally is real knowledge. Under the influence of this reduction of reason, Catholic university administrators and faculty have tended to find their Catholic commitments burdensome and annoying, and liable to lose them prestige among the upper echelons of American universities. They have viewed their Catholicism as largely an impediment to their institutional aspirations, one that needs to be minimized, even if not abandoned altogether. The result has been to exclude the Catholic philosophic vision from the classroom and to claim Catholicity through campus ministry and other extracurricular activities. This has often proven enervating for these institutions, both as regards their Catholicity and their intellectual coherence and excellence. By mimicking the intellectual wounds of secular academia without being able to reproduce their resources, many Catholic universities have risked becoming third-rate secular schools, rather than aspiring to become first-rate Catholic ones.

A more compelling alternative than this process of minimization is to see that Catholicity is an excellent advantage for our institutions, specifically as intellectual endeavors. Our goal should not be to reduce or explain away the Catholic element, but rather to nurture its full expression, thus allowing it to function as the great advantage it is. We should be looking to find the right balance of elements that will further genuine intellectual creativity and therefore human benefit. It is not a question of making a choice between *either* an academically sound institution *or* one that is spiritually vital. A genuinely Catholic university should naturally tend to both excellences at the same time. Rather than maintaining a dichotomy that pits technically successful academic programs imbued by secular modes of thought against a strong devotional community gathered around nonintellectual activities, a true Catholic project will result in a deeper integration of all the university's facets. It will see an invigorated Catholic mind pursuing the various disciplines with an understanding of their coherence and their relations to each other. It will see the intellectual pursuits of the university organically influencing ways of living and worshiping, and a spiritual communion constantly fertilized and enhanced by serious Catholic thinking. Such an environment has an attraction and a potency all its own and tends to have a natural formative effect on students and faculty.

Secular universities have come largely to abandon their most profound intellectual tasks. In the absence of a clear and impressive metaphysical orientation that could provide a coherent anthropology and therefore an integrated educational philosophy, they have little to say about the most important questions facing the students who attend them. They are good at one thing: teaching techniques. They are not places to become wise, or good, or humanly whole, or more mature, or even intelligent except in rather narrow ways. Quite the opposite is true: a student is lucky if he or she has not been seriously wounded in mind and conscience after four years spent in the typical modern academic environment. Catholic universities thus have a special role to play, certainly for our own students and communities but also for the wider academic world: namely, to keep alive a magnificent thousands-year-old educational tradition that has been instrumental in the growth of civilization and that has been productive of so much excellence, but that is now in danger of disappearing.

Such an effort is unlikely to bring the applause of the wider academic world. There will no doubt be a price to pay along the way. But it is a noble and a much-needed service, this *diakonia* of truth. For America, this is the hour of the Catholic university; at least, if our universities do not rise to the challenge of the time, it is not clear who else would or could.

[13]

Embracing the Gift of *Ex corde Ecclesiae* to Challenge the Culture

Sean O. Sheridan, TOR

"Born from the heart of the Church, a Catholic University is located in that course of tradition which may be traced back to the very origin of the University as an institution. It has always been recognized as an incomparable center of creativity and dissemination of knowledge for the good of humanity."[1] St. Pope John Paul II began with these words his 1990 apostolic constitution *Ex corde Ecclesiae*, his "Magna Carta" on Catholic universities. John Paul understood that Catholic universities face an abundance of challenges from the secular world and wanted to encourage them to remain true to the mission for which they were established. "My hope is that these prescriptions, based on the teaching of Vatican Council II and the directives of the Code of Canon Law, will enable Catholic Universities and other Institutes of higher studies to fulfill their indispensable mission in the new advent of grace that is opening up to the new Millennium."[2]

Nearly ten years ago, Melanie Morey and Fr. John Piderit of the

1. John Paul II, apostolic constitution *Ex corde Ecclesiae* (hereafter *EcE*) 1, August 15, 1990: *Acta Apostolicae Sedis* 82 (1990). Translation in English by National Conference of Catholic Bishops in *Origins* 20, no. 17 (October 4, 1990): 265–76. See also Committee on Catholic Education, United States Conference of Catholic Bishops, *Catholic Mission and Culture in Colleges and Universities: Defining Documents: 1965–2014* (Washington, DC: United States Conference of Catholic Bishops, 2014) 69–89.

2. *EcE*, 11.

Society of Jesus considered the ongoing development of Catholic higher education and the current issues that Catholic educators face. They maintained that the evolving culture of Catholic universities had neared the point of crisis and called for a renewed dedication to this ministry. They submitted:

> A crisis is looming within American Catholic higher education. As Catholic colleges and universities analyze their position and set a course for the future, they are faced with a structural reality that threatens their ability to continue as institutions with vibrant religious cultures . . . Much has been said and written about such questions as: What constitutes the "Catholic identity" of Catholic colleges and universities? Is it inevitable for Catholic colleges and universities to follow the historical trend and lose their religious identity? What does it mean to be an authentically Catholic institution and is there only one way to do that? What is the appropriate balance between the secular and religious missions of Catholic colleges and universities? Will the loss of nuns, brothers, and priests as a vital and visible presence on campus prove fatal for institutional Catholic character? These are important questions to define carefully, describe accurately, and confront effectively.[3]

Arguably, Pope John Paul II also envisioned this looming crisis among Catholic universities when he, too, called for a rededication of Catholic educators to their mission and particularly to remain Catholic while providing a quality education.

There have been many discussions about *Ex corde Ecclesiae*, especially on issues such as the need for a mandate to teach the theological disciplines in a Catholic university[4] and to maintain Catholic identity.[5] Twenty-five years have now elapsed since the Holy Father promulgated his apostolic constitution on Catholic universities and invited the various episcopal conferences to assist with its implementation. Yet challenges continue to be raised regarding how to implement *Ex corde*

3. Melanie M. Morey and John J. Piderit, *Catholic Higher Education: A Culture in Crisis* (New York: Oxford University Press, 2006), 3.

4. *Codex Iuris Canonici auctoritate Ioannis Pauli PP. II promulgatus* (Vatican City: Libreria Editrice Vaticana, 1983), c. 812: "Those who teach theological disciplines in any institutes of higher studies whatsoever must have a mandate from the competent ecclesiastical authority." English translation from *Code of Canon Law*, Latin-English ed., new English trans. [reprint] (Washington, DC: CLSA, 2012). *EcE*, art. 4, §3.

5. *EcE*, art. 2.

Ecclesiae, for example, how to ensure that a majority of the faculty is Catholic.[6] Moreover, while the Church expects Catholic universities to comply with *Ex corde Ecclesiae*'s provisions, these same universities are immersed within a civil structure with its own legal requirements. As a result, some maintain that adhering to these civil law requirements and remaining competitive with their secular counterparts make it difficult to implement the apostolic constitution.

Yet the experience of Franciscan University has demonstrated that it is possible to thrive as an institution that is both Catholic and a university. In large part, Franciscan University's success can be attributed to its culture. In daily practice, the culture at Franciscan University is based on the principles that St. John Paul II set forth in *Ex corde Ecclesiae.* Its culture is noteworthy because it enables all members of the university family, students in particular, to be immersed in their academic endeavors while focusing on the pursuit of holiness and the deepening of their relationship with Christ. As a result, they are empowered to live their faith and to pass their faith on to others through their words and their actions. Their own experience with Christ transforms their lives so that they can become the presence of Christ to others. Their transformed lives give witness to Christ in all that they say and do.

In this essay, I describe the various elements of culture here at Franciscan University, framed and supported by references to St. John Paul II's *Ex corde Ecclesiae*, as a way of demonstrating how the gift of *Ex corde Ecclesiae* as envisioned by John Paul can equip a Catholic university with the tools to challenge the culture and therefore to transform the world.

As Morey and Piderit recognized, the challenges that Catholic universities face today are diverse and significant. Yet Catholic universities provide an essential ministry for the Church, and they are needed for the education of future generations. As John Paul said, "The mission that the Church, with great hope, entrusts to Catholic Universities holds a cultural and religious meaning of vital importance because it concerns the very future of humanity. The renewal requested of Catholic universities will make them better able to respond to the task of bringing the message of Christ to man, to society, to the various cultures."[7]

6. *EcE*, art. 4, §4.

7. *EcE*, Conclusion.

Embracing the gift of *Ex corde Ecclesiae* provides a road map for the success of Catholic universities.

The University Community

Pope John Paul II described the university community as an essential component of life within a Catholic university. The community of a Catholic university is unique in that it is united in its focus on Christ, through which the community promotes the Catholic identity of the university.

> A Catholic university pursues its objectives through its formation of an authentic human community animated by the spirit of Christ. The source of its unity springs from a common dedication to the truth, a common vision of the dignity of the human person, and ultimately, the person and message of Christ, which gives the institution its distinctive character. As a result of this inspiration, the community is animated by a spirit of freedom and charity; it is characterized by mutual respect, sincere dialogue and protection of the rights of individuals. It assists each of its members to achieve wholeness as human persons; in turn, everyone in the community helps in promoting unity, and each one, according to his or her role and capacity, contributes towards decisions which affect the community, and also towards maintaining and strengthening the distinctive Catholic character of the institution.[8]

Many people are part of the community of a Catholic university. They include teachers, students, directors and administrators, clerics, members of a religious congregation, and laypeople. Within the context of these various roles, each member of a university community has his or her own duties to participate in the university community. For example, "all teachers are to be inspired by academic ideals and by the principles of an authentically human life."[9] Students come to a Catholic university to pursue truth and meaning in their lives, thus enabling them to more deeply live a Christian way of life. "They should realize the responsibility of their professional life, the enthusiasm of being the trained 'leaders' of tomorrow, of being witnesses to Christ in whatever

8. *EcE*, 21.
9. *EcE*, 22.

place they may exercise their profession."[10] Directors and administrators of a Catholic university seek to promote the university community through their ministry of service.[11]

Ex corde Ecclesiae also recognizes that although many Catholic universities were founded originally by institutes of consecrated life, members of the laity have today increasingly come to play a more prominent role in these institutions.

> The future of Catholic universities depends to a great extent on the competent and dedicated service of lay Catholics. The church sees their developing presence in these institutions both as a sign of hope and as a confirmation of the irreplaceable lay vocation in the church and in the world, confident that lay people will, in the exercise of their own distinctive role, "illumine and organize these (temporal) affairs in such a way that they always start out, develop, and continue according to Christ's mind, to the praise of the Creator and the Redeemer."[12]

Moreover, the Catholic university community extends to men and women of different faith traditions and also to those who may not profess any religious beliefs. Yet the training and experience provided to these individuals also further the ministerial outreach of a Catholic university.[13]

Here at Franciscan University, while we do have what *Ex corde Ecclesiae* describes as a university community, I prefer to describe those of us who participate in this great adventure known as Franciscan University of Steubenville as the Franciscan University family. Each of us does our part to support the mission of the university. We all have different gifts to share. But the Lord has brought us together and entrusted to us his university so that we might continue to build up his kingdom here on earth. Together, under the guidance of the Holy Spirit, the Franciscan University family can and will do amazing things to promote a Christian culture that will challenge and renew the secular culture in which we live.

10. *EcE*, 23.
11. *EcE*, 24, emphasis original.
12. *EcE*, 25.
13. *EcE*, 26.

The Faculty

The Lord's Great Commission to the Apostles is set forth in the final verses of Matthew's Gospel: "Go, therefore, and make disciples of all nations, baptizing them in the name of the Father, and of the Son, and of the holy Spirit, *teaching them to observe all that I have commanded you.* And behold, I am with you always, until the end of the age."[14] Thus the ministry of teaching is an extension of Jesus's ministry to the sheep who were without a shepherd and whom he taught many things.[15] At any educational institution, teaching is an important component of the daily lives of the members of the community, particularly for those who have dedicated their lives to the classroom setting. But each one of us has the additional obligation to teach about Jesus Christ. Each one of us has the obligation to preach the Good News.

The Catholic university is described as an "academic community" that seeks to protect and advance the dignity of the human person through research, teaching, and other activities in communities at the local, national, and international levels.[16] Each Catholic university, because it is in fact Catholic, must embrace the following essential characteristics:

> 1. a Christian inspiration not only of individuals but of the university community as such;
> 2. a continuing reflection in the light of the Catholic faith upon the growing treasury of human knowledge, to which it seeks to contribute by its own research;
> 3. fidelity to the Christian message as it comes to us through the Church; and
> 4. an institutional commitment to the service of the people of God and of the human family in their pilgrimage to the transcendent goal which gives meaning to life.[17]

In *Ex corde Ecclesiae*, John Paul acknowledged that a Catholic university is a community of scholars that advances the various branches

14. Mt 28:19–20.
15. Cf. Mk 6:34.
16. *EcE*, 12.
17. *EcE*, 13.

of academic studies. But it is also an educational institution that embraces and promotes the teachings of the Catholic Church as a defining component of what it was established to be as a "Catholic university." Consequently, as John Paul urged, Catholic ideals ought to permeate all activities of a Catholic university.

Certainly, any academic institution is dependent upon the members of its faculty to carry out classroom instruction. But at an institution "born from the heart of the Church," the faculty fulfills a special calling or vocation to witness to the Gospel in their own lives as well. The need to support the Catholic mission at all levels of a Catholic university provides the members of the faculty with the opportunity to integrate faith into their daily lives in the classrooms, in their interactions with students and their colleagues, and within a variety of service related activities. There are many opportunities throughout the course of the day, particularly for faculty members, to bring Christ to each other.

At a Catholic university, there are also numerous daily occasions for prayer and reflection, for example, praying with the faith community within the celebration of the mass, and praying with students as class begins. By engaging in such opportunities, faculty members bring to prayer the challenges they experience in their teaching and, in turn, to bring back to the classroom the insights that they receive in prayer. John Paul said, "Catholic members of this community will be offered opportunities to assimilate Catholic teaching and practice into their lives and will be encouraged to participate in the celebration of the sacraments, especially the Eucharist as the most perfect act of community worship."[18] Through their words and example, faculty members are especially equipped to encourage other members of the university community to engage in these various spiritual opportunities.

John Paul II stated that because members of the faculty share in promoting the Catholic mission of the university, this "calls for the recruitment of adequate university personnel, especially teachers and administrators, who are both willing and able to promote that identity."[19] Of particular importance in this regard is the quality of those recruited to teach and their respect for Catholic doctrine. In addition to their pedagogical obligations, Catholic faculty members "are called to be witness-

18. *EcE*, 39.

19. *EcE*, art. 4, §1.

es and educators of authentic Christian life, which evidences attained integration between faith and life, and between professional competence and Christian wisdom."[20] Thus they should lead authentically human lives that are also authentically Christian.

Members of the faculty are poised to help their students and colleagues to live out their faith. At Franciscan University, for example,

- The families of many of our faculty members are part of our faith community. They participate together in the numerous daily faith-based activities on campus, including the celebration of the sacraments. Students and other members of the university family observe and learn from these families. This is especially evident when faulty members form long-lasting faith-based relationships with their colleagues and the students that they mentor.
- Faculty members may serve as advisors to households within our household life system, helping to promote these faith-based communities. Students look to these leaders for guidance and direction on how to incorporate the teachings of the faith into their daily lives and how to remain true to their identity as baptized children of God.
- Faculty members might also accompany our students on various mission trips to areas of the United States, Central America, and even parts of Europe to minister to our brothers and sisters in need—to bring to them the Gospel, the sacraments, and catechesis and to help these students to better understand themselves as a child of God and how they can bring Christ to others. Thus, through the witness of their professors, students "become more aware of their responsibility towards those who are suffering physically or spiritually."[21]
- Faculty members may also serve as advisors for student clubs, and work with our Center for Leadership to foster development of leadership skills. They lead Bible study groups. They present numerous nonacademic talks on a variety of topics, such as promoting marriage and family.

20. *EcE*, 22.
21. *EcE*, 40.

At a Catholic university, faculty members are essential to promoting the Catholic mission. Faith is constitutive of a Catholic university. A Catholic university's focus on the spiritual development of all members of the university community, with the assistance of the faculty, is of primary importance in promoting the Catholic character of the institution.

Yet a Catholic education, particularly a Franciscan Catholic education, directs each of the academic disciplines to a charity that is always oriented toward God. The Franciscan theologian St. Bonaventure wrote:

> This is the fruit of all sciences, that in all, faith may be strengthened, *God may be honored*, character may be formed, and consolation may be derived from union of the Spouse with his beloved, a union which takes place through charity, to the attainment of which the whole purpose of sacred Scripture, and thus of every illumination descending from above, comes to rest—a charity without which all knowledge is vain.[22]

Thus the study of all academic disciplines should be directed to turning the mind to God so that there is no "investigation without wonder," no "observation without joy," and no "understanding without humility."[23]

Article 4, §3 of *Ex corde*'s General Norms reiterates the need for all Catholic teachers to be faithful to Catholic doctrine and for those who teach the theological disciplines to have a mandate to teach from the competent ecclesiastical authority:

> In ways appropriate to the different academic disciplines, all Catholic teachers are to be faithful to, and all other teachers are to respect, Catholic doctrine and morals in their research and teaching. In particular, Catholic theologians, aware that they fulfill a mandate received from the Church, are to be faithful to the Magisterium of the Church as the authentic interpreter of Sacred Scripture and Sacred Tradition.[24]

In 1989, with the encouragement of Fr. Michael Scanlan, TOR, then president of Franciscan University, the university's theology professors

22. Bonaventure, *De reductione artium ad theologiam* 26. Zachary Hayes, trans., *On the Reduction of the Arts to Theology*, vol. 1, *The Works of St. Bonaventure* (St. Bonaventure, NY: Franciscan Institute, 1996), 61.

23. Bonaventure, *The Soul's Journey into God*, trans. Ewert Cousins (New York: Paulist Press, 1978), prologue, 4, 55–56.

24. *EcE*, art. 4, §3. Cf. cc. 810, 812.

became the first of the Catholic theology faculties in the United States to make a public Profession of Faith and Oath of Fidelity to the Magisterium. Each year thereafter, our new theologians, priests, and ministry personnel have done the same. Members of Franciscan University's Board of Trustees also make the Profession and Oath. And in 2013, my entire president's cabinet along with members of the Sacred Music Department and the Philosophy Department made the Profession and Oath. Numerous other Catholic universities have also seen the importance of the fidelity of faculty members to the Magisterium and have similarly taken up the charge to make the public Profession of Faith and Oath of Fidelity. These public acts express the heart of who we are as a university that is in fact Catholic.

Pope Francis, in his 2013 apostolic exhortation *Evangelii gaudium*, also pointed to the importance of a Catholic university's role in evangelization. He said, "Universities are outstanding environments for articulating and developing this evangelizing commitment in an interdisciplinary and integrated way."[25] The encounter with Jesus Christ brought about through evangelization further enhances the mission of a Catholic university, where all teachers are to be informed about the university's Catholic identity at the time of their appointment. They are also to be advised of the implications of the university's Catholic identity for their teaching and research.

The Role of Pastoral Care to Support the Students

Franciscan University of Steubenville is first and foremost an educational institution. But with pastoral care, we engage our students to develop a personal relationship with Jesus Christ. And this outreach extends to many other people who may never be enrolled as Franciscan students.

Ex corde Ecclesiae addresses both pastoral care and evangelization—

25. Francis, apostolic exhortation *Evangelii gaudium* (*EG*) 134, November 24, 2013: *Acta Apostolicae Sedis* (*AAS*) 105 (2013): 1019–137, http://w2.vatican.va/content/francesco/en/apost_exhortations/documents/papa-francesco_esortazione-ap_20131124_evangelii-gaudium.html.

topics that are also treated in Pope Francis's apostolic exhortation *Evangelii gaudium*. Both documents provide to those who minister within a Catholic university guidance on how pastoral care and evangelization ought to be incorporated into their daily activities. Again, Catholic ideals ought to permeate all activities of a Catholic university.

To promote the university's Catholic identity, the Catholic university focuses on Christ. John Paul said:

> A Catholic university pursues its objectives through its formation of an authentic human community animated by the spirit of Christ. The source of its unity springs from a common dedication to the truth, a common vision of the dignity of the human person, and ultimately, the person and message of Christ, which gives the institution its distinctive character. As a result of this inspiration, the community is animated by a spirit of freedom and charity; it is characterized by mutual respect, sincere dialogue and protection of the rights of individuals. It assists each of its members to achieve wholeness as human persons; in turn, everyone in the community helps in promoting unity, and each one, according to his or her role and capacity, contributes towards decisions which affect the community, and also towards maintaining and strengthening the distinctive Catholic character of the institution.[26]

John Paul went on to broadly define pastoral ministry as "that activity of the University which offers the members of the university community an opportunity to integrate religious and moral principles with their academic study and non-academic activities, thus integrating faith with life."[27] Because of their accessibility to students, those who provide pastoral care are in a position to help them to integrate "faith with life," giving a "practical demonstration of its faith in its daily activity."

Pastorally delivered care at all levels of a Catholic university provides the members of the university community with the opportunity to integrate faith into their daily lives through participation in the sacraments; in the residence halls; in the many and various activities that are student oriented, such as athletics, clubs, or associations; or even in dealing with issues of student discipline. Residence hall directors and assistants physically live with the students and see them engage their spiritual highs and lows. Athletic coaches also meet the members of

26. *EcE*, 21.

27. *EcE*, 38.

their teams on a daily basis for practice or on long bus trips for away games. Even the person at a Catholic university charged with meeting with students who have participated in some action that might lead to discipline has the opportunity to bring Christ to that student through their encounter.

Students of a Catholic university encounter the struggles of the poor and those that society has forgotten. They "become more aware of their responsibility towards those who are suffering physically or spiritually,"[28] beginning with those within their own academic community and extending to our brothers and sisters beyond the university community. Through various formation or missionary activities, students are prepared to actively participate in the life of Church.

Students can also be assisted in becoming more aware of their vocation in life, whether it is to be married or to remain single, to be ordained or to be consecrated as a religious. There are many opportunities for students to be formed about the various vocations in the Church and to help students hear and respond to God's special call for their lives.

At Franciscan University of Steubenville, we are blessed to have chapels in our residence halls where the Blessed Sacrament is reserved. This allows the residents the opportunity throughout the course of the day—and even into the late hours of the night—for quiet time and reflection to discern God's plan for them. Each residence hall also has a chaplain who is available at designated times throughout the week to offer spiritual direction or, in the case of priest chaplains, the sacrament of reconciliation. Forming faith-sharing groups and encouraging participation in devotional exercises are just a few additional ways that a Catholic university can assist students with their discernment.

At a Catholic university, pastoral care is not limited to the activities that go on in the university chapel. Pastoral care is integral to the university community and enhances the totality of a student's university experience because faith is not an ancillary activity. Faith is constitutive of a Catholic university. Pastoral care is essential to the life of the university that is Catholic. The university's focus on the spiritual development of the members of the university community is of primary importance for promoting the Catholic character of the institution.

28. *EcE*, 40.

All Members of the University Family as Evangelizers

Throughout the pontificates of Popes John Paul II and Benedict XVI, and now Francis, we have learned much about the new evangelization. In *Ex corde Ecclesiae*, Pope John Paul II said: "The primary mission of the Church is to preach the Gospel in such a way that a relationship between faith and life is established in each individual and in the socio-cultural context in which individuals live and act and communicate with one another."[29] In *Evangelii gaudium*, Pope Francis indicates that "the primary reason for evangelizing is the love of Jesus which we have received."[30] Evangelization according to these principles should also be a goal of a Catholic college or university because "each Catholic university makes an important contribution to the Church's work of evangelization."[31]

In trying to describe the various components of the new evangelization, one commentator suggested:

> In essence, New Evangelization is comprised of three things: First, New Evangelization includes renewed spiritual devotion as well as renewed efforts in catechesis. We must know Jesus, and we must understand Christianity and the Catholic faith in particular. This renewed knowledge enables the second element, living our faith. And third, a natural extension of knowing and living our faith is to share it with others.[32]

Thus the new evangelization embraces personal renewal or conversion, living the faith, and sharing the faith with others. Each is important to the life of a Catholic university. As agents of evangelization, the members of a Catholic university community have a wonderful opportunity to evangelize through their own renewal, through their actions, and through the faith they share with each other.

At Franciscan University, we are familiar with the conversion of St. Francis of Assisi. Later in his life, Francis wrote in his testament:

29. *EcE*, 48.

30. *EG*, 264.

31. *EG*, 49.

32. Greg Willits, *The New Evangelization and You: Be Not Afraid* (Cincinnati, OH: Servant Books, 2013), 14.

> The Lord gave me, Brother Francis, thus to begin doing penance in this way: for when I was in sin, it seemed too bitter for me to see lepers. And then the Lord Himself led me among them and I showed mercy to them. And when I left them, what had seemed bitter to me was turned into sweetness of soul and body. And afterwards I delayed a little and left the world.[33]

According to Francis, it was his encounters with the lepers that led to his conversion. Showing mercy and compassion to the men and women whom society had forgotten caused Francis to reflect on his life. This reflection led to the deepening of his relationship with Christ.

In being merciful, Francis came to understand what Christ was asking him to do. He left behind his possessions and attachments to preach the Good News.

But his conversion did not end there. Francis continued daily in his quest to encounter Christ more deeply. Every day he sought to redirect himself toward God and to bring others to Christ. He even took on the wounds of Christ in his own body.

Each of us has a story to tell about our encounter with Christ. Our own ongoing conversion must include the act of "turning away" from sin and those things that distract us from our pursuit of holiness. Going to confession and to mass, or participating in Holy Hours, can only be effective for us if we are in fact "turning away" from those things that keep us from God. Members of a Catholic university community should focus their daily activities on Christ and turning toward Christ. Ongoing conversion is at the heart of being an authentic agent of the new evangelization and, for that matter, at the heart of being Christian.

Our own encounter with Christ would lose its significance if we did not allow it to transform us in a way that leads us to Christ. Conversion demands a response. Conversion demands the transformation of our lives. Conversion causes us to share the fruits of conversion with others.

Pope Francis reminds us that:

> An evangelizing community knows that the Lord has taken the initiative, he has loved us first, and therefore we can move forward, boldly take the initiative, go out to others, seek those who have fallen away, stand at the crossroads and welcome the outcast. Such a community has an endless desire to show

33. Francis of Assisi, "The Testament," in *Francis of Assisi: Early Documents*, vol. 1, *The Saint*, ed. Regis J. Armstrong et al. (New York: New City Press, 1999), 1–3, 124.

mercy, the fruit of its own experience of the power of the Father's infinite mercy.[34]

Personal conversion causes the follower of Christ to live the faith more authentically. And it demands that faith be shared with others. We may never encounter a leper as part of our conversion, but the focus on personal conversion enables us to live the faith and hand it on to others. *Nemo dat quod non habet*—"You cannot give what you do not have."

Some people are influenced by secularism in our society. It becomes challenging to identify any teaching as an absolute truth. And even if a person might personally believe in some truth, under the influence of secularism, he or she may become unwilling to commit to the absolute nature of that truth as it affects other people. They become reluctant to impose their beliefs on others and expect all persons to make their own assessment of what is truth and what is not. Secularism often leads to the privatization of one's faith.

Pope Francis acknowledges in his encyclical *Lumen fidei*[35] that our society is drifting away from the recognition of absolute truths to the point that, for many people, "truth" has become what is most convenient for them. In *Lumen fidei* 25, Pope Francis writes:

> Today more than ever, we need to be reminded of this bond between faith and truth, given the crisis of truth in our age. In contemporary culture … truth is what makes life easier and more comfortable. In the end, what we are left with is relativism, in which the question of universal truth—and ultimately this means the question of God—is no longer relevant.[36]

In our culture today, we encounter the emergence of seemingly "more comfortable" truths when society advances a distorted view on contraception, abortion, marriage, and euthanasia—which are all contrary to the teachings of the Church.

If Catholic universities do not connect faith with daily life, if we fail to infuse academics, residence life, athletics, student activities, and the like with the truths of the Catholic faith, then we are unwittingly reduc-

34. *EG*, 24.

35. Francis, encyclical *Lumen Fidei* (*LF*), June 29, 2013: *AAS* 105 (2013): 555–96, http://w2.vatican.va/content/francesco/en/encyclicals/documents/papa-francesco_20130629_enciclica-lumen-fidei.html.

36. *LF*, 25.

ing our God-given and constitutionally guaranteed right to "freedom of religion" to a mere "freedom of worship," thereby buying into the very premise of secularism. In fact, if the culture—and, ultimately, all men and women of faith—do not embrace the teachings of the Church—the absolute truths of the faith—and maintain the voice of faithful Catholics in the public square, the potential arises for much more serious consequences than secularism and relativism. We run the risk of rejecting Christ himself, and at that point our lives become meaningless.

At first glance, many people might think that the younger members of our Church are the ones who are in need of learning the truth. But this is not always the case. At Franciscan University, I see our students and alumni as the ones who are in the best position to bring the new evangelization to fruition.

Conclusion

In *Ex corde Ecclesiae*'s conclusion, St. John Paul II recognized the important task entrusted to Catholic colleges and universities. In the twenty-five years since St. John Paul II issued *Ex corde Ecclesiae*, engaging the culture in a dialogue about the truths of the faith has become even more relevant. Engaging the culture, which necessarily includes aspects of challenging and influencing the culture through dialogue about truths of the faith, is different than "embracing" or "accepting" the culture through which the Church might become just an extension of the culture. As John Paul pointed out, a Catholic college or university is a highly appropriate place for this dialogue to occur.

In his recent book *Seeds of the Word: Finding God in the Culture*, now Most Reverend Robert Barron, auxiliary bishop of the Archdiocese of Los Angeles, commented on the place of a Catholic university within the culture of our society. His comments relate to two Catholic universities and how they engaged President Barack Obama on their campuses. Barron noted that the University of Notre Dame "presented an honorary degree (in law, of all things) to the most radically pro-abortion president in history."[37] He also recalled that "shortly thereafter, Georgetown [Uni-

37. Robert Barron, *Seeds of the Word: Finding God in the Culture* (Skokie, IL: Word on Fire, 2015), 187.

versity], the most prominent Jesuit university in the country, in order to satisfy the demands of the Obama White House, covered up all the religious symbols in Gaston Hall when the President spoke there."[38]

Bishop Barron stated:

What a Catholic university should never do is to surrender its own identity or to make apologies for its own deepest commitments. A Catholic center of higher learning should never acquiesce in its own secularization in order to participate in the public conversation.[39]

He went on to recall the tradition of the great Catholic universities that provided the foundation for engaging the teachings of the secular world through the lens of Catholicism.

This is why the first universities—Bologna, Paris, Oxford, Cambridge—emerged precisely out of the milieu of the Church. In the thirteenth century, St. Bonaventure, professor at the University of Paris, composed an extraordinary text called *Christ the Center*, the gravamen of whose argument is that Jesus the *Logos* is at the heart of physics, mathematics, history, and metaphysics. In the mid-nineteenth century, John Henry Newman, in a series of lectures entitled *The Idea of a University*, made much the same assertion. The Jesus reverenced by the great tradition belongs, therefore, very much in the public sphere and around the table of intellectual conversation. In that context, he poses no threat to legitimate expressions of reason, and he serves as a trump to the unreason that can surface easily enough in the sciences, in politics, or in philosophy. A Catholic university worthy of the name is a place where Jesus the *Logos* has this essential regulating role.[40]

Here at Franciscan University, we strive to follow the example of these early Catholic universities in the way we embrace the search for truth in the dialogue between faith and reason, while recognizing that the source of all truth is God himself. As Pope John Paul II recognized in *Ex corde Ecclesiae*, a Catholic university places itself in the middle of the dialogue between faith and reason, an interaction that would not be found in a typical secular university. Moreover, as centers for the new evangelization, Catholic universities and members of the university family are compelled to embark on the lifelong commitment to ongo-

38. Ibid.
39. Ibid., 188.
40. Ibid., 188–89.

ing conversion as authentic witnesses to the faith. Catholic universities should continue to promote the teachings of our faith in the public square, in scholarship, and in the many decisions that are made for a Catholic university. Education, catechetics, and theology are key to the new evangelization. All of us have a role to play in educating ourselves, in living our faith, and in drawing others to Christ. And, as Pope Francis has modeled for us, we must strive to do so with great joy.

APPENDIX

Practical Suggestions for the Implementation of *Ex corde Ecclesiae*

Sean O. Sheridan, TOR

While this collection of essays advances the discussion around *Ex corde Ecclesiae* and Catholic universities—in its treatment of both theoretical and practical questions—there are a number issues related to the implementation of *Ex corde Ecclesiae* that did not receive sustained attention. But these issues are important because they help to explain the reluctance of some Catholic universities, particularly in the United States, to implement the provisions of *Ex corde Ecclesiae* and those of the National Conference of Catholic Bishops. Having previously written on this question, I thought it might be useful here to recapitulate those findings on five prominent themes:

1. The need for a canonical juridic link between a Catholic university and the Church before these canonical norms can be operative.
2. What is included within the concept of a university's Catholic identity.
3. The ability of a Catholic university to give preference in hiring decisions such that a critical mass of the faculty will be baptized Catholics.

This appendix is drawn from the author's previous work. See "*Ex corde Ecclesiae*: A Canonical Commentary on Catholic Universities, 'From the Heart of the Church' to Catholic Universities" (JCD diss., Catholic University of America, 2009).

4. The role of contracts with faculty members in a Catholic university, including the need to comply with canon law, particularly Canons 810 and 812.

5. An understanding of how a Catholic university relates with the local and universal Church.[1]

We offer a brief explanation of each of these issues together with some practical guidance for those universities that wish to promote themselves as Catholic universities. Although the focus here is the United States, to the extent that similar laws, arguments, or circumstances in other countries can be raised, we endeavor to do so such that consideration might be given throughout the world to the implementation of *Ex corde Ecclesiae* and the provisions of the code dealing with Catholic universities.

Catholic Universities and Canonical Juridic Personality

At the outset, we should first consider those concerns that have been raised regarding the applicability of *Ex corde Ecclesiae* and other canonical provisions regarding Catholic universities to those Catholic universities that do not have their own distinct canonical juridic personality. This issue raises the question of whether *Ex corde Ecclesiae* and similar provisions in the code of canon law regulate the way Catholic education is to be provided in many Catholic institutions of higher learning, particularly those in the United States.[2]

1. See Sean O. Sheridan, "*Ex corde Ecclesiae*. A Canonical Commentary on Catholic Universities, 'From the Heart of the Church' to Catholic Universities" (JCD diss., Catholic University of America, 2009).

2. Numerous scholars have made significant contributions on this issue. See James A. Coriden, "Catholic Universities and Other Institutes of Higher Studies (cc. 807–814)," in *The Code of Canon Law: A Text and Commentary*, ed. James A. Coriden et al. (New York: Paulist Press, 1985), 571; James Coriden and Frederick R. McManus, "Appendix A: The Present State of Roman Catholic Canon Law Regarding Colleges and Sponsoring Religious Bodies," in Philip R. Moots and Edward McGlynn Gaffney Jr., *Church and Campus: Legal Issues in Religiously Affiliated Higher Education* (Notre Dame, IN: University of Notre Dame Press, 1979); Eduardo Molano, "Juridical Persons," in *Code of Canon Law Annotated*, ed. Ernesto Caparros et al. (Montreal: Wilson & Lafleur, 1993), 97–123; Ladislas Örsy, "The Mandate to Teach Theological Disciplines: Glosses on Canon 812 of the New Code,"

Throughout the discussion and drafting process that led to the promulgation of the new code, representatives of Catholic universities in the United States raised objections on numerous occasions. For example, in 1976, in response to an early proposal for an apostolic constitution that would govern ecclesiastical faculties and universities, the College and University Department of the National Catholic Educational Association stated, "we do not consider appropriate nor legally feasible the extension of jurisdiction over noncanonically established institutions, at the expense of existing rights of local bishops or the institutions themselves."[3] This document also argued that "since the colleges and universities in the United States have received their charters from the respective state governments and have independent legal existence as private, non-profit educational institutions, the notion of canonical establishment by the Holy See has never been thought of as typical or standard in the United States."[4]

Yet the comments that the Board of the Association of Catholic Colleges and Universities (ACCU) and the Bishops and Presidents' Committee submitted in response to the 1978 Draft Schema for the proposed canons that would address Catholic universities stated no objection to the applicability of the proposed canons on the basis of a lack of juridic personality.[5] It was not until the ACCU responded to the 1980 Draft

---

Theological Studies 44 (1983): 476–88; Ladislas Örsy, *The Church: Learning and Teaching. Magisterium, Assent, Dissent, Academic Freedom* (Wilmington, DE: Michael Glazier, 1987); James Conn, *Catholic Universities in the United States and Ecclesiastical Authority*, Canon Law Studies 259 (Rome: Pontificia Universita Gregoriana, 1991); Francis Joseph Hoffman, *The Apostolic Constitution Ex Corde Ecclesiae and Catholic Universities in the United States of America*, Canon Law Studies 567/95 (Rome: Pontificium Athenæum Sanctae Crucis, 1996); Archbishop J. Michael Miller, "Catholic Universities and Their Catholic Identity," *Origins* 35, no. 27 (December 15, 2005): 451–58.

3. National Catholic Educational Association, College and University Department, "Relations of American Catholic Colleges and Universities with the Church: Position Paper of the College and University Department, National Catholic Educational Association," in *American Catholic Higher Education: Essential Documents, 1967–1990*, ed. Alice Gallin (Notre Dame, IN: University of Notre Dame Press, 1992), 83.

4. Ibid., 81.

5. See, generally, Board of the Association of Catholic Colleges and Universities and the Bishops and Presidents' Committee, "Revision of the Code of Canon Law: Canons on Higher Education: Critique Endorsed by the Board of the Association of Catholic Colleges and Universities and the Bishops and Presidents' Committee," in Gallin, *American Catholic Higher Education*, 159–64.

Schema that the objection based on lack of juridic personality was specifically raised. This response asserted that "the present and traditional relationships of the Catholic colleges and universities to the local churches and the religious institutes largely avoid the formalities of direct juridical or canonical bonds."[6] Nevertheless, the response did not contend specifically that the absence of distinct canonical bonds between Catholic universities and the Church prevented the proposed legislation from being applicable to institutions without such formal bonds. The argument seemed to be more that any canonical legislation that would govern Catholic universities would be detrimental to their operation.[7] Further, the ACCU response argued that the absence of a juridical relationship might in some ways strengthen the mission of Catholic universities. "The absence of the formal juridical requirements of the proposed canons—in other words, the present relationship of Church and institutions—in no way weakens the authentically Catholic mission or witness of the colleges and universities."[8]

Ex corde Ecclesiae

Juridic Personality

Despite arguments regarding the nonapplicability of canonical legislation to most of the Catholic universities in the United States, in his 1990 apostolic constitution *Ex corde Ecclesiae*, Pope John Paul II stated at Article 1, section 1 of the constitution's General Norms that the norms "are valid for *all* Catholic Universities and other Catholic Institutes of Higher Studies throughout the world."[9] The apostolic constitution does not distinguish between those Catholic universities that the

6. Association of Catholic Colleges and Universities, "Canons 762–770 on Catholic Higher Education Recommendations: A Response from the Association of Catholic Colleges and Universities," in Gallin, *American Catholic Higher Education*, 167.

7. Ibid., 168–69.

8. Ibid., 169.

9. John Paul II, apostolic constitution *Ex corde Ecclesiae* (hereafter *EcE*) 1, §1, August 15, 1990: *Acta Apostolicae Sedis* 82 (1990). Translation in English by National Conference of Catholic Bishops in *Origins* 20, no. 17 (October 4, 1990): 265–76. See also Committee on Catholic Education, United States Conference of Catholic Bishops, *Catholic Mission and Culture in Colleges and Universities: Defining Documents: 1965–2014* (Washington, DC: United States Conference of Catholic Bishops, 2014), 69–89 (emphasis added).

Church established as legal persons and those that have a bond of communion with the Church. The Holy Father did, however, acknowledge that "many Catholic Universities were founded by Religious Congregations, and continue to depend on their support."[10] He urged those congregations to "assist these Institutions in their renewal of their commitment"[11] to higher education.

Further, *Ex corde Ecclesiae* seems to indicate that if a university wants to present itself as a "Catholic" university, then the university and those associated with it must remain faithful to the teachings of the Church and be regulated by those canonical provisions that address the operation of Catholic universities. This is premised on a "special bond" that exists between a Catholic university and the Church. Thus in Article 27 of Part I of the apostolic constitution, the Holy Father argued:

> Every Catholic University, without ceasing to be a University, has a relationship to the Church that is essential to its institutional identity. As such, it participates most directly in the life of the local Church in which it is situated; at the same time, because it is an academic institution and therefore a part of the international community of scholarship and inquiry, *each institution participates in and contributes to the life and the mission of the universal Church, assuming consequently a special bond with the Holy See by reason of the service to unity which it is called to render to the whole Church.* One consequence of its essential relationship to the Church is that *institutional* fidelity of the University to the Christian message includes a recognition and adherence to the teaching authority of the Church in matters of faith and morals. Catholic members of the university community are also called to a personal fidelity to the Church with all that this implies. Non-Catholic members are required to respect the Catholic character of the University, while the University in turn respects their religious liberty.[12]

Pope John Paul II continued by arguing that "every Catholic University is to maintain communion with the universal Church and the Holy See; it is to be in close communion with the local Church and in particular with the diocesan Bishops of the region or nation in which it is to be located."[13]

10. *EcE*, 25.
11. *EcE*, 25.
12. *EcE*, 27, emphasis added in part.
13. *EcE*, art. 5, §1.

Article 2, section 2 of the General Norms also points to the bond that exists between a Catholic university and the Church. "A Catholic University ... *is linked with the Church either by a formal, constitutive and statutory bond or by reason of an institutional commitment made by those responsible for it.*"[14]

Thus it seems that the Holy Father suggested several arguments that can be raised for the applicability of those canonical provisions that regulate Catholic universities even if they are not recognized as legal persons with a juridic link to the Church. First, because many Catholic universities were founded by religious institutes as part of their apostolic works, the Church does have a juridic bond with these religious institutes that could be relied upon to promote institutional fidelity to the Church.[15] Second, all Catholics who participate in the life of the Catholic university are independently obligated to maintain communion with the Church by virtue of their baptisms. Thus, even if the university does

14. *EcE*, art. 2, §2, emphasis added.

15. The significance of this argument was reiterated with the 1997 proposed sale of St. Louis University Hospital to Tenet Health System Hospitals, Inc. The hospital claimed that it was a distinct civilly incorporated entity that was not subject to the provisions of canon law. The Holy See disagreed on the basis that, as an apostolate of the Missouri Province of the Society of Jesus, the hospital was subject to canon law. This result was reached despite the hospital's invalid attempts to distance itself from ecclesiastical control in a way that many other Catholic colleges and universities in the United States have attempted to do by altering the composition of its board of trustees from members of the religious institute to lay trustees.

> This issue became apparent in late 1997 when the university proposed to sell its teaching hospital. The Archbishop of St. Louis notified the president of the university that the sale of the hospital would require the permission of the Holy See. The university president responded that the university was not an entity subject to Church control and that it had been alienated in 1967, after which, it was a university operated in the Catholic tradition, but not subject to control by either the Jesuits or the Holy See.
>
> This issue was presented by the leadership of the Society of Jesus to the Holy See for clarification. The Holy See, through the Prefect of the Congregation for Catholic Education and the Prefect for the Congregation for Institutes of Consecrated Life and Societies of Apostolic Life, in early 1998, stated that the authorization of the Holy See was necessary for the sale of Saint Louis University Hospital. This was because the Province had not alienated the university which remained subject to the requirements of Canon Law and the authority of the Jesuits.

Bernard C. Huger, "Canon Law Issues of Sponsorship, Governance Control and Alienation as They Relate to Catholic Church Entities in the United States: A Diocesan Attorney's Perspective," *Catholic Lawyer* 41 (2001–2): 21.

not have a formal link with the Church, those persons who are baptized Catholics and members of the university community do have such a link.[16] Third, the Holy Father suggested that all Catholic universities have assumed a "special bond" with the Church owing to the nature of their mission and participation in the ministry of the Church.

Ex corde Ecclesiae asserted the applicability of the canonical provisions that regulate Catholic universities. If a university desires its university community, the Church, and the general public to consider the university to be a Catholic university, then it ought to acknowledge the assumption of a special bond with the Church such that the Church has canonical authority over the university as provided in the canons of the code of canon law and the provisions of *Ex corde Ecclesiae*. If a university were not to do so, then it really is not a Catholic university.

Application to the United States

When the National Conference of Catholic Bishops promulgated the ordinances to implement *Ex corde Ecclesiae* that would apply in the United States, they followed suit with Article 1 of the General Norms and stated that the norms would apply to all Catholic universities. "These particular norms are applicable to all Catholic colleges, universities and institutions of higher learning within the territory encompassed by the National Conference of Catholic Bishops, contrary particular laws, customs or privileges notwithstanding."[17]

16. Reliance upon the 1988 authentic interpretation of Canon 1737, which indicated that a group of the faithful that lacked juridical personality could not seek hierarchical recourse as a group but could do so individually, would be tenuous. First, the issue of hierarchical recourse is not at issue here. Moreover, the action proposed in the request for authentic interpretation is precluded by Canon 310, which provides: "A private association which has not been established as a juridic person cannot, as such, be a subject of obligations and rights. Nevertheless, the members of the Christian faithful associated together in it can jointly contract obligations and can acquire and possess rights and goods as co-owners and co-possessors; they are able to exercise these rights and obligations through an agent or a proxy."

17. National Conference of Catholic Bishops (NCCB), "The Application of *Ex corde Ecclesiae* for the United States," *Origins* 29, no. 25 (December 2, 1999): 402–9, Part II, art. 1, §1. See also Committee on Education, Bishops' and Presidents' Subcommittee, United States Conference of Catholic Bishops (USCCB), *Catholic Identity in Our Colleges and Universities: A Collection of Defining Documents* (Washington, DC: USCCB, 2006) 75–94; Alice Gallin, ed., *Ex corde Ecclesiae: Documents Concerning Reception and Implementation* (Notre Dame, IN: University of Notre Dame Press, 2006), 388–406. See Monika Hellwig,

The NCCB ordinances also responded to the Congregation for Catholic Education's Directive regarding the specific identification of the relationship between a Catholic university and the Church. In 1991, the Congregation for Catholic Education had issued certain directives[18] to assist the various episcopal conferences with the implementation of the provisions of *Ex corde Ecclesiae*. Included within the requirements that the congregation set forth is a directive that the ordinances of the episcopal conferences would require each Catholic university to identify its relationship with the Church. The directives provided:

> In accord with Article 1, §§1, 2, and 3 of the General Norms, a listing of the different types of Catholic Universities and other Catholic Institutes of Higher Studies to be found in the region or country and the exact nature of the relationship of each type with the Church and with ecclesiastical authorities. On the basis of this listing, each Catholic institution should be asked to specify the category to which it belongs and the conditions under which it has received the consent of competent ecclesiastical Authority (cf. General Norms, Article 3, §3).[19]

Thus, at Article 3, the NCCB ordinances provide:

> 1. A Catholic university may be established, or an existing university approved, by the Holy See, the National Conference of Catholic Bishops, other hierarchical assemblies or individual diocesan bishops. It may also be established by a religious institute or some other public juridic person, or by individual Catholics, acting singly or in association, with proper ecclesiastical approval.
>
> 2. At the time of its establishment the university should see to it that its canonical status is identified, including the ecclesiastical authority by which it has been established or approved or to which it is otherwise related.

"What Makes Our Colleges Catholic?," in *Mission and Identity: A Handbook for Trustees of Catholic Colleges and Universities*, ed. Association of Governing Boards of Universities and Colleges, Association of Catholic Colleges and Universities and Association of Jesuit Colleges and Universities (Washington, DC: Association of Governing Boards of Universities and Colleges, 2003), 111.

18. Congregation for Catholic Education, "Directives to Assist in the Formulation of the Ordinances for the Apostolic Constitution *Ex Corde Ecclesiae*," in Gallin, *Ex corde Ecclesiae*, 66–68.

19. Ibid., 67.

3. The statutes of Catholic universities established by hierarchical authority or by religious institutes or other public juridic persons must be approved by competent ecclesiastical authority.

4. No university may assume the title Catholic without the consent of the competent ecclesiastical authority.[20]

After nearly fifty years of drafting and implementing the canons dealing with Catholic universities and the apostolic constitution *Ex corde Ecclesiae*, including implementation at the level of the episcopal conference for the United States, the questions that initially surrounded the applicability of these provisions to Catholic universities in the United States have been addressed at many different levels.

The more specific arguments upon which this line of reasoning in favor of recognizing a link between the Church and a Catholic university include the following:

1. The legislator has clearly stated that these provisions apply to all universities that want to be considered to be "Catholic universities," upon the conditions established by the Holy Father rather than those conditions selected by individual universities.

2. Many Catholic universities were founded by religious institutes as part of their apostolic works, and the Church does have a juridic bond with these religious institutes that extends to their Catholic universities and can be relied upon to promote institutional fidelity to the Church.

3. All Catholics who participate in the life of the Catholic university are independently obligated to maintain communion with the Church by virtue of their baptisms. Thus, even if the university does not have a formal link with the Church, those persons who are baptized Catholics and members of the university community do have such a link.

4. All Catholic universities have assumed a "special bond" with the Church due to the nature of their mission and participation in the ministry of the Church.

5. While it is the general practice that the code does not impose obligations nor afford rights to those who are neither baptized Catholics nor juridic persons, there are exceptions to this general rule. Although these persons are generally not subject to the Church's merely ecclesias-

20. NCCB, "Application of *Ex corde Ecclesiae* for the United States," Part 2, Art. 3.

tical laws, they choose to subject themselves to such laws by the actions they want to take, e.g., to marry a Catholic or to receive a sacrament from a Catholic minister. Thus a university that wants to be a Catholic university chooses to subject itself to the applicable ecclesiastical laws.

6. The behavior of Catholic universities in the United States throughout the process of drafting and implementing the code provisions on Catholic universities and the apostolic constitution *Ex corde Ecclesiae* suggests that they believe that they are subject to these provisions. Otherwise, why would they have been so extensively involved in the process if these provisions did not apply to them in the absence of a juridic link with the Church?

7. Additionally, the Congregation for Catholic Education has continued to assert its authority over these universities in the United States as evidenced by the listing of 218 Catholic universities in the United States that are within the competence of the Congregation and subject to the provisions of *Ex corde Ecclesiae*.[21]

Whether the Catholic universities in the United States have been recognized as legal persons in canon law, derived their canonical status by their sponsoring institutions, or have assumed a special bond with the Church owing to their participation in the ministry and teaching office of the Church, they are subject to the canonical provisions embodied in the code of canon law (cc. 807–14), the provisions of *Ex corde Ecclesiae* and the NCCB's "*Ex corde Ecclesiae*: An Application to the United States."

Catholic Identity

Ex corde Ecclesiae devotes eighteen paragraphs to describing the identity of a Catholic university.[22] Yet some have asked, "what does Catholic identity entail?" Some representatives of Catholic universities are unclear as to the expectations of the Church with regard to the identity of a Catholic university. We will attempt to address those concerns

21. See Congregation de Institutione Catholica (de Seminariis at que Studiorum Institutis), *Index Editio 2005: Universitates et alia Instituta Studiorum Superiorum Ecclesiae Catholicae* (Vatican City: Libreria Editrice Vaticana, 2005), 82–123.

22. *EcE*, 12–29.

to better enable Catholic universities to understand and promote their Catholic identity.[23]

Pope Benedict XVI's 2008 Address to Catholic Educators

In his April 17, 2008, address to Catholic educators at the various levels of their respective institutions in the United States, Pope Benedict XVI commented on his interpretation of the role that Catholic identity should play in Catholic education.

A university or school's Catholic identity is not simply a question of the number of Catholic students. It is a question of conviction—do we really believe that only in the mystery of the Word made flesh does the mystery of man truly become clear (cf. *Gaudium et Spes*, 22)? Are we ready to commit our entire self-intellect and will, mind and heart—to God? Do we accept the truth Christ reveals? Is the faith tangible in our universities and schools? Is it given fervent expression liturgically, sacramentally, through prayer, acts of charity, a concern for justice and respect for God's creation? Only in this way do we really bear witness to the meaning of who we are and what we uphold.[24]

The Holy Father continued:

Clearly, then, Catholic identity is not dependent upon statistics. Neither can it be equated simply with orthodoxy of course content. It demands and inspires much more: namely that each and every aspect of your learning communities reverberates within the ecclesial life of faith. Only in faith can truth become incarnate and reason truly human, capable of directing the will along the path of freedom (cf. *Spe Salvi*, 23). In this way our institutions make a vital contribution to the mission of the church and truly serve society. They

23. For some of the scholarly debate, see James H. Provost, "The Sides of Catholic Identity," in *Enhancing Religious Identity: Best Practices from Catholic Campuses*, ed. John Wilcox and Irene King (Washington, DC: Georgetown University Press, 2000), 18–25; Monika K. Hellwig, "Emerging Patterns among Roman Catholic Colleges and Universities," in *The Future of Religious Colleges*, ed. Paul J. Dovre (Grand Rapids, MI: Eerdmans, 2002), 110–11; Roch Pagé, "From the Really Catholic to the Legally Catholic University," *Concilium* (1994): 91–99; J. Malone, "Reflections of Applying the Apostolic Constitution," *Origins* 23, no. 27 (December 16, 1993): 472–74; Miller, "Catholic Universities and Their Catholic Identity," 451–58; Archbishop Donald Wuerl, "The Marks of a Catholic College or University," *Origins* 37, no. 37 (February 28, 2008): 592–96.

24. Pope Benedict XVI, "Speech to Educators," *Origins* 37, no. 46 (May 1, 2008): 742.

become places in which God's active presence in human affairs is recognized and in which every young person discovers the joy of entering into Christ's "being for others" (cf. ibid., 28).[25]

Pope Benedict's remarks to Catholic educators were certainly intended to motivate Catholic educators to rededicate themselves and their institutions to the promotion of Catholic identity in all aspects of the lives of their institutions. Nevertheless, they did not give specific or concrete steps for Catholic educators to undertake to promote Catholic identity. In this setting, it would not have been appropriate for the Holy Father to do so, given the broad context of the audience, which ranged from diocesan directors of religious education to presidents of the largest Catholic universities in the United States. What can and should be done to promote Catholic identity would vary at the different levels of these institutions. Even so, it is apparent that the Holy Father, himself a former university professor, remained concerned that Catholic identity should pervade all aspects of the life of a university that promotes itself as a "Catholic university."

Reflections on and Proposed Solutions for Addressing Catholic Identity

A university that promotes itself as "Catholic" is meant to stand apart from other universities. That which distinguishes a Catholic university is its Catholic identity, which is important to the mission and purpose for which a Catholic university was founded. The Catholic identity of a university should pervade the university at all levels. Moreover, it should be evident from how the university operates and decisions are made that the university is in fact a "Catholic university."

To the extent that Catholic universities throughout the world have looked for guidance on how to promote their Catholic identity, certain concrete examples have been provided. These might include:

1. A Catholic university ought to further the Church's teachings on social ethics and protect the dignity of the human person. This should be manifested in all aspects of the operations of a Catholic university, particularly in the way representatives of the university interact with faculty, students, and members of the staff.

25. Ibid., 743.

2. A Catholic university should include Catholic identity in the discussions on hiring decisions of higher-level officials that are charged with promoting the Catholic identity of the university. This would enable the university to further its Catholic identity by hiring persons who are aware of its identity and committed to promoting the identity along with the university.

3. The Catholic identity of the university should also be a consideration in decisions regarding curriculum. This would not only include which courses are offered, such as theology and philosophy courses, but also decisions regarding how the university's Catholic identity ought to be incorporated into other courses, such as literature or fine arts. The university concerned about promoting its Catholic identity should consider offering courses dedicated to the writings of Catholic authors or the musical compositions of Catholic composers.

4. A Catholic university should also dialogue with external sources, such as its board of trustees, the Church's hierarchy, and canonical norms to promote its Catholic identity.

5. A Catholic university should support the Church's teaching on social justice issues and serve the preferential option for the poor.

6. Collaboration among Catholic universities is also important, especially with Catholic universities in underprivileged areas that might not have an abundance of resources available to them to promote their Catholic identity.

7. A Catholic university should look back to the reasons for which it was founded, particularly because most were founded to provide higher education from the perspective of the teachings of the Catholic Church.

These suggestions should be helpful for a Catholic university that wishes to promote its Catholic identity and ought to be considered. Nevertheless, they should not serve as benchmarks to identify all that a Catholic university should do to promote its Catholic identity. The university that wants to promote itself as "Catholic" should seek to incorporate its Catholic identity in all aspects of its life as a university, rather than just doing what is required of them. The goal of promoting Catholic identity should be such that the university is recognized as a truly Catholic university, rather than a Catholic-lite university.

Further, a university should promote its Catholic identity by comporting with the canonical requirements that the Church has established for such universities. Even in the absence of a juridic link, the relationship between a Catholic university and the Church and the willingness of a Catholic university to incorporate into its governing regulations the norms of the Church further demonstrate the Catholic identity of a university.

Hiring Practices

Article 4, section 4 of Part II of *Ex corde Ecclesiae* states that a majority of the faculty of a Catholic university should be baptized Catholics. "In order not to endanger the Catholic identity of the University or Institute of Higher Studies, the number of non-Catholic teachers should not be allowed to constitute a majority within the Institution, which is and must remain Catholic."[26] The intention of this provision is to assist a Catholic university with the preservation of its Catholic identity.

> The right to exercise religious preference in employment, at least with respect to some employees of [religiously affiliated colleges], is regarded by many administrators and members of governing boards of [religiously affiliated colleges] as crucial to preserving the distinct religious character of those institutions. This need has been voiced by leaders in church-related higher education.[27]

Yet a plain reading of this provision of *Ex corde Ecclesiae* indicates that the provision is merely suggestive in nature, rather than a mandatory requirement that a majority of the faculty at a Catholic university must be baptized Catholics. As a result, some Catholic universities may not feel compelled to implement the recommendation. This reluctance has also been supported by the argument that absent a juridic link with the Church, a Catholic university is not required to comply with this

26. *EcE*, art. 4, §4. Cf. NCCB, "Application of *Ex corde Ecclesiae* for the United States," Part 2, Art. 4, §4(a), emphasis added.

27. Fernand N. Dutile and Edward McGlynn Gaffney Jr., *State and Campus: State Regulation of Religiously Affiliated Higher Education* (Notre Dame, IN: University of Notre Dame Press, 1984), 14–15. See Giuseppe Pittau, "The Catholic College and University in the 21st Century," *Origins* 29, no. 35 (February 17, 2000): 564. See also James Heft and Fred P. Pestello, "Hiring Practices in Catholic Colleges and Universities," *Current Issues in Catholic Higher Education* 20, no. 1 (Fall 1999): 92.

provision.[28] Moreover, owing to concerns with the possibility for a discrimination lawsuit, some commentators have recommended against making any attempts to hire a majority of baptized Catholics as faculty members.[29]

In the following sections, I consider the effects of compliance with *Ex corde Ecclesiae*'s recommendation that a majority of the faculty should be baptized Catholics, particularly from the perspective of the antidiscrimination laws for the United States.

Preferential Hiring Practices at a Catholic University

Burling and Moffatt cautioned against implementing the critical mass provision of *Ex corde Ecclesiae* based on the potential for a lawsuit premised on the antidiscrimination laws of the United States. They based their argument on Title VII of the Civil Rights Act of 1964, 42 U.S.C. §2000e et seq., which was made applicable to public and private educational institutions in 1972 and prohibits certain types of discrimination in the employment context. The general prohibition provides at 42 U.S.C. §2000e–2(a):

It shall be an unlawful employment practice for an employer –

To fail or refuse to hire or to discharge any individual, or otherwise to discriminate against any individual with respect to his compensation, terms, conditions, or privileges of employment, because of such individual's race, color, religion, sex, or national origin; or

To limit, segregate, or classify his employees or applicants for employment in any way which would deprive or tend to deprive any individual of employment opportunities or otherwise adversely affect his status as an employee, because of such individual's race, color, religion, sex, or national origin.[30]

28. See Philip Burling and Gregory T. Moffatt, "Notes from the Other Side of the Wall: University Counsel's Reflections on Potential Interactions between the Civil Law and the Apostolic Constitution," in *Catholic Universities in Church and Society: A Dialogue on Ex corde Ecclesiae*, ed. John P. Langan (Washington, DC: Georgetown University Press, 1993), 153–75.

29. Ibid., 156. Cf. Gerard Bradley, "Legal Beagle: ECE's Best Friend May Be the Civil Law," in *Ex corde Ecclesiae: A Conversation "From the Heart of the Church" September 18, 1999*, ed. David O'Connell (Washington, DC: Catholic University of America, 1999), 30.

30. See 42 U.S.C. §2000e–2(a).

Thus the discrimination that the act is intended to prohibit is limited to the categories of race, color, religion, sex, and national origin. "It applies to all employers, public or private, who have more than a minimal number of employees, and thus it is probably the most sweeping and significant federal nondiscrimination statute."[31] Apparently the reason for making Title VII applicable to institutions of higher education was because of the assessment that a significant amount of discrimination was occurring in these institutions. "The legislative record supporting this amendment [in 1972] reflected the sense of Congress that a considerable amount of discrimination was occurring in higher education and that the previously sanctioned practice of deferring to purportedly 'academic decisions' about faculty employment was not serving the public interest."[32]

An allegation premised on antidiscrimination in the employment context can be based on two different types of claims: the "disparate treatment" claim and the "disparate impact" or "adverse impact" claim.[33]

> In the former type of suit, an individual denied a job, promotion, or tenure, or subjected to a detrimental employment condition, claims to have been treated less favorably than other applicants or employees because of his or her race, sex, national origin, or religion. In the "disparate impact" or "adverse impact" type of suit, the claim is that some ostensibly neutral policy of the employer has a discriminatory impact on the claimants or the class of persons they represent. Of the two types of suits, disparate treatment is the more common for postsecondary education. The disparate treatment and disparate impact theories are also sometimes used when claims are litigated under other nondiscrimination laws, such as the Equal Pay Act and Title IX of the Education Amendments of 1972.[34]

Burling and Moffatt cautioned a Catholic university against implementing *Ex corde Ecclesiae*'s critical mass provision because of their perceived threat of an antidiscrimination lawsuit against the university. Similarly, they argued that "attempting to attain compliance with this

31. Steven G. Poskanzer, *Higher Education Law: The Faculty* (Baltimore, MD: Johns Hopkins University Press, 2002), 160.

32. Ibid.

33. William A. Kaplan and Barbara A. Lee, *The Law of Higher Education*, 4th ed., vol. 1 (San Francisco: Jossey-Bass, 2006), 375.

34. Ibid., 375–76 (citations omitted). See also Poskanzer, *Higher Education Law*, 160–61.

requirement through the termination of non-Catholic faculty members (tenured or not) would involve civil lawsuits or de facto abandonment of secular status. Therefore, compliance can only be maintained (or, if necessary, attained) through attrition and/or hiring."[35]

Nevertheless, Burling and Moffatt also offered an alternative plan for a Catholic university that wishes to implement voluntarily the critical mass provision.

> An institution willing to take a risk by complying with section 4 would be advised to use a postemployment request that faculty list their religious faith for purposes of identifying resources for the student body. Disclosure in this instance would be voluntary and for a permitted purpose. Then, by abstracting anonymous data on numbers of Catholics in the faculty, the school can begin to comply with section 4. Maintaining data on the religious demography of the university community is not illegal if the names of particular persons are not included, so the numerical basis for compliance with the second sentence can be obtained without difficulty, as long as a reasonable number of the faculty provide the data requested. Since only the number of Catholics is needed to determine a majority, and the Catholic faculty are more likely to be willing to identify themselves in a Catholic university, this approach offers some hope of a nondiscriminatory solution to the compliance dilemma.[36]

Burling and Moffatt's argument recognized that there are viable solutions available to a Catholic university that wants to attempt to implement the critical mass provision of *Ex corde Ecclesiae.* Moreover, in addition to the argument that Burling and Moffatt made to circumvent the antidiscrimination prohibition, Title VII provides for an exemption from its requirements for religious employers.[37] In the next section, I

35. Burling and Moffatt, "Notes from the Other Side of the Wall," 157.

36. Ibid.

37. A religious exemption for discrimination is found in the European context as well. For example, Council Directive 2000/78/EC for the European Union provides at Article 23: "In very limited circumstances, a difference of treatment may be justified where a characteristic related to religion or belief, disability, age or sexual orientation constitutes a genuine and determining occupational requirement, when the objective is legitimate and the requirement is proportionate. Such circumstances should be included in the information provided by the Member States to the Commission." "Council Directive 2000/78/EC of 27 November 2000," in *Religion Related-Norms in European Union Law,* ed. Gerhard Robbers (Trier: Institut für Europäisches Verfassungsrecht Fachbereich Rechtswissenschaft Universität Trier, 2001), 17. For further consideration of employment discrimination in the

turn to the application of the religious exemption provision to claims of antidiscrimination to further assist Catholic universities that want to implement this provision.

Religious Exemption

Despite concerns that might have been raised when Congress amended Title VII to include employers of educational institutions within its purview of antidiscrimination, section 702(a) of Title VII, 42 U.S.C. §2000e–1(a) exempts religious employers from the antidiscrimination provisions under certain conditions. Section 2000e–1(a) of Title 42, U.S.C., provides:

> This title shall not apply to an employer with respect to the employment of aliens outside any State, or to a religious corporation, association, educational institution, or society with respect to the employment of individuals of a particular religion to perform work connected with the carrying on by such corporation, association, educational institution, or society of its activities.[38]

"The plain meaning of this provision is that Congress granted legal authority to support an employment policy whereby religious corporations, associations, or societies could legally exercise religious preference in job categories related to the religious activities of the groups."[39] Thus a religious educational institution is exempt from Title VII's antidiscrimination provisions with regard to employment decisions if the persons concerned are hired to perform work that is connected with the activities of the educational institution.

In addition to the religious exemption provision embodied in section 702, section 703 embodies two similar religious exemption provisions. Thus all employers are entitled "to take into account an individual's religion, sex, or national origin in cases where one or more of those categories might be a 'bona fide occupational qualification reasonably

---

European context, see M. Bell, *Anti-Discrimination Law and the European Union* (Oxford: Oxford University Press, 2002); M. D. Evans, *Religious Liberty and International Law in Europe* (Cambridge: Cambridge University Press, 1997); P. Van Dijk, F. Van Hoof, A. Van Rijn, and L. Zwaak, eds., *Theory and Practice of the European Convention on Human Rights* (Antwerp: Intersentia, 2006).

38. See 42 U.S.C. §2000e–1(a).

39. Moots and Gaffney, *Church and Campus*, 41. For a discussion of the legislative history of this religious exemption provision, see ibid., 40–47.

necessary to the normal operation of [a] particular business or enterprise.'"[40] Thus an individual must meet the recognized qualifications for both the position and also the institution where employed. This exemption is commonly referred to as the BFOQ exception, or the Bona Fide Occupational Qualification exception. Similarly, an amendment to the BFOQ exception was added to make the exemption specifically applicable to religiously affiliated colleges and universities. Section 703(e)(2) provides that

> it shall not be an unlawful employment practice for a school, college, university, or other educational institution or institution of learning to hire and employ employees of a particular religion if such school, college, university, or other educational institution or institution of learning is, in whole or in substantial part, owned, supported, controlled, or managed by a particular religion or by a particular religious corporation, association, or society, or if the curriculum of such school, college, university, or other educational institution or institution of learning is directed toward the propagation of a particular religion.[41]

Each of these religious exemption provisions may be available to a Catholic university in the employment context.[42]

The federal antidiscrimination law does not define what is included within the "activities" of the religious educational institution. But the US Supreme Court has broadly interpreted the meaning of the activities of a religious institution. For example, in *Church of Jesus Christ of Latter-Day Saints v. Amos*,[43] the court upheld a challenge to a decision by the Mormon church that required all employees of a gymnasium owned and operated by the church to be church members. The court considered whether the religious exemption provision that protected the gymnasium's employment requirement violated the First Amendment's establishment clause. Dismissing the challenge, the court applied the three-prong test previously announced in *Lemon v. Kurtzman*.[44] The Lemon test requires a secular legislative purpose, with a principal or primary

40. Ibid., 47, quoting Section 703(e)(1) [42 U.S.C. §2000e–2(e)(1)].

41. See 42 U.S.C. §2000e–2(e)(2). For a discussion of the legislative history of Section 703(e)(2), see Moots and Gaffney, *Church and Campus*, 52–54.

42. See Dutile and Gaffney, *State and Campus*, 16–17.

43. *Church of Jesus Christ of Latter-Day Saints v. Amos*, 483 U.S. 327 (1987).

44. *Lemon v. Kurtzman*, 403 U.S. 602 (1971).

effect that neither advances nor inhibits religion, and a substantial relationship between the activity and the sponsoring religious institution.[45] The court held that the gymnasium satisfied the requirements of the Lemon test. Further, the court noted that the purpose of the exemption "was to minimize governmental interference with the decision-making process in religions."[46] Kaplan and Lee saw this as an extension of the religious exemption to the antidiscrimination laws to all job positions of the religious institution.[47]

Numerous other cases have been litigated regarding the religious exemption to Title VII antidiscrimination claims. For example, in *Killinger v. Samford University*,[48] the issue involved whether Samford University was in fact a religious institution entitled to the exemption. The court considered the application of section 703(e)(2),[49] the Title VII exemption for religiously affiliated schools. Factors that the court found persuasive as evidence of the university's religious status included: the university's board of trustees, composed of members of the Baptist church, controlled the university; the university required students to attend religious convocations; the university promoted itself as a religious university in its advertising materials; the Baptist church provided a substantial portion of the university's budget; the university required all faculty to subscribe to the Baptist Statement of Faith and Message; and the Internal Revenue Service and the US Department of Education also considered the university to be a religious institution.[50] The court con-

45. *Church of Jesus Christ of Latter-Day Saints*, 483 U.S. at 335–36.

46. Ibid., at 336.

47. Kaplan and Lee, *Law of Higher Education*, 457: "The Supreme Court held that Section 702 does not distinguish between secular and religious job activities, and that the Section 702 exemption could apply to all job positions of a religious organization without violating the establishment clause."

48. *Killinger v. Samford University*, 917 F.Supp. 773 (N.D. Ala. 1996), *aff'd*, 113 F.3d 196 (11th Cir. 1997).

49. See 42 U.S.C. 2000e–2(e)(2): "it shall not be an unlawful employment practice for a school, college, university, or other educational institution or institution of learning to hire and employ employees of a particular religion if such school, college, university, or other educational institution or institution of learning is, in whole or in substantial part, owned, supported, controlled, or managed by a particular religion or by a particular religious corporation, association, or society, or if the curriculum of such school, college, university, or other educational institution or institution of learning is directed toward the propagation of a particular religion."

50. *Killinger*, 113 F.3d at 198. See *Hall v. Baptist Memorial Health Care Corporation d/b/a*

cluded: "to us, a teaching job in a divinity school of a religious educational institution is at the core of the section 702 exemption: the inherent purpose of such schools is the study of God and God's attributes."[51]

In *Pime v. Loyola University of Chicago*,[52] the question presented whether a religious university could reserve faculty positions for members of a certain religious institute. The appellate court considered the application of section 703(e)(1) of Title VII,[53] the more general exemption provision. In *Pime*, the court upheld a philosophy department's decision to reserve for Jesuit priests seven of the department's thirty-one tenure track positions. The court found the historical relationship between the university and the Jesuits to be significant and important to its operation.[54] Thus the religious exemption provision at issue in *Pime* protected this Catholic university from the claim of discrimination in

---

Baptist Memorial College of Health Sciences, 215 F.3d 618 (6th Cir. 2000): "The College atmosphere is permeated with religious overtones. It recruits students in Baptist publications and at Baptist Conventions. Prospective students are informed of the religious mission of the College at open houses. Incoming students are informed of this mission at orientation. The College seal includes a picture of the Bible and the words 'higher education with a higher purpose.' All students are required to take three hours of religious studies and must comply with a dress code that reflects 'Christian principles of appropriateness.' The College holds numerous prayer breakfasts and chapel programs. It has held several commencements at Baptist churches and hosted Baptist-sponsored programs. The fact that the College trains its students to be nurses and other health care professionals does not transform the institution into one that is secular. See, e.g., *Mississippi College*, 626 F.2d 477 (four-year co-educational liberal arts college owned and operated by the Mississippi Baptist convention is a 'religious educational institution'); *Siegel v. Truett-McConnell College, Inc.*, 13 F.Supp. 2d 1335 (N.D. Ga. 1994) (private co-educational college of liberal arts and sciences founded by the Georgia Baptist Convention is a 'religious educational institution' under Title VII)." Ibid. at 625. See also Kaplan and Lee, *Law of Higher Education*, 457–58.

51. *Killinger*, 113 F.3d, at 200.

52. *Pime v. Loyola University of Chicago*, 803 F.2d 251 (7th Cir. 1986).

53. See 42 U.S.C. §2000e–2(e)(1): "it shall not be an unlawful employment practice for an employer to hire and employ employees, for an employment agency to classify, or refer for employment any individual, for a labor organization to classify its membership or to classify or refer for employment any individual, or for an employer, labor organization, or joint labor-management committee controlling apprenticeship or other training or retraining programs to admit or employ any individual in any such program, on the basis of his religion, sex, or national origin in those certain instances where religion, sex, or national origin is a bona fide occupational qualification reasonably necessary to the normal operation of that particular business or enterprise."

54. Kaplan and Lee, *Law of Higher Education*, 458.

choosing to give preference to the Jesuit Catholic priests rather than to the Jewish philosophy teacher who challenged the decision.

Also of significance in this area is a case that involved a decision by the Catholic University of America to not grant tenure to a Dominican Sister who taught in the Department of Canon Law. In *EEOC v. Catholic University*,[55] the appellate court for the District of Columbia held in favor of the Catholic University of America on Dominican Sister Elizabeth McDonough's claim of sex discrimination under Title VII involving the university's decision not to grant tenure. Sister McDonough argued that because she was not an ordained minister and did not perform a religious function at the university, the religious exemption to Title VII should not apply. The appellate court disagreed and ruled that it was irrelevant whether Sister McDonough was an ordained minister. The appellate court also ruled that, despite her assertion to the contrary, Sister McDonough did perform religious duties because part of the function of the Department of Canon Law was to instruct students, including men who were studying for ordained ministry, about the laws of the Church. Thus the university was entitled to raise the religious exemption to preclude judicial review of its decision not to grant tenure to Sister McDonough.[56]

Reflections on and Proposed Solutions for Addressing Hiring Practices

In making voluntary rather than obligatory the provision of *Ex corde Ecclesiae* with regard to striving to hire baptized Catholics to be faculty members at a Catholic university, Pope John Paul II indirectly acknowledged that some Catholic universities might be located within areas where the laws of the jurisdiction could affect the ability of the university to comply with the provision. Although some commentators have urged Catholic universities to use caution and discretion when deciding whether to implement the provision, they have also recognized that efforts can be made to implement the provision without contravening laws that might prohibit this activity, such as the antidiscrimination laws in the United States. For example, we looked at a proposal that Burling and Moffatt made that would allow a Catholic university to gather

55. *EEOC v. The Catholic University of America*, 83 F.3d 455 (D.C. Cir. 1996).

56. Kaplan and Lee, *Law of Higher Education*, 461–62.

data about the faith dimension of faculty members without requesting such information as a prescreening employment device. Nevertheless, if the proposal is only for collecting data, it is not really a policy to achieve the goal of hiring baptized Catholics to serve as faculty members. Thus their proposal is not beneficial to a Catholic university that is trying to comply with these canonical requirements.

In addition to other similar efforts that might be made to get around the laws that prohibit antidiscrimination, because a Catholic university should be considered a religious educational institution, it would also be entitled to raise as a defense the various religious exemption provisions embodied in Title VII. As shown above, these provisions have been interpreted broadly to protect the activities of a religiously affiliated university that wishes to further its religious affiliation.

Similarly, Moots and Gaffney concluded that a Catholic university "would not by the exercise of religious preference in selection of its faculty and administrative staff forfeit eligibility to receive public institutional assistance, and that such a policy would not endanger the eligibility of its students for public financial assistance."[57]

Nevertheless, a university that considers itself to be Catholic but picks and chooses how to demonstrate its Catholicity might find itself in the precarious position of facing the possibility of obtaining a juridical ruling that the university is not entitled to the religious exemption defense because the extent of its Catholicity might be questioned. As demonstrated in *Killinger*, challenges have been made to the availability of the religious exemption provisions of Title VII based on the university's religious affiliation. A university that chooses to distance itself from the Church's teachings and canonical requirements runs the risk of being unprotected by the religious exemption provisions if a discrimination claim were to be brought. Thus a university that claims to be a de facto Catholic university, but not subject to the laws of the Church because it has no juridic link with the Church, might be subject to discrimination challenge if it engaged in the practice of preferentially hiring Catholics. It is reasonable to conclude that, in evaluating the evidence to support whether a university that claims to be Catholic and thus entitled to a religious exemption, a court would look to whether

57. Moots and Gaffney, *Church and Campus*, 70.

such a university attempts to comply with the laws of the Church as well as to other ways in which it aligns itself with the Church to which it claims to be religiously affiliated. In such a situation, a university that purports to be Catholic might be handed a judicial decision that, at least for purposes of the civil law, it is not entitled to religious exemption because in fact it is not a Catholic university. Further, it would seem reasonable to conclude that the Holy See might be persuaded by such a decision and pronounce also that the university is not Catholic and not entitled to promote itself as a Catholic university.

In contrast, it seems that the more a university that considers itself to be Catholic aligns itself with the teachings of the Church, including the laws of the Church with regard to Catholic universities, the more likely that the religious exemption provisions would protect such a university for preferentially hiring baptized Catholics as faculty members.[58]

Pope John Paul II stated that "the identity of a Catholic University is essentially linked to the quality of its teachers and to respect for Catholic doctrine."[59] A Catholic university promotes its Catholic identity by hiring baptized Catholics to be members of its faculty. Archbishop Pittau argued for ongoing education efforts for faculty members to assist them with promoting the Catholic identity of the institution and engaging the dialogue with non-Catholic faculty members.

> The same Catholic Church which asks us to be faithful to our Catholic tradition and our Catholic roots asks us also to entertain an ongoing and mutually enriching dialogue with Christians of other denominations and with people of other religions and with modern culture. In order to establish a meaningful dialogue, which goes beyond an atmosphere of general good will and nondenominationalism, it is extremely important that the "Catholic core" be well prepared and well versed in the Catholic tradition. Programs should be offered for the initial and continuing faith formation of Catholic faculty and administrators. The founding religious congregations and the sponsoring dioceses made great sacrifices in the formation of sisters, brothers

58. See Moots and Gaffney, *Church and Campus*, 70; Hellwig, "Emerging Patterns among Roman Catholic Colleges and Universities," 112; and Arthur Gross Schaefer and Dan Van Bogaert, "The Changing Legal Landscape for Clergy," *Catholic Lawyer* 42 (2002): 117.

59. *EcE*, art. 4, §1.

and priests who could carry on the difficult but indispensible apostolate of higher education.[60]

Thus a well-prepared critical mass of baptized Catholic faculty members is essential to a Catholic university.

As argued above, the more a Catholic university comports with the laws of the Church, the more likely it will be that the religious exemption provisions of Title VII would protect a university that practices preferential hiring. But the more a university distances itself from the Church and her laws, the more it exposes itself to liability because the extent of its religious affiliation is more remote. A Catholic university that opts to distance itself from the laws of the Church ought to be careful in this regard.

Contracts in Institutions of Catholic Higher Education

The relationship that exists between a Catholic university and its professors is a contractual one. "This is a realm in which contract law is king. One must always remember that faculty are employees bound to their employer colleges or universities by written or unwritten contract and that the rights and obligations flowing between the parties are determined by those contracts."[61] The laws of the jurisdiction in which the Catholic university is located would typically dictate the interpretation of the contract, whether written or oral, that exists between a university and its employees. The parties could also agree as part of the contract that the laws of another jurisdiction could be used to address the relationship, provided that the jurisdiction selected has some connection with the relationship and could adequately protect the parties. More specifically, at a Catholic university, the parties to the contract could agree to incorporate the laws of the Church into the contract in addition to the laws of a jurisdiction agreed upon as controlling. Thus, as Kaplan and Lee pointed out, "some religiously affiliated institutions require their faculty to observe the code of conduct dictated by the doc-

60. Pittau, "Catholic College and University in the 21st Century," 564.

61. Poskanzer, *Higher Education Law*, 182.

trine of the religious sponsor; others incorporate church law or canon law into their contracts."[62] Many universities have incorporated standard university policies and procedures into the terms of an agreement with individual faculty members, particularly when formal written contracts might not be used.[63] Thus it would not be uncommon for a Catholic university to incorporate the provisions of canon law into its contracts with employees. To do so would also help the university to promote or make efforts to promote its Catholic identity.

Moreover, because a Catholic university is a religiously affiliated university, in the United States, the provisions of the First Amendment to the US Constitution would be at issue in interpreting the contract.[64] The protection that a Catholic university would be afforded in a breach of contract claim could be of assistance in dealing with claims that arise out of circumstances that suggest that an individual professor has acted contrary to the provisions of canon law. In the following sections, I consider some of the challenges associated with application of Canons 810 and 812 at a Catholic university and reflect on the likelihood that a Catholic university could address the dictates of these canonical norms without violating the civil laws of the jurisdiction in which the university is located.

Canon 810: Causes for Termination

Canon 810 states:

> §1. The authority competent according to the statutes has the duty to make provision so that teachers are appointed in Catholic universities who besides their scientific and pedagogical qualifications are outstanding in integrity of doctrine and probity of life and that they are removed from their function when they lack these requirements; the manner of proceeding defined in the statutes is to be observed.
>
> §2. The conferences of bishops and diocesan bishops concerned have the duty and right of being watchful so that the principles of Catholic doctrine are observed faithfully in these same universities.[65]

62. Kaplan and Lee, *Law of Higher Education*, 485.

63. See Poskanzer, *Higher Education Law*, 184.

64. See Kaplan and Lee, *Law of Higher Education*, 485–86.

65. Canon 810.

Burling and Moffatt offered three scenarios involving the dismissal of tenured[66] faculty members that may be likely to occur at a Catholic university and involve the application of Canon 810.[67] For example, they presented the dilemma of a faculty member who has an affair with a student, the situation of those Catholics who have been divorced and remarried outside of the Church without first obtaining a declaration of nullity from the Church, and the case of a priest who was granted tenure at the university but later abandoned his priestly duties without obtaining a decree of laicization and then attempted marriage outside of the Church. Each of these scenarios by that Burling and Moffatt has two things in common. First, Burling and Moffatt, both civil attorneys, advised against relying solely on the provisions of canon law for resolving employment issues. Second, the proposed solution that they offered to address each of these scenarios involved including language in the contractual agreement between the parties or the faculty handbook,[68] which would be incorporated into a faculty employment contract. The provisions of the contract would enable a Catholic university to dismiss a faculty member who has violated the provisions of Canon 810 and the parallel provisions in *Ex corde Ecclesiae*. Thus even Burling and Moffatt have not advised against dismissing offending faculty members, but rather they advised to proceed with caution in dismissing them for breaching their contract with the university rather than dismissing them for violating canon law.

Canon 812: Mandate to Teach the Theological Disciplines

Canon 812 requires that "those who teach theological disciplines in any institutes of higher studies whatsoever must have a mandate from the competent ecclesiastical authority."[69] A plain reading of Canon 812 suggests that a Catholic university has no direct role in obtaining the mandate for one who teaches the theological disciplines. The obligation

66. Cf. Poskanzer, *Higher Education Law*, 202.

67. Burling and Moffatt, "Notes from the Other Side of the Wall," 159–62.

68. Charles H. Wilson, "Catholic Campus Trustees and American Civil Law," in *Mission and Identity: A Handbook for Trustees of Catholic Colleges and Universities* (Washington, DC: Association of Governing Boards of Universities and Colleges, 2003), 89: "Civil courts generally consider a college's faculty handbook to be part of a faculty member's contract."

69. Canon 812.

falls to the individual professor.[70] Yet, as Wilson pointed out, "the *Application* does provide for a role for the university: 'If a particular professor lacks a *mandatum* and continues to teach a theological discipline, the university must determine what further action may be taken in accordance with its own mission and statutes.'"[71]

It would seem prudent that if a Catholic university wishes to act on such a decision, it should also address this requirement in its faculty handbook or contract with faculty members in a manner similar to what Burling and Moffatt advocated for challenges involving Canon 812. As stated above, if such a situation were to arise, the university is supposed to act in accord with its mission and statutes. Wilson also acknowledged the need for the university to act to modify its governing documents in this regard.

> The *mandatum* requirement is an obvious example of a provision of the Apostolic Constitution and the Application that will require changes in the faculty handbook, should the governing board endorse that requirement. In that case, the faculty handbook would have to be amended to state the *mandatum* requirement, to explain how the *mandatum* is obtained, and to delineate the consequences for failing to seek or obtain a *mandatum*. In addition, the contracts signed by Catholic members of the theology department also should be amended to contain that information. Finally, advertisements recruiting new members for the theology department would have to describe adequately the *mandatum* requirement for Catholic applicants for vacancies in that department.[72]

Similar to the situation with regard to the enforcement of Canon 810, if a university decided to take disciplinary action against a theologian who was denied a mandate by the bishop or the bishop withdrew the mandate, the university would be well advised to act on its governing documents or contracts with faculty members to support its reliance upon canon law.

70. See Wilson, "Catholic Campus Trustees and American Civil Law," 86.

71. Ibid.

72. Ibid., 89.

Judicial Review of Employment Contracts in Catholic Institutions

Numerous cases have been litigated that illustrate how a Catholic university can limit the potential for liability on a breach of contract claim that involve principles of canon law. For example, in *Curran v. Catholic University of America*,[73] a professor of theology who had been granted tenure at the university alleged a claim for breach of contract because the university refused to allow the plaintiff professor to continue to teach courses that considered Catholic theology. The impetus for the university's decision arose because the Holy See had informed the university that the professor was no longer able to teach Catholic theology because he had publicly objected to certain teachings of the Magisterium. As a result, the university's board of trustees withdrew the professor's canonical mission to teach in university departments that awarded ecclesiastical degrees. The court considered controlling the question of whether the parties intended to be bound by canon law, which in this case was not incorporated specifically into the contract that was at issue. The court found that the professor knew that the Holy See could dictate the requirements for ecclesiastical faculties and that the university was bound by those requirements. Moreover, the court considered the fact that members of an ecclesiastical faculty were bound by the provisions of *Sapientia Christiana* and were not to oppose the teachings of the Magisterium. Kaplan and Lee summarized the court's ruling:

> The court ruled that the university had the right to require faculty who taught theology to meet the requirements of the Holy See, since that body could withdraw the university's authority to award ecclesiastical degrees if the university failed to comply with its requirements. Because the university had a special relationship with the Holy See, the court found implied in Curran's contract with the university an obligation to abide by the Holy See's requirements. The court also found that, whatever academic freedom Curran was due, his academic freedom could not limit the Holy See's authority to determine which ecclesiastical faculty were qualified to teach theology.[74]

73. *Curran v. The Catholic University of America*, Civ. No. 1562–87, 117 *Daily Wash. L.R.* 656 (D.C. Super. Ct., February 28, 1987).

74. Kaplan and Lee, *Law of Higher Education*, 486–87. See also Robert K. Poch, *Ac-*

The court in the *Curran* case held that the provisions of canon law were intended to be incorporated into the contract between the parties even though the requirement was not specifically included in a document reflecting that intent. Once the court reached that conclusion, it refrained from interpreting the provisions of canon law.

In *Alicea v. New Brunswick Seminary*,[75] the court considered a decision that the Reform Church's Board of Theological Education had made to reserve to itself all decisions on the hiring and retention of faculty. The court refused to consider whether the seminary had breached an implied contract with the plaintiff, who was a nontenured professor at the seminary. Kaplan and Lee described the basis for the court's ruling: "Governmental interference with the polity, i.e., church governance, of a religious institution could also violate the First Amendment by impermissibly limiting the institution's options in choosing those employees whose role is instrumental in charting the course for the faithful."[76] Alternatively, the court considered controlling the fact that the plaintiff performed a ministerial function in the teaching of theology to and the counseling of future ministers. This was an additional reason for the court to abstain from exercising jurisdiction in the matter.[77]

Similarly, in *McEnroy v. St. Meinrad School of Theology*,[78] a professor who taught Catholic theology and doctrine at a seminary that trained candidates for priesthood brought a claim for breach of contract. The plaintiff's contract had not been renewed because he signed a public statement that opposed the Holy Father's teaching on the ordination of women to the priesthood. The trial court abstained from considering the matter because "judicial review of the complaint would require

---

ademic Freedom in American Higher Education: Rights, Responsibilities and Limitations, ASHE-ERIC Higher Education Report No. 4 (Washington, DC: George Washington University, School of Education and Human Development, 1993), 64–67.

75. *Alicea v. New Brunswick Theological Seminary*, 608 A.2d 218 (N.J. 1992).

76. Kaplan and Lee, *Law of Higher Education*, 487, citing *Alicea*, 608 A.2d, at 222.

77. *Alicea*, 608 A.2d, at 223. See also *Petruska v. Gannon University*, 462 F.3d 294 (3d Cir. 2006), at 312: "The First Amendment protects a church's right to decide matters of faith and to declare its doctrine free from state interference. A church's ability to select who will perform particular spiritual functions is a necessary corollary to this right. The function of Petruska's position as University Chaplain was ministerial in nature, and therefore, her Title VII, civil conspiracy, and negligent retention and supervision claims—each of which directly turns on the propriety of Gannon's personnel decisions—must be dismissed."

78. *McEnroy v. St. Meinrad School of Theology*, 713 N.E.2d 334 (Ct. App. Ind. 1999).

the court to decide religious issues regarding the Church's good faith motivation and doctrinal basis for removing the plaintiff under canon law."[79]

In *Patterson v. Southwestern Baptist Theological Seminary*,[80] a faculty member brought a claim against a Baptist seminary after he was discharged for failing to comport his lifestyle and behavior with what was expected of a seminary faculty member. The court found significant the requirement included in the seminary's faculty handbook that members of the faculty were to be active and faithful members of a Baptist church and to profess fidelity to the Articles of Faith of the Southern Baptist Convention. "The explicit inclusion of these requirements in the faculty handbook made it evident that the seminary 'makes employment decisions regarding faculty members largely upon religious criteria,' rendering judicial review of the discharge decision a violation of the Constitution's First and Fourteenth Amendments."[81]

In *Hartwig v. Albertus Magnus College*,[82] a former priest taught in the department of religious studies and philosophy. The university dismissed him after someone had sent to the university president newspaper articles that identified the plaintiff as a former priest who had purportedly attempted to marry another man. The court agreed with the university that the plaintiff's defamation claim would require the court to ascertain whether a priest remains a priest forever after leaving active ministry as a priest. Nevertheless, the court allowed the plaintiff to pro-

79. Kaplan and Lee, *Law of Higher Education*, 489. See *McEnroy*, 713 N.E.2d, at 336–37.

80. *Patterson v. Southwestern Baptist Theological Seminary*, 858 S.W.2d 602 (Tex. Ct. App. 1993).

81. Kaplan and Lee, *Law of Higher Education*, 489–90. See *Patterson*, 858 S.W.2d, at 606: "The current case is most similar to *Milivojevich*, in which the court concluded that the civil court may not decide whether the church complied with the procedural rules contained in the church constitution and penal code in defrocking one of its bishops. *Milivojevich*, 426 U.S. 722–23, 96 S. Ct. 2386–87, 49 L. Ed. 2d 170–71. The court also announced the trial court may not use the guise of the 'neutral principles' approach to delve into issues concerning whether the general church acted beyond its authority under the church constitution in declaring a reorganization of the Dioceses. *Id.* Just as the church constitution concerns the internal governance of the Diocese, the bylaws concern the internal governance of the Southwestern Baptist Theological Seminary. Therefore, the trial court could not delve into issues concerning whether Patterson's employment was terminated in accordance therewith."

82. *Hartwig v. Albertus Magnus College*, 93 F.Supp. 2d 200 (D. Conn. 2000).

ceed on his claim for breach of contract against the university, presumably because the contract claim did not involve issues of canon law.[83]

Nevertheless, given the proper facts, courts have also ruled against the university employer. For example, in *Welter v. Seton Hall University*,[84] two Ursuline Sisters brought claims for breach of contract when the university did not renew their contracts to teach computer science. Because the Sisters taught computer science, the court did not consider them to be fulfilling a ministerial function. The court was further persuaded that the claim did not involve teachings of the Magisterium or matters of Church governance. The court was persuaded that there was substantial evidence that the university terminated the Sisters' contracts because they had not performed their job duties in the manner that was expected. Thus the court found that the provisions of canon law were not implicated in these particular circumstances.[85]

In 2012, the US Supreme Court unanimously approved a "ministerial exception" to federal antidiscrimination law. *Hosanna-Tabor Evangelical Lutheran Church & School v. EEOC*[86] interpreted the religious exemption embodied in the Americans with Disabilities Act (ADA) and Title VII of the Civil Rights Act of 1964 that permit faith-based institutions to discriminate on the basis of religion. The Equal Employment Opportunity Commission sued on behalf of Cheryl Perich, a teacher at an elementary school teacher sponsored by the Lutheran Synod. The school employed two categories of teachers: lay teachers and those teachers who had been "called." Lay teachers were not required to have any specific theological training or even be practicing Lutherans. But a "called" teacher was required to be a practicing Lutheran with theological training, pass a theological examination, and receive the endorsement of the Lutheran Synod. A "called" teacher was commissioned and received the title "Minister of Religion, Commissioned." Perich began

83. Kaplan and Lee, *Law of Higher Education*, 490. See *Hartwig*, 93 F.Supp. 2d, at 215.

84. *Welter v. Seton Hall University*, 608 A.2d 206 (1992).

85. See *Welter*, 608 A.2d 206, at 216. See generally Bruce N. Bagni, "Discrimination in the Name of the Lord: A Critical Evaluation of Discrimination by Religious Organizations," *Columbia Law Review* 79 (1979): 1539–41 (discussing the factors relevant to the determination of whether the religious institution performs a secular or nonsecular function).

86. *Hosanna-Tabor Evangelical Lutheran Church & School v. EEOC*, 565 US 171, 132 S.Ct. 694 (2012).

working at the school as a lay teacher, but after completing the necessary requirements was commissioned as a "called" teacher. Although she taught primarily secular subjects, she also taught religion. She led her students in prayer, and she led worship services. Following a leave of absence for narcolepsy, school officials asked Perich to resign because they believed her narcolepsy could be harmful to students. When she refused to do so, the school rescinded her "call" and terminated her employment.

Writing for a unanimous Supreme Court, Chief Justice John Roberts said, "the Establishment Clause prevents the Government from appointing ministers, and the Free Exercise Clause prevents it from interfering with the freedom of religious groups to select their own."[87] Because the ministerial exception is grounded in both clauses, the court recognized that a religious employer has the right to determine whom to employ as a minister. The government is not to interfere with these decisions.

In his concurring opinion, Justice Samuel Alito proposed that the court should concentrate more on the functions that a minister performed rather than being tied to a particular title. He maintained that the ministerial exception

> should apply to any "employee" who leads a religious organization, conducts worship services or important religious ceremonies or rituals, or serves as a messenger or teacher of its faith. If a religious group believes that the ability of such employee to perform these key functions has been compromised, then the constitutional guarantee of religious freedom protects the group's right to remove the employee from his or her position.[88]

Thus it is important in assessing contractual disputes to consider the nature of the function that the plaintiff employee performed, that is, the extent to which their job duties entailed ministerial functions rather than purely secular duties. The more remote the association with ministry, the less likely the courts will abstain from exercising jurisdiction.

These cases have demonstrated the courts' reluctance to get involved in interpreting matters of canon law or Church governance. The more the relationship between a Catholic university and its employee can be

87. *Hosanna-Tabor*, 132 S. Ct., at 703.
88. *Hosanna-Tabor*, 132 S. Ct., at 713 (J. Alito, concurring).

described as a ministerial one, the more likely the court will abstain from considering the propriety of the university's action if a dismissed plaintiff were to bring a claim for breach of contract. In contrast, if the person is performing a purely secular role at a Catholic university, it seems more probable that a court would intervene and adjudicate the issues pursuant to the law of the jurisdiction in which the university is located.

Additionally, although some courts have ruled in favor of a Catholic university even in the absence of a specific provision in the employment contract at issue, it would be prudent, as Burling and Moffatt have advised, for a Catholic university to address issues of contract interpretation in sufficient detail so as to incorporate the provisions of canon law and Church governance within the agreement of the parties.

Dealing with Non-Catholic Employees

In Part I of *Ex corde Ecclesiae*, Article 27, Pope John Paul II stated that "non-Catholic members [of a Catholic university] are required to respect the Catholic character of the University, while the University in turn respects their religious liberty."[89] Similarly, in Article 4, section 4 of the apostolic constitution's General Norms, the Holy Father indicated that "those university teachers and administrators who belong to other Churches, ecclesial communities, or religions, as well as those who profess no religious belief, and also all students, are to recognize and respect the distinctive Catholic identity of the University."[90]

Questions might be raised as to whether these provisions would be limited to baptized Catholics who are employed at Catholic universities or whether they can be extended to non-Catholic employees. In *Little v. Wuerl*,[91] a teacher who was not Catholic brought a claim against the Roman Catholic Diocese of Pittsburgh and Bishop Donald Wuerl, who was the bishop of the diocese at the time. The plaintiff was employed at a parish elementary school within the diocese, but "was not given responsibility for teaching religion ... and participated in the school's programs for teachers that were intended to strengthen their ability to

89. *EcE*, 27.

90. *EcE*, art. 4, §4.

91. *Little v. Wuerl*, 929 F.2d 944 (3d Cir. 1991).

impart 'Catholic' values to students."[92] She based her claim on discrimination when her employment contract was not renewed because she divorced and remarried. The diocese argued that even though the teacher had performed well and had even been granted tenure, she violated her employment contract when she remarried. The relevant portion of the contract stated:

> Teacher recognizes the religious nature of the Catholic School and agrees that Employer has the right to dismiss a teacher for serious public immorality, public scandal, or public rejection of the official teachings, doctrine or laws of the Roman Catholic Church, thereby terminating any and all rights that the Teacher may have hereunder, subject, however, to the personal due process rights promulgated by the Roman Catholic Church.[93]

In addition to the "Cardinal's Clause," the contract incorporated the diocese's *Handbook of Personnel Policies and Procedures*, which provided examples of cause for employment termination. The *Handbook* provided:

> One example of termination for just cause is a violation of what is understood to be the Cardinal's Clause. The Cardinal's Clause requires the dismissal of the teacher for serious public immorality, public scandal or public rejection of the official teachings, doctrine or laws of the Catholic Church. *Examples of the violation of this clause would be the entry of a teacher into a marriage which is not recognized by the Catholic Church*, or the support of activities which espouse beliefs contrary to Church teaching, e.g., advocacy of a practice such as abortion.[94]

The court also made an interesting observation that the diocese "took very seriously its mission to be a Catholic presence in a secular world … [and] changed its policy in 1984 to favor hiring only Catholics and to require that any school hiring a non-Catholic get special permission."[95] This policy did not, however, affect the plaintiff's status because she began working for the diocese prior to the policy change.

At the time that the diocese initially hired the plaintiff, she had recently been married in a Protestant religious ceremony. She later di-

92. Ibid., at 945.
93. Ibid.
94. Ibid., at 946, emphasis original.
95. Ibid.

vorced her husband from that marriage and attempted to marry a man who had been baptized in the Catholic Church, although he purportedly did not practice any particular religion. The plaintiff did not seek a declaration of nullity of her prior marriage before attempting to marry the baptized Catholic. The diocese did not rehire the plaintiff "because she had remarried … without pursuing the proper canonical process available from the Roman Catholic Church to obtain validation of her second marriage."[96] The court acknowledged that "Little makes no claim to be Catholic. Nevertheless, if this court were to review the Parish's decision, it would be forced to determine what constitutes 'the official teachings, doctrine of laws of the Roman Catholic Church' and whether plaintiff has 'rejected' them."[97] Thus the *Little* court concurred with the jurisprudence of other courts to abstain from reviewing a decision of an ecclesiastical nature even though the plaintiff was not a baptized Catholic but chose to subject herself to the canonical laws of the Church by attempting to marry a baptized Catholic. Moreover, the conduct in which she engaged was prohibited by her employment contract.

The example of *Little* significantly points to the importance of including in employment contracts and employee handbooks the terms and conditions for employment at a Catholic university. These terms should address the various circumstances that would promote the university's Catholic identity as well as point to the circumstances that would detract from the university's Catholic identity and serve as just cause for termination. If these terms are properly included in the university's governing documents and employment contracts, *Little* suggests that a Catholic university would be protected in its relationships with all employees, including those who are not baptized Catholics.

Reflections on and Proposed Solutions for Addressing Contracts in Catholic Universities

The relationship between a Catholic university and its employees is based on a contract, whether oral or written. The provisions of a written contract may be specifically set forth in a single document or embodied in multiple documents, such as an employee handbook, that are incorporated by reference into the contract. Nevertheless, it would seem pru-

96. Ibid.

97. Ibid., at 948.

dent for a Catholic university that intends to take action to enforce the provisions of canon law as they affect employment decisions, specifically Canons 810 and 812, to protect itself from liability on multiple levels.

First, it would seem wise for a Catholic university to include in its employment contracts a specific incorporation of the provisions of canon law such that the parties are reasonably on notice that these provisions, in addition to civil laws, would control the interpretation of the contract. Second, a Catholic university ought to address in a contract provision specific examples of conduct that would violate canon law, indicating potential reasons for just cause for termination. Lastly, as demonstrated above, courts have been reluctant to get involved with the interpretation of employment contracts that would require the court to interfere with matters of Church governance or the interpretation of canon law.[98] These principles would be particularly appropriate to the extent that the employee performed a ministerial duty such as teaching theology. The further removed that they might be from a ministerial function to a purely secular role, the more difficult it would be for a Catholic university to prevail. Nevertheless, it seems that these principles could be extended to relationships with non-Catholic employees, provided that they are sufficiently addressed in their employment contracts as well.

The Catholic University's Role in the Catholic Church

Ex corde Ecclesiae invited Catholic universities to become more involved in the Church and to assist the Church with her various missions. In this section, I consider various ways in which a Catholic university might be involved in the Church at both the universal and local levels. I also consider how disputes between theologians and the local bishop might be addressed as suggested in the NCCB's *Application*.

The Universal and Local Church

In Part I of *Ex corde Ecclesiae*, Catholic universities are reminded that they are part of both the universal Church and the local church in which

98. See "Judicial Review of Employment Contracts in Catholic Institutions" above.

it is situated. Because of this relationship, Pope John Paul II maintained that the Catholic university assumed a special bond with the Holy See. "One consequence of its essential relationship to the Church is that the institutional fidelity of the University to the Christian message includes a recognition and adherence to the teaching authority of the Church in matters of faith and morals."[99] The Holy Father also reminded bishops throughout the world that they have a responsibility to promote Catholic universities and to dialogue with theologians. "Because of their interrelated roles, dialogue between Bishops and theologians is essential; this is especially true today, when the results of research are so quickly and so widely communicated through the media."[100]

Ex corde Ecclesiae extends into its General Norms the concern for the relationship that should exist between a Catholic university and the Church. These Norms are embodied in Article 5 of *Ex corde Ecclesiae*'s Part II. Specifically, regarding the obligations of the Catholic university, section 1 provides:

> Every Catholic University is to maintain communion with the universal Church and the Holy See; it is to be in close communion with the local Church and in particular with the diocesan Bishops of the region or nation in which it is located. In ways consistent with its nature as a University, a Catholic University will contribute to the Church's work of evangelization.[101]

To assist in keeping ecclesiastical authorities aware of the activities of a Catholic university, Catholic universities are to periodically report to the competent ecclesiastical authority. Catholic universities that were established by the Holy See, an episcopal conference, diocesan bishop, or a religious institute or other public juridic person are to submit their reports to the competent ecclesiastical authority. Catholic universities established by others are to submit their report to the local ordinary.[102]

While *Ex corde Ecclesiae* charged Catholic universities to be involved in the universal and local Church, the apostolic constitution does not provide specific details on how a Catholic university ought to go about doing this. This may have been intentional on the Holy Father's

99. *EcE*, 27.
100. *EcE*, 29.
101. *EcE*, art. 5, §1.
102. *EcE*, art. 5, §3.

part so that the episcopal conferences, when drafting their ordinances to implement *Ex corde Ecclesiae*, could consider more particular aspects of how Catholic universities can fulfill their role in the Church.[103]

Accordingly, the NCCB's *Application*[104] does provide some guidance on how a Catholic university ought to fulfill its role in the Church. The *Application*'s Article 5 speaks to the topic. But the *Application* could be considered to be rather general. Again, this may have been intentional to allow individual Catholic universities to be creative in developing ways most appropriate for them to fulfill their role in the Church. For example, section 1(a) directs a Catholic university to "develop and maintain a plan for fulfilling its mission that communicates and develops the Catholic intellectual tradition, is of service to the Church and society, and encourages the members of the university community to grow in the practice of the faith."[105] Section 1(b) further suggests that this plan should consider such issues as "intellectual and pastoral contributions to the mission of communicating Gospel values, service to the poor, social justice initiatives, and ecumenical and inter-religious activities."[106] At the level of the local church, the *Application* directs a Catholic university and the local bishop to be in dialogue and collaboration. For example, section 2(c) directs mutual commitment "to regular dialogues to achieve the goals of *Ex corde Ecclesiae* according to local needs and circumstances."[107] Collaboration should be practical and "harmonious with the university's structure and statutes. Similar forms of collaboration should also exist between the university and the religious institute to which it is related by establishment or tradition."[108]

For a Catholic university looking for more concrete suggestions on how to fulfill its role in the Church, much of what was considered above regarding how to promote the university's Catholic identity would also

103. See *EcE*, art. 1, §2.

104. NCCB, "Application of *Ex corde Ecclesiae* for the United States," 402–9. See also Committee on Education, Bishops' and Presidents' Subcommittee, USCCB, *Catholic Identity in Our Colleges and Universities*, 75–94; Gallin, *Ex corde Ecclesiae*, 388–406.

105. NCCB, "Application of *Ex corde Ecclesiae* for the United States," Part 2, Art. 5, §1(a).

106. Ibid., Part 2, Art. 5, §1(b).

107. Ibid., Part 2, Art. 5, §2(c).

108. Ibid., Part 2, Art. 5, §2(d).

be helpful here.[109] Additionally, in his 2008 speech to the Association of Catholic Colleges and Universities, Archbishop Donald Wuerl gave several tangible examples of ways in which a Catholic university could engage the Church and how these universities can work together with the local bishops.

> Let me cite but a few examples. The Alliance for Catholic Education program at Notre Dame University is designed to support, through collaborative efforts, Catholic elementary schools and now Catholic parish religious education programs as well … Another example of programmatic support for inner-city schools is found in the collaboration with The Catholic University of America and St. Anthony of Padua Parish in the northeast section of the city.
>
> Still another example of a Catholic university offering programmatic support for inner-city schools is found in the Extra Mile Education Foundation schools in Pittsburgh, with their integrated collaboration with Duquesne University, Carlow College and La Roche College.
>
> In this way the involvement of university students in the mission of the church allows them to participate in the effort to reach out to those in need and at the same time to support Catholic education, which is a distinctly effective Catholic contribution to the wider community.[110]

Archbishop Wuerl subsequently gave another example in which he personally collaborated with the three Catholic universities in the Diocese of Pittsburgh while he was their local ordinary.

> I invited the three Catholic institutions of higher learning, Duquesne University, Carlow University and LaRoche College, to do something for the Year of the Eucharist that would be faithful both to the church's teaching and to the unique academic institution that is a college or university. The results were varied in the manifestation and positive in approach. While each university chose a different format, what resulted were symposia, lecture series and seminars on all three campuses presenting a deeper and academically

109. See "Catholic Identity" above.

110. Wuerl, "Marks of a Catholic College or University," 593–94. Similarly, the Catholic University of America has an agreement with the Brothers of Charity to help provide education during their novitiate. The Brothers of Charity were founded in the nineteenth century in Gent, Belgium, but have now assumed an international character and draw from developing countries for the majority of their vocations. See also William J. Byron, "Collaboration or Competition: How Should Catholic Universities Relate to the Wider World of Higher Education?," *Seminarium* (1990): 722–29.

qualified and intellectually profound discussion of the church's understanding of the great gift of the Eucharist.[111]

Archbishop Wuerl's examples certainly help to elaborate on the more general statements in *Ex corde Ecclesiae* and the *Application* with regard to how a Catholic university could pursue its role in the Church. Other examples are evident and will be discussed below.[112] Nevertheless, like the three universities that Archbishop Wuerl used in his example, each Catholic university should ultimately consider how it is best equipped to pursue this role.

Handling Disputes: Doctrinal Responsibilities

At times, concerns might arise regarding the substance of teaching that a theologian presents at a Catholic university, and it seems prudent to have a method to address those concerns. To handle such disputes in the dioceses of the United States, in 1989, the NCCB approved the document titled *Doctrinal Responsibilities: Approaches to Promoting Cooperation and Resolving Misunderstandings between Bishops and Theologians.*[113] Commenting on *Ex corde Ecclesiae*, Euart suggested that the procedures contained within *Doctrinal Responsibilities* should be used to address disputes in connection with the mandate to teach the theological disciplines. Quoting from *Doctrinal Responsibilities*, Euart argued:

> The apostolic constitution ought not to "presuppose a situation of tension or envisage adversarial relations between bishops and theologians in the United States, as if the rights of one had to be protected against the other." Rather,

111. Wuerl, "Marks of a Catholic College or University," 595. See Jude Butcher, Kristin Johnson, Elizabeth Labone, Peter Howard, and Mark McFadden, "Community Engagement as a Core Focus for Education at Australian Catholic University," *Current Issues in Catholic Higher Education* 23, no. 2 (Summer 2003): 3–44.

112. See the above list of examples of how a Catholic university can engage the Church.

113. NCCB, *Doctrinal Responsibilities: Approaches to Promoting Cooperation and Resolving Misunderstandings between Bishops and Theologians, Origins* 19, no. 7 (June 29, 1989): 97–110; See also Committee on Education, Bishops' and Presidents' Subcommittee, USCCB, *Catholic Identity in Our Colleges and Universities*, 131–58. For a comprehensive report that preceded the preparation of *Doctrinal Responsibilities*, see Leo J. O'Donovan, ed., *Cooperation between Theologians and the Ecclesiastical Magisterium: A Report of the Joint Committee of the Canon Law Society of America and the Catholic Theological Society of America* (Washington, DC: Canon Law Society of America, 1982).

it ought "to encourage increased communication and collaboration between bishops and theologians, to forestall disputes and if such disputes arise to promote their resolution for the good of the faithful."[114]

Subsequently, the NCCB identified *Doctrinal Responsibilities* in *The Application of Ex corde Ecclesiae for the United States* as a possible approach to be used to address disputes that arise within the local church. The *Application* states at Part II, Article 5, section 2(e):

> *Doctrinal Responsibilities: Approaches to Promoting Cooperation and Resolving Misunderstandings between Bishops and Theologians*, approved and published by the National Conference of Catholic Bishops, June 17, 1989, can serve as a useful guide for diocesan bishops, professors of the theological disciplines and administrators of universities to promote informal cooperation and collaboration in the Church's teaching mission and the faithful observance within Catholic universities of the principles of Catholic doctrine.[115]

The document is also referenced in the conference's *Guidelines Concerning the Academic Mandatum in Catholic Universities* (*Canon 812*)[116] for disputes over the granting or withdrawal of the mandate to teach the theological disciplines. The guidelines provide: "For the resolution of disputes about the withholding or withdrawal of the *mandatum*, there should be that contact between the Bishop and the professor as urged in canon 1733 § 1. The process set forth in *Doctrinal Responsibilities* should be followed. The right of all parties to good reputation must always be honored (cf. canon 220)."[117]

Doctrinal Responsibilities is divided into three parts:

114. Langan, *Catholic Universities in Church and Society*, 143.

115. NCCB, "Application of *Ex corde Ecclesiae* for the United States," Part 2, Art. 5, §2(e).

116. USCCB, *Guidelines Concerning the Academic Mandatum in Catholic Universities, Origins* 31, no. 7 (June 28, 2001): 128–30. See also Committee on Education, Bishops' and Presidents' Subcommittee, USCCB, *Catholic Identity in Our Colleges and Universities*, 115–19.

117. USCCB, *Guidelines Concerning the Academic Mandatum in Catholic Universities*, §6(c). See also Sharon Euart, "Canonical Reflections on *The Application of Ex corde Ecclesiae for the United States*," in *Mission and Identity: A Handbook for Trustees of Catholic Colleges and Universities*, ed. Association of Governing Boards of Universities and Colleges, Association of Catholic Colleges and Universities and Association of Jesuit Colleges & Universities (Washington, DC: AGB Publications, 2003), 75–82.

I. *The Context of Ecclesial Responsibilities* presents a general statement of the ecclesial framework, the operative principles, and the responsibilities and rights of bishops and theologians … II. *Promoting Cooperation and Informal Dialogue* recommends ways in which bishops and theologians can enhance cooperation in their common service of the gospel and the Church, especially through personal contacts and informal dialogue. This section focuses on positive efforts to promote cooperation, and also makes suggestions for actions by which bishops or theologians can screen complaints from third parties so that unnecessary disputes might be avoided. III. *A Possibility for Formal Doctrinal Dialogue* sets out a suggested procedure designed specifically to deal with doctrinal disputes between bishops and theologians in dioceses.[118]

It is beyond the scope of this essay to consider in detail the procedures embodied within *Doctrinal Responsibilities.* Nevertheless, the purpose of the document appears to be to promote a spirit of cooperation and dialogue between theologians and their local ordinaries. This would be particularly important when the circumstances involve the granting or withdrawal of a mandate to teach the theological disciplines. It seems that while bishops are concerned with protecting the integrity of the teachings that are presented at Catholic universities within their dioceses, they are also concerned with undertaking that task in a spirit of collaboration with those who teach within their dioceses. *Doctrinal Responsibilities* could be of assistance to bishops who see the need to formally address disputes regarding what is taught within their dioceses.

It is also noteworthy that the regulations[119] issued by the Congregation for the Doctrine of the Faith in 1997 should also be used for these purposes in all dioceses throughout the world. As noted above,[120] these regulations also involve the local bishop in the process of handling disputes with a theologian and safeguard the rights of the theologian in the process in a manner similar to that which the NCCB's *Doctrinal Responsibilities* attempt.

118. USCCB, *Doctrinal Responsibilities*, Preface.

119. Congregation for the Doctrine of the Faith, "Regulations for Doctrinal Examination," *Origins* 27, no. 13 (September 11, 1997): 221–24.

120. See the above discussion of Archbishop Wuerl.

Reflections on and Proposed Solutions for Addressing the Role of a Catholic University in the Church

Ex corde Ecclesiae and the NCCB's *Application* call on Catholic universities to play an active role in the life of the Church. Although these documents provide certain general principles to assist Catholic universities with this role, the way they do so really ought to be determined by the individual universities, since only they can ascertain their strengths and the abilities of their students and faculty. Moreover, many Catholic universities may have a unique charism that they have inherited from the religious institute that founded them and sought to extend their charism into the realm of education. For example, a Catholic university founded by one of the members of the Franciscan family might be particularly drawn to prayer, service, or evangelization in many different ways. Numerous examples could be ascertained by looking to the respective charism of other religious institutes such as the Society of Jesus, the Benedictines, or the Augustinians. Each of their Catholic universities may bring their own vision to the manner in which they fulfill their role in the Church.

In addition to the examples that Archbishop Wuerl provided in his speech to the Association of Catholic Colleges and Universities, numerous other examples might be suggested as ways in which a Catholic university could engage the Church.

1. A Catholic university could coordinate sending groups of students to mission countries to provide an example of Christian kindness and to plant the seeds for helping them to understand better the Gospel.

2. A Catholic university could coordinate pilgrimages for students, alumni, or other interested participants to locations, such as the Holy Land or the Vatican, in which significant spiritual events have occurred to reinvigorate their faith journeys.

3. A Catholic university could sponsor educational conferences to present the teachings of the Church or to help other Catholic universities to understand better what it means to be a Catholic university.

4. A Catholic university could partner with another Catholic university in an underdeveloped country that could benefit from the sharing of ideas on how to be a Catholic university.

5. A Catholic university could establish a satellite campus in another country to share with the people of that country the Christian values to which the university's students and faculty aspire.

6. A Catholic university could invite the local ordinary to be an active participant in the life of the university, whether as a member of the university's board of trustees, an adjunct faculty member, or frequent guest lecturer.

7. A Catholic university could incorporate into its core curriculum required courses that include the Catholic tradition in areas such as Church history, music, and literature.

8. A Catholic university that trains students in the healthcare professions could endeavor to place student interns in underprivileged areas to assist with providing healthcare to the poor and marginalized.

9. A Catholic university could encourage its students and faculty members to volunteer in the local parishes surrounding the university and serve as lectors, extraordinary ministers of Holy Communion, members of the choir, or in whatever way they see their gifts and talents.

10. A Catholic university could sponsor an association that assists underprivileged persons with obtaining government assistance with paying for their utility bills, obtaining needed medications and other healthcare services, or just meeting their daily needs.

11. A Catholic university could coordinate students who visit those in prison or assist the elderly who are unable to do their own grocery shopping.

12. A Catholic university could sponsor a literacy clinic to help people to learn to read.

There are many different things that a Catholic university could do to fulfill its role in the Church.[121] The important thing for representatives of a Catholic university to remember as they guide these discussions in this area is that the university is not isolated. It has a special relationship with the universal Church, particularly the Holy See, to which it owes institutional fidelity. Additionally, the Catholic university is embodied within the territory of a local Church and ought to play a vital role in assisting with the promotion of Catholic teachings and

121. See Melanie M. Morey and John J. Piderit, *Catholic Higher Education: A Culture in Crisis* (New York: Oxford University Press, 2006), 21.

values and the Church's mission of evangelization. How a Catholic university does that can best be ascertained by looking to the individual university to determine how the university can make its unique contribution. I hope the examples provided herein might stir their thinking and assist them with finding the special way in which each Catholic university can fulfill its role in the Church.

Conclusion

Presented here are five challenges to the implementation of *Ex corde Ecclesiae* and the canons dealing with Catholic universities, and I offered suggestions to address the challenges:

1. *Catholic Universities and Juridic Personality.* Although most Catholic universities in the United States do not have their own distinct canonical juridic personality, numerous arguments were presented to support the competence of the Church to regulate them. These included: the legislator's specific application of the concerned canonical provisions to all Catholic universities; the juridic link of the religious institutes that established the various Catholic universities; the need for Catholics associated with a Catholic university to maintain communion with the Church; a special bond that Catholic universities have assumed with the Holy See; the assumption of rights and responsibilities by those who wish to be a Catholic university; the behavior of Catholic universities in the drafting and implementation processes; and the practice of the Congregation for Catholic Education in exercising competence over Catholic universities.

2. *Catholic Identity.* Each Catholic university needs to assess the ways in which it can best promote its Catholic identity so that it permeates all aspects of the university's life. Nevertheless, several suggestions include: furthering the Church's teaching on social ethics and protecting the dignity of the human person; involving in hiring decisions high-level personnel who are responsible for promoting Catholic identity; incorporating Catholic identity into curriculum choices; dialoguing with external sources, such as boards of trustees and the Church's hierarchy; embracing the Church's canonical norms; supporting social justice issues and the preferential option for the poor; collaborating with

other Catholic universities to promote Catholic identity; or revisiting the vision of the university's founders to promote Catholic identity.

3. *Hiring Practices. Ex corde Ecclesiae* suggests a preference for hiring baptized Catholics to comprise a majority of the faculty. Additionally, the religious exemption provisions would likely protect a Catholic university faced with a discrimination claim based on preferential hiring practices.

4. *Contracts in Institutions of Catholic Higher Education.* The relationship that exists between a Catholic university and its faculty members is a contractual one. As a result, it would seem prudent for a Catholic university that intends to implement the provisions of the code dealing with Catholic universities and *Ex corde Ecclesiae* to incorporate into its employment contracts and faculty handbook the provisions of canon law as controlling and also to identify violations of canon law as grounds for termination.

5. *A Catholic University's Role in the Church.* A Catholic university has a role to play in the Church at both the universal level and the level of the local Church. Numerous examples were provided to assist a Catholic university with ascertaining how it can best fulfill its role. Additionally, I briefly considered an option of how to address disputes between theologians and the local ordinary.

I hope these discussions and observations to address these concerns will be helpful to a Catholic university seeking to implement the provisions of *Ex corde Ecclesiae* and its related canonical provisions.

In his April 2008 meeting with the Catholic educators of the United States, Pope Benedict XVI put forth several pointed questions to challenge his audience. "Is the faith tangible in our universities and schools? Is it given fervent expression liturgically, sacramentally, through prayer, acts of charity, a concern for justice and respect for God's creation? Only in this way do we really bear witness to the meaning of who we are and what we uphold."[122] The Holy Father also acknowledged that the Catholic identity of an institution is not determined merely by size of the institution or the numbers of students enrolled. Nevertheless, his questions, if considered seriously, should have challenged all those

122. Pope Benedict XVI, "Speech to Educators," *Origins* 37, no. 46 (May 1, 2008): 742.

involved in delivering Catholic education to be renewed in their commitment to their ministry. And the Church continues its commitment to assisting Catholic universities with their ministry. *Ex corde Ecclesiae* and the canons in the code of canon law that address Catholic universities are intended to help these institutions with their mission.

The Church has always exercised some degree of supervision over the operation of Catholic universities and since the medieval period has required the permission of the competent ecclesiastical authority to teach. The *licentia docendi* embodied the ecclesiastical permission to teach. Thus, although the inclusion of a separate chapter on Catholic universities may be new to the 1983 code, the specific canons that regulate Catholic universities have a respected tradition in the law of the Church. This was also demonstrated by the inclusion in the 1917 code of canon law canons that addressed schools in general, and Catholic universities in particular.

Catholic universities who seek to implement the provisions of *Ex corde Ecclesiae* and its related canonical requirements face numerous competing forces that might make compliance difficult at times because of the need to consider each of these competing forces. Theologians, Catholic universities, and those who administer them are to be commended for their dedication and ministry in service to the Church. In promulgating *Ex corde Ecclesiae*, Pope John Paul II expressed his profound respect for Catholic universities and expressed his great appreciation for the work that they do.[123] As they continue to address the challenges that present themselves, may they find some assistance in these comments, but always be led by the Holy Spirit in implementing them.

123. See *EcE*, 2.

Afterword

Sean O. Sheridan, TOR

In November 2015, after we completed the oral presentations of the papers for the "Fidelity and Freedom Series: *Ex corde Ecclesiae* at 25," I had the opportunity to participate in the World Congress on Catholic Education, sponsored by the Congregation for Catholic Education of the Roman curia. The Congress, titled "Educating Today and Tomorrow: A Renewing Passion," was called to celebrate the fiftieth anniversary of Vatican II's 1965 decree *Gravissimum educationis* and the twenty-fifth anniversary of Pope John Paul II's 1990 apostolic constitution *Ex corde Ecclesiae.* We focused on four principal themes: identity and mission of Catholic institutions, the various stakeholders in education, the formation of formators, and today's challenges affecting the field of education. At times, the participants gathered to address the themes, but also spent time in focused groups of leaders of Catholic schools, Catholic universities, and legal scholars. Throughout the congress, there was a shared desire to collaborate and to listen to each other about common experiences to advance Catholic education.

At the conclusion of the congress, Pope Francis addressed the participants at an audience in Paul VI Hall, with a brief prepared address followed by a question-and-answer session. While Pope Francis recognized the importance of Catholic education, he also challenged Catholic educators on many different levels. Because his thinking on Catholic education has not been gathered in a single authoritative source, it is worthwhile to set forth below a few excerpts from his remarks at this gathering.[1] Francis said:

1. "Pope's Q-and-A on the Challenges of Education," *Zenit*, November 23, 2015, https://zenit.org/articles/pope-s-q-and-a-on-the-challenges-of-education/.

- "One cannot speak of *Catholic education* without speaking of *humanity*, because, precisely, the Catholic identity is God who became man.... To educate in a Christian way is to lead young people, children, in human values in the whole of reality, and one of these realities is *transcendence*.... For me, the greatest crisis of education, in the Christian perspective, is being closed to transcendence."[2]
- "Leave places where there are so many educators and go to the peripheries.... Seek there the needy, the poor. And they have something that young people of the richer neighborhoods don't have ... they have the experience of surviving, also of cruelty, also of hunger, also of injustices. They have a wounded humanity. And I think that our salvation comes from the wounds of a man wounded on the cross. Those, of those wounds, bring wisdom, if there is a good educator that leads them forward."[3]
- "The greatest failure an educator can have is to educate 'within walls.' To educate within walls: the walls of a selective culture, the walls of a culture of security, the walls of a social sector that is well-off and does not go further."[4]
- "In this Year of Mercy, is mercy only to give alms?—or, in education, how can I do the works of mercy? They are, namely, the works of the Love of the Father ... How can I have this Love of the Father, which is especially stressed in this Year of Mercy, come to our educational endeavors?"[5]

Pope Francis's remarks to Catholic educators reminded me that leaders in Catholic education have additional responsibilities to those that they serve to assist them in their development as fully authentic human persons and on their journey to the persons that God created them to be. These are important themes that, perhaps not coincidentally, were also advanced to Catholic educators in both *Gravissimum educationis* and *Ex corde Ecclesiae*, the documents that we were there to celebrate, and the documents upon which we should rely as we deliver Catholic higher education.

2. Ibid.
3. Ibid.
4. Ibid.
5. Ibid.

Although much can be, and has been, said about Catholic universities, *Ex corde Ecclesiae*, and the delivery of Catholic higher education, those who have dedicated their lives to this unique ministry must always remain focused on the source of everything that flows from a Catholic university that is "born from the heart of the Church." It is God himself who leads and guides a Catholic university. As the great Franciscan theologian St. Bonaventure once reasoned, all studies should lead us to God, so that there is no "investigation without wonder," no "observation without joy," and no "understanding without humility."[6]

In *Ex corde Ecclesiae*, Pope John Paul II maintained:

> A Catholic university pursues its objectives through its formation of an authentic human community animated by the spirit of Christ. The source of its unity springs from a common dedication to the truth, a common vision of the dignity of the human person, and ultimately, the person and message of Christ, which gives the institution its distinctive character. As a result of this inspiration, the community is animated by a spirit of freedom and charity; it is characterized by mutual respect, sincere dialogue and protection of the rights of individuals. It assists each of its members to achieve wholeness as human persons; in turn, everyone in the community helps in promoting unity, and each one, according to his or her role and capacity, contributes towards decisions which affect the community, and also towards maintaining and strengthening the distinctive Catholic character of the institution.[7]

All who respond to the Lord's invitation to teach, in imitation of his witness and following his example, must never lose sight of this sacred obligation.

Morey and Piderit[8] predicted a crisis in Catholic higher education and urged Catholic universities to remain faithful to the purpose for which they were established. Higher education, in general, has recently gone through significant changes and will likely continue to experience much more transformation in the future. Some are predicting

6. Bonaventure, *The Soul's Journey into God*, trans. Ewert Cousins (New York: Paulist Press, 1978), prologue, 4, 55–56.

7. *EcE*, 21.

8. Melanie M. Morey and John J. Piderit, SJ, *Catholic Higher Education: A Culture in Crisis* (Oxford: Oxford University Press, 2006).

that higher education will not resemble what we now see in traditional "brick-and-mortar" four-year undergraduate institutions.

But while the future delivery of higher education remains to be revealed, we do know that the Lord promised to remain steadfast in his love for us. May we who engage in the delivery of education within a Catholic college or university be comforted by that promise.

CONTRIBUTORS

Mark L. Bartchak attended St. Mark Seminary and Gannon University, where he received a bachelor's degree in philosophy in 1977. He also studied for the priesthood at Christ the King Seminary, receiving a master's degree in theology in 1981. He studied canon law at the Catholic University of America, where he received a licentiate degree in 1989 and a doctorate degree in 1992. Bishop Bartchak was ordained a deacon at Christ the King Seminary on September 22, 1980, and served as deacon at St. Joseph Parish in Warren, Pennsylvania. He was ordained a priest for the Diocese of Erie on May 15, 1981. In 2000, he received papal honors from Pope John Paul II with the title of Chaplain to His Holiness. He was ordained a bishop and installed as the eighth Bishop of the Diocese of Altoona-Johnstown on April 19, 2011. Bishop Bartchak has been involved in various roles in the Church on the state, national, and international level. He has authored various journals articles on canon law topics. Bishop Bartchak has been a member of the teaching faculty of the Institute on Matrimonial Tribunal Practice, held each summer at the Catholic University of America, and he has taught canon law for the permanent diaconate formation program in the Diocese of Erie.

James J. Conn, SJ, is a native of Philadelphia, and since 1974 has been a priest of the Maryland Province of the Society of Jesus. After serving for fifteen years as Ordinary Professor of Canon Law at the Pontifical Gregorian University in Rome, where he earned his doctorate, Father Conn is now professor of the practice of canon law at the School of Theology and Ministry at Boston College and St. John's Seminary in Brighton, Massachusetts. He is a consultor of the Holy See's Congregation for the Clergy, and a commissioner of the matrimonial section of the Congregation for the Doctrine of the Faith. Prior to his assignment in Rome, he was a teacher and administrator at several Jesuit-sponsored secondary schools and universities in the United States, and *praeses* of the ecclesiastical faculty of theology at St. Mary's Seminary and University in Baltimore as well as dean of its School of Theology. He serves as a canonical advisor to episcopal conferences, diocesan bishops, and institutes of consecrated life. A graduate of Fordham Law School, he is a member of the bar in Maryland and the District of Columbia.

Scott W. Hahn is a bestselling author of over forty titles, including *The Lamb's Supper* and *Reasons to Believe*. Professor Hahn has taught at Franciscan University of Steubenville since 1990 and holds the Fr. Michael Scanlan Chair of Biblical Theology and the New Evangelization. He is founder and president of the St. Paul Center for Biblical Theology and editor-in-chief of Emmaus Road Publishing. Scott and his wife, Kimberly, have six children and fifteen grandchildren. They live in Steubenville, Ohio.

Anne Hendershott is a professor of sociology and the director of the Veritas Center at Franciscan University in Steubenville, Ohio. She is the author of *Status Envy: The Politics of Catholic Higher Education*; *The Politics of Abortion*; *The Politics of Deviance*; and *The Reluctant Caregivers*. Her most recent coauthored book is *Renewal: How a New Generation of Catholic Priests and Bishops Are Revitalizing the Church*.

Stephen M. Hildebrand is a professor of theology and chair of the Department of Theology at Franciscan University of Steubenville. He is the author of *The Trinitarian Theology of Basil of Caesarea* (Catholic University of America Press, 2007) and *Basil of Caesarea* (Baker, 2014), and translator of St. Basil, *On the Holy Spirit* (St. Vladimir's, 2007), and Robert Grosseteste, *On the Cessation of the Laws* (Catholic University of America Press, 2012).

Reinhard Hütter is presently an ordinary professor of fundamental and dogmatic theology at the Catholic University of America's School of Theology and Religious Studies. He previously taught for eighteen years systematic theology at Duke University Divinity School. He was a visiting fellow at the Institute for Advanced Studies of Religion of the University of Chicago, a visiting fellow at the Center of Theological Inquiry in Princeton, and a visiting professor at the University of Jena, Germany. He held the Robert J. Randall Distinguished Chair in Christian Culture at Providence College in Rhode Island, and the Chester and Margaret Paluch Chair of Theology at the University of St. Mary of the Lake/Mundelein Seminary. He is a distinguished fellow at the St. Paul Center for Biblical Theology, a member of the American Theological Society, was a founding member and served as president of the Academy of Catholic Theology, is an ordinary academician of the Pontifical Academy of St. Thomas Aquinas, and is a faculty fellow of the Institute for Human Ecology of the Catholic University of America. He is the author of numerous books, most recently *Dust Bound for Heaven: Explorations in the Theology of Thomas Aquinas* (2012) and *Bound for Beatitude: A Thomistic Study in Eschatology and Ethics* (2019).

Richard Jusseaume, sixth president of Walsh University, has led Walsh to unprecedented achievement over the past seventeen years. Ohio's second longest-serving president of a four-year private university, Jusseaume became president of Walsh in 2001. Under his leadership and guidance, Walsh has experienced phenomenal growth in almost every facet of its operations, including enrollment, academic programming, faculty and staff, financial resources, and physical facilities.

Jeffrey Monforton received a bachelor's in sacred theology from Sacred Heart Major Seminary in Detroit in 1992. While studying at the Pontifical North American College in Rome, he obtained a licentiate in sacred theology and was later awarded a doctorate in sacred theology from Pontifical Gregorian University in Rome. He served in the Archdiocese of Detroit as associate pastor at the National Shrine of the Little Flower, Royal Oak, from 1994 to 1996, while also serving the faculty at the parish high school for two academic years in the department of religion. In 2005, he was named pastor of St. Therese of Lisieux Church, Shelby Township, Michigan, and that same year was conferred the title of monsignor by Pope Benedict. He was named Bishop of Steubenville, Ohio, on July 3, 2012. He was ordained to the episcopate and installed on September 10, 2012.

Peter F. Ryan, SJ, is a professor of theology and the college spiritual director at Sacred Heart Major Seminary in Detroit. He holds a doctorate in moral theology from the Gregorian University in Rome, serves on the executive board of the Fellowship of Catholic Scholars, and is a past president of the Jesuit Philosophical Society. His work has been published in a variety of journals, including *Gregorianum* and *Theological Studies*, on such topics as the indissolubility of marriage, contraception, embryo adoption, discernment, and the relationship between moral action and ultimate human fulfillment.

James P. Shea became the youngest college or university president in the United States in 2009. During his tenure as the sixth president of the University of Mary, he has spearheaded several groundbreaking initiatives, including new campuses for the university in Rome and Peru, an unprecedented collaborative agreement with Arizona State University, and Year Round Campus—a new way of conceiving higher education to elevate student achievement and reduce debt. A farm boy from Hazelton, North Dakota, he has studied at the Catholic University of America in Washington, DC, the Vatican's North American College, the University of Chicago, and Harvard. He was ordained a Catholic priest in 2002.

Sean O. Sheridan, TOR, began serving as president of Franciscan University of Steubenville on June 1, 2013. A Third Order Regular Franciscan Friar, Province of the Most Sacred Heart of Jesus, he was ordained a priest in 2006. Father Sean obtained a doctorate in Canon Law from the Catholic University of America in 2009, writing a dissertation titled "*Ex corde Ecclesiae*: A Canonical Commentary on Catholic Universities 'From the Heart of the Church' to Catholic Universities." Before entering the Franciscan Third Order Regular, Father Sean obtained a bachelor of science degree in pharmacy from the University of Pittsburgh in 1985, and a juris doctor from the University of Pittsburgh School of Law in 1990. His law practice in Sacramento and Pittsburgh focused on healthcare litigation, primarily with the representation of hospitals and physicians. As an assistant professor in the School of Canon Law at the Catholic University of America (2009 to 2012) and a professor of theology at Franciscan University (2012 to present), Father Sean concentrates his research and canonical consulting in the areas of Consecrated Life and the Teaching Office of the Church.

Terrence W. Tilley is the Avery Cardinal Dulles, SJ, Professor Emeritus of Catholic Theology at Fordham University. He holds a PhD from the Graduate Theological Union in Berkeley, California, and taught previously at Georgetown University, St. Michael's College (Vermont), Florida State University, and the University of Dayton. He is a past president of the Catholic Theological Society of America, the College Theology Society, and the Society for Philosophy of Religion; author of ten books, editor of three books, author of scores of articles and reviews; and the recipient of numerous awards, including the John Courtney Murray Award for Distinguished Achievement in Theology from the Catholic Theological Society of America in 2012.

Susan K. Wood, SCL, is professor of systematic theology and chair of the Department of Theology at Marquette University. She received her doctorate in systematic theology from Marquette University. She is an associate editor of *Pro Ecclesia* and serves on the editorial advisory board of the journal *Ecclesiology*. Most of her writing explores the connections between ecclesiology and sacramental theology. In addition to numerous articles, she has published *Spiritual Exegesis and the Church in the Theology of Henri de Lubac* (Eerdmans, 1998), *Sacramental Orders* (Liturgical Press, 2000), which has also been translated into Spanish, and *One Baptism: Ecumenical Dimensions of the Doctrine of Baptism* (Liturgical Press, 2009), and coauthored with Timothy J. Wingert *A Shared Spiritual Journey: Lutherans and Catholics Traveling toward Unity* (Paulist Press, 2016). She is the editor of *Ordering the Baptismal Priesthood* (Liturgical Press, 2003) and coeditor with Alberto Garcia of *Critical Issues in Ecclesiology* (Eerdmans, 2011). She served as president of the Catholic Theological Society of America 2014–15.

INDEX

Index

Index